THE QUOTABLE MARK TWAIN

THE QUOTABLE MARK TWAIN

His Essential Aphorisms, Witticisms, & Concise Opinions

EDITED BY R. KENT RASMUSSEN

CB

CONTEMPORARY BOOKS

Library of Congress Cataloging-in-Publication Data

Twain, Mark, 1835–1910.
    The quotable Mark Twain : his essential aphorisms, witticisms & concise
opinions / edited by Kent Rasmussen ; foreword by Shelley Fisher Fishkin.
        p.   cm.
    Includes bibliographical references and index.
    ISBN 0-8092-3088-7 (cloth)
    ISBN 0-8092-2987-0 (paper)
    1. Twain, Mark, 1835–1910—Quotations—Dictionaries.   2. Quotations,
American—Dictionaries.   I. Rasmussen, R. Kent.
    IN PROCESS   PS1303.R
    818′.4′409—dc21   97-43653
                                    CIP

Cover design by Nick Panos
Image enhancement by Todd Petersen
Interior design by Nick Panos
Interior production by Betsy Kulak

Published by Contemporary Books
An imprint of NTC/Contemporary Publishing Company
4255 West Touhy Avenue, Lincolnwood (Chicago), Illinois 60646-1975 U.S.A.
Copyright © 1997 by R. Kent Rasmussen
All rights reserved. No part of this book may be reproduced, stored in a retrieval system,
or transmitted in any form or by any means, electronic, mechanical, photocopying, recording,
or otherwise, without the prior permission of NTC/Contemporary Publishing Company.
Printed in the United States of America
International Standard Book Number: 0-8092-3088-7 (cloth)
                                       0-8092-2987-0 (paper)
20   19   18   17   16   15   14   13   12   11   10   9   8   7   6   5   4   3   2   1

To the staff of the Mark Twain Project in Berkeley,
in appreciation of the exemplary work they do.

Reasonable people may disagree on what makes an edition
"definitive"—but what reasonable person will deny that the
Project's editions come closer to that elusive goal than any others?

Contents

Picture Credits

Page numbers of illustrations appearing in this volume are followed by the pictures' original sources, keyed to the bibliography. Names of illustrators who can be confidently identified are given in parentheses.

Acknowledgments

The greatest of all inventors, according to Mark Twain, is accident. This book surely proves that to be true. One evening in 1967, as I sat in an African history seminar at UCLA, a fellow student named Dick Ralston casually mentioned Mark Twain's hilarious description of the Book of Mormon. Over the next twenty-five years I never forgot that remark, for I certainly repeated it often enough. Eventually I decided to find exactly where it came from. Well, Dick, it's now thirty years later, and I can report that I found that quote—as well as several thousand others. Thanks for the tip. If you hadn't given it to me, neither this book nor two others would exist.

Dick Ralston has not heard of this book before now. Others have, however, and I must thank them, too, for their contributions. Dahlia Armon, formerly an editor at the Mark Twain Project in Berkeley, read primitive drafts and convinced me that even Mark Twain experts would appreciate a book such as this. She also put me on to Robert Hirst, the Project's general editor, who reinforced that idea. More recently he somehow found time to answer my numerous queries and provide tangible help in ways that meticulous readers of this book should recognize.

Recently someone dubbed Kevin Bochynski the "angel" of Mark Twain studies. It must be true, because he's always on deck when there's a miracle to the fore and people like me need help. I also appreciate the advice I've gotten from Mark Dawidziak, whose own recent book, *Mark My Words: Mark Twain on Writing* (St. Martin's Press), must certainly be the most entertaining writer's handbook ever assembled, as well as a most useful collection of Mark Twain quotes. To Michael Kiskis go my thanks for so readily giving me permission to quote from *Mark Twain's Own Autobiography*. How many years ago were we all marveling at the sensational impact that Shelley Fisher Fiskhin's book *Was Huck Black? Mark Twain and African-American Voices* was having on the nation as a whole? It's hard to believe that she now reads *my* manuscripts and offers barrels of facts and ideas that have helped improve the book in dozens of subtle ways.

Others who have provided valued encouragement and help include JoDee Benussi, Julie Castiglia, Chris Ehret, Gerilee Hundt, Michael

vii

Patrick, Barbara Schmidt, Susan Schwartz, Barbara Staton, and Tom Tenney. My fondest thanks go, of course, to my wife, Kathy. She performed the painstaking tasks of locating more than 2,000 quotes and checking them against their original sources. Without her help, I'd probably still be minding my *P*s and *Q*s and wondering what had become of my *R*s.

The staff of the Mark Twain Project did not participate directly in the preparation of this book, but the fine editions that they have produced have made it possible for this book to stake a claim to being the most authoritative collection of Mark Twain quotes yet published. In appreciation of this, and in gratitude for the contributions that the Project staff have made to Mark Twain studies generally, I dedicate this book to them. And, as always, I encourage all those who treasure Mark Twain to support the Project's vitally important future work.

Foreword

Reading Mark Twain is not quite like reading anybody else. First of all, the frequency of our "I wish I'd said that" response per page is higher than for other authors. Second, he makes us laugh even when he seems to be trying not to. Third, he makes us wince when he sounds like he's just being matter-of-fact. And fourth, he manages to shock us, more often than any other author I can think of, with his perfect rendering of some deep, dark corner of our psyche we may not have even visited yet ourselves, and certainly hadn't opened for public view. Mark Twain's aphorisms, witticisms, insights, and epiphanies are part of what keeps us coming back for more.

But they are also a snare and a delusion. For they never turn out to be where we remember them being, and we can lose hours (sometimes most of a night's sleep) trying to find the "somewhere else" they have mysteriously transported themselves to. We ransack our bookshelves and our memories. We race to the library. No quote. The hunt for a beloved phrase or witty truth from a cherished old friend begins as a pleasure trip but ends (like Mark Twain's *Quaker City* excursion) in exasperation.

R. Kent Rasmussen can help. Long personal acquaintance with this debilitating syndrome, combined with years of helping others cope with the disease, has led him to develop a highly effective cure: *The Quotable Mark Twain*.

Didn't Mark Twain write something about inspiration that began with the phrase "when the tank runs dry"? And didn't he call patriotism "the refuge of the scoundrel" somewhere? Where did he say that the Emancipation Proclamation "not only set the black slaves free, but set the white man free also"? And where did he refer to German as "the language which enables a man to travel all day in one sentence without changing cars"? These are the kinds of questions *The Quotable Mark Twain* can answer promptly, efficiently, and in the privacy of your own home.

But be forewarned: While *The Quotable Mark Twain* has been proved to reduce the frequency of sleepless quote-hunting nights, it is not without side effects. Even random, purposeless browsing through this book may prove addictive. Sleep interference may result. Readers are therefore urged to proceed with caution.

In *The Quotable Mark Twain*, Rasmussen draws not only on works published in Mark Twain's lifetime but on posthumously published material, uncollected pieces, letters, journals, and interviews. He pulls this unwieldy mass of material together with the good judgment we might expect from the author of the magisterial *Mark Twain A to Z*. In the book's pages we see Mark Twain's quirks and contradictions emerge. We witness the range of tones he evoked in his public and private writings, and are reminded of the themes that exercised his intellect, triggered his emotions, and animated his life. We see Mark Twain being maudlin and sentimental, acerbic and trenchant. And throughout it all, the man's inimitable energy, elan, and irreverence tease us out of our complacency and myopia and force us to look at our world in new ways.

What a treat to be able to flip through Mark Twain's witty comments on lies, civilization, citizenship, compliments, courtship, adversity, and bliss, all helpfully sorted and sourced and indexed and cross-referenced amidst apt illustrations from Mark Twain's books. He emits quirky unassailable bits of sensibleness such as "Clothes make the man. Naked people have little or no influence in society." He gives us useful rules for living such as "When angry, count four; when very angry, swear." We see him being pithy and playful, angry and incisive, kind, smart, wise—and always precise. We see his generosity of spirit as well as the petty vanities and vendettas that remind us that he was not, after all, that different from the rest of us.

Mark Twain's aphorisms and quips are carefully crafted: "It is more trouble to make a maxim than it is to do right" he tells us. But he has taken the trouble to make many a maxim, and Rasmussen shares a raft of the best of them with the reader. The result is a fascinating portrait of the author's preferences and prejudices interlarded with testimony to Mark Twain's inimitable modesty: "I like a good story well told," he once said. "That is the reason I am sometimes forced to tell them myself." *The Quotable Mark Twain* is both useful and fun: a valuable reference work and a terrific book to curl up with on a cold night.

"To get the right word in the right place is a rare achievement," Mark Twain wrote. "To condense the diffused light of a page of thought into the luminous flash of a single sentence is worthy to rank as a prize composition just by itself." Lucky for us, Mark Twain turned out "prize compositions" of this order by the truckload. And lucky for us that so many of them can be found between the covers of this book!

—Shelley Fisher Fishkin

Introduction

With the possible exception of the singularly prolific Anon., Mark Twain must surely be the most frequently quoted writer in American literature. His words turn up everywhere: in advertisements, textbooks, novels, newspapers, and magazines, as well as on radio and television. *Reader's Digest* alone has quoted him so frequently that a scholar once quipped that it was merely a matter of time before that magazine would begin imitating the Bible by printing Mark Twain's words in red ink.

During Mark Twain's later years, as he campaigned for copyright reform, he observed that of the 220,000 American books published since the nation's founding, "not a bathtub-full of them are still alive and marketable." The contrast between the fates of those now forgotten books and his own work is stunning. In 1998—nearly nine decades after Mark Twain died—virtually everything he published in book form is still in print. Some of his books—such as *Tom Sawyer* and *Huckleberry Finn*—have never been out of print since their first copies came off the presses well over a century ago. To date, more than 5,000 separate editions of his books have been published throughout the world, and the flow is increasing.

Why so much attention for one long-dead writer, when so many others are forgotten? One need not look far to find answers. Mark Twain left a vast body of work that remains as fresh today as it was in his own time. Within his surprisingly diverse writings he seems to have commented on almost every issue of his time, and he was so forward-looking that much of what he wrote remains alive and relevant. Since his death in 1910 his stature as a writer has steadily climbed. This rise has not been without some controversy, but at least one thing about his writing seems immune to serious challenge: he introduced a naturalness and authenticity to literature by writing much as people actually spoke. Indeed, this may have been what Ernest Hemingway had in mind when he wrote:

All modern American literature comes from one book by Mark Twain called *Huckleberry Finn.* . . . it's the best book we've had.

> All American writing comes from that. There was nothing before.
> There has been nothing as good since.
>
> (The Green Hills of Africa, *1935*)

Mark Twain wrote with a vigor, honesty, and courage that few writers of his or any other time could match, and he enlivened his work with such wit and imagination that his best writing only grows stronger with repeated readings. Moreover, he used his considerable powers as a writer to articulate ideas that others dared not express openly. He questioned everything that smacked of what today would be called "conventional wisdom." He was never afraid to attack orthodoxies and conventions of every kind—from oppressive religious dogmas to ideas about how to dress. If a single theme pervades his writings it is his ceaseless quest for liberation from sham and from every form of human shackles.

Almost all of Mark Twain's work—even his inferior writings—contains something memorable: a sharp eye for a fascinating detail, a profound idea in an unexpected place, a fresh and vivid image, or a superbly turned phrase. Although he wrote voluminously, it is remarkable how infrequently he repeated himself. To appreciate the full dimensions of that achievement, one must read through the bulk of his work. Not everyone can do that, of course—hence the value of quote collections such as this.

Mark Twain's love of language and his respect for its forms and nuances are evident in everything he wrote. Despite his limited formal schooling, he was a serious student of the English language and of the craft of writing. He meant exactly what he said when he wrote that

> the difference between the almost-right word & the right word is really a large matter—it's the difference between the lightning-bug & the lightning.

His "lightning-bug" metaphor may owe something to his fellow humorist Josh Billings, but the idea that it illuminates so brightly was very much his own. His sincerity can easily be tested by reading his work, in countless passages of which alteration of a single word would turn something special into something ordinary.

The Quotable Mark Twain is an outgrowth of my personal admiration for Mark Twain's writing. It began almost by accident seven years ago, when I decided to find the source of Mark Twain's caustic opinion of the Book of Mormon, which I had heard quoted many years earlier. I began my search in *Roughing It*, which describes his visit to Salt Lake City, the center of Mormondom. I happened to do this at a moment when Leonard Louis Levinson's *Left Handed Dictionary* (1963) and *Webster's Unafraid Dictionary* (1967) were on my mind. Filled with ironic and often wickedly humorous quotes from scores of people, these books invited comparison with what I was finding in *Roughing It*. Almost immediately, however, I sensed the superiority of Mark Twain's wit, and particularly the brilliance of his language. Often his imagery lifted the mundane to lofty heights, as in this description:

> The cayote is a living, breathing allegory of Want. He is *always* hungry. He is always poor, out of luck and friendless. The meanest creatures despise him, and even the fleas would desert him for a velocipede. He is so spiritless and cowardly that even while his exposed teeth are pretending a threat, the rest of his face is apologizing for it.

As I read on, I wondered if it were possible to assemble a collection of quotes solely from Mark Twain's writings that would match Levinson's collections in size, while outdoing them in wit. I then set myself the goal of reading all of Mark Twain and creating just such a book. It has taken seven years for that book to reach maturity, but much of my time went into two other books on Mark Twain that I could not have imagined when I began my original quest. Through these years I read almost everything by Mark Twain that has found its way into print—and most of that I read several times over and expect to read again and again.

I have my doubts that anyone other than Mark Twain himself has actually read everything that he wrote. After all, most of his correspondence and many other manuscripts still wait to see print. Furthermore, one can only guess at how many of his early newspaper articles have been lost to history because he published them anonymously, or because copies of the papers in which they appeared no longer exist. One can, nevertheless, come close to reading "all of Mark Twain." For my part, reading all of his books and virtually all of his published stories, sketches, essays, speeches, letters, and memoirs was much like what I experienced the first time I read *Tom Sawyer* at age nine: immediately after finishing, I wanted to turn back to the beginning and start again. Perhaps this sounds strange, but I have come to learn that I am not the only person on whom Mark Twain has this effect. It seems impossible to grow bored with the man.

There are cogent reasons why it is so difficult to tire of Mark Twain. First is the fact that his writings encompass almost every topic one can imagine—from the inner person to humanity's place in the universe. Moreover, his own life is a vast subject in itself. During his lifetime he saw the world undergo more changes than it had experienced during several preceding centuries, thanks to the coming of the industrial age, the end of slavery, the beginnings of universal suffrage, and the advent of modern imperialism and mechanized warfare. Mark Twain observed and commented on all these changes. Everything interested him, and he traveled exceptionally widely. He lived in every section of the United States, visited most of its present states (including Hawaii), and slept in hundreds of its cities and villages. He also crossed the Atlantic twenty-five times, went around the world, and lived outside the United States for more than a dozen years. His travels and voluminous correspondence brought him into direct touch with an extraordinary number of the leading literary, cultural, and political figures of his time. On top of all this, his interests extended deeply into history, and he had a lively imagination about the future. To read the works of this true man of all seasons is to explore a very large part of the human experience in the company of one of the wittiest and most stimulating guides to the world who has ever lived. Samuel Johnson once said that "when a man is tired of London, he is tired of life; for there is in London all that life can afford." The same might be said of Mark Twain.

Any collection of one writer's quotations is necessarily a selection built on certain emphases and principles. *The Quotable Mark Twain* is a distillation of Mark Twain's entire works that emphasizes his aphoristic writings and opinions. Several other collections of his quotes have been published, but none closely resembles *The Quotable Mark Twain*, either in content or in form. At least half of its material appears in no other collection, and the form in which it is presented is also different. This book differs partly because it draws on a wider range of sources than earlier collections, but more importantly because it emphasizes content over style. In selecting quotes, I looked more at the substance of passages than at their wording, though the latter also weighed heavily in my choices.

It sometimes seems that Mark Twain is credited with every witty

remark in circulation that cannot be confidently connected with someone else. The Mark Twain Project in Berkeley—which is painstakingly
preparing new editions of Mark Twain's writings—answers so many
queries about the sources of quotes attributed to him that one might
think it the heft of their business. However, despite the efforts of the
Project and other authorities to dispense correct information, many
unattested quotes are still so closely identified with Mark Twain's name
that petrifaction has set in.

In the interest of achieving the greatest possible authenticity for *The
Quotable Mark Twain*, I do not include any quotes of doubtful or
unproven origin—however famous they may be. My rule for excluding
doubtful material is simple: if I find no compelling evidence that Mark
Twain himself wrote or uttered a passage, it does not go in. Every quote
in this book is referenced to a text that Mark Twain is known to have
written or spoken. (One partial exception is a quote about the Philippines taken from Albert Bigelow Paine's biography; there is good reason to believe it comes from a Mark Twain manuscript.) If I have
accidentally omitted a worthy quote or two, readers will doubtless find
them in other collections. However, since sins of omission are less damaging than sins of commission in these matters, I doubt that any great
harm will have been done.

To spare readers some of the frustration of looking for familiar passages that are not in this book, I will mention several here. I cannot defin-
itively claim that Mark Twain never said or wrote these things; I merely
say that I am unaware of any satisfactory evidence that he did so. It is
quite possible that some of these quotes derive from words he uttered
that acquaintances heard and later recorded. Even if this is so, however,
how accurately his words were recorded is another question that makes
me hesitate to use such quotes. Like oral contracts, personal recollections are often not worth the paper on which they are written. (To be
fair, I should add that the same charge might be leveled against some
transcriptions of Mark Twain speeches quoted in this book.) These
qualms aside, it can be added that some unattested quotes that have
found their way into the modern Mark Twain canon are highly suspect
at face value. For example, the *Reader's Digest* (September 1937) once
credited Mark Twain with this:

When I was a boy of fourteen, my father was so ignorant I could
hardly stand to have the old man around. But when I got to be

twenty-one, I was astonished at how much he had learned in seven years.

It is a clever passage but one scarcely likely to have been written by someone who was only eleven when he lost his father.

Another, more famous quote has been of special interest to me because finding it was one of the reasons that I picked up *Roughing It* seven years ago: "The coldest winter I ever spent was a summer in San Francisco." Since *Roughing It* describes the time when Mark Twain lived in San Francisco, it seemed the best place to look for that particular quote. I went through the book with a fine-tooth comb, turned it upside down and shook it, but not only could I not find the quote, everything I did find about San Francisco weather expressed exactly opposite views. Later I learned that the Mark Twain Project (which is just across the bay from San Francisco) is asked about that particular quote so often that it printed a special flyer to save time explaining its true history—which has almost nothing to do with Mark Twain.

"Golf is a good walk spoiled" is another famous Mark Twain quote; it is good enough, in fact, to have inspired the title of a recent book on golf. However, Mark Twain probably never uttered those words. The same can probably be said of: "A banker is a fellow who lends you his umbrella when the sun is shining and wants it back the minute it begins to rain." Another example, "It's better to keep your mouth shut and appear stupid than to open it and remove all doubt," has often been attributed to both Mark Twain and Abraham Lincoln; this may explain why William Dean Howells called Mark Twain "the Lincoln of our literature," but it is possible that neither man ever made that remark. Even better known is: "Everybody talks about the weather, but nobody does anything about it." This line has been elevated from a mere quote attributed to Mark Twain to a modern-day cliché. The jury is not fully in on its authorship, but it appears to have been the invention of Mark Twain's friend Charles Dudley Warner, not Mark Twain himself.

A number of other famous quotes that originated with other people have also come to be associated with Mark Twain. In some cases, however, their fame has developed because Mark Twain repeated them, so they are in this book. Perhaps the best known example is Bill Nye's remark, "I have been told that Wagner's music is better than it sounds" (see "Wagner").

A danger intrinsic to all quote books is the ease with which words taken out of context can be misinterpreted. In selecting and editing extracts for *The Quotable Mark Twain*, I have tried to be careful about not presenting them in ways that might invite misunderstanding; however, the danger is impossible to eliminate entirely. Readers need only exercise some common sense in allowing for the likely contexts of passages in this book. They should also keep in mind that Mark Twain, like anyone else, did not always intend for his words to be taken literally. Often he wrote with deliberate sarcasm, or for ironic effect. Further, what he wrote privately did not necessarily match what he wrote publicly on the same subjects, and what he wrote in fiction did not always agree with what he wrote in essays. To understand his true intentions more fully, there can be no substitute for reading his original texts. Finally, allowance should always be made for the fact that he occasionally changed his mind. *The Quotable Mark Twain* does not contain extracts of every opinion that he had on every subject, but its chronological arrangement of related quotes should help to point up the evolution of his thinking on many topics.

If there is such a thing as a "definitive" collection of Mark Twain quotes, I do not know what it might be—other than his complete works. In assembling *The Quotable Mark Twain* I have tried to keep in mind Mark Twain's own prescription: "a successful book is not made of what is in it, but of what is left out of it." After collecting more than 2,500 quotes, it took me some time to appreciate that something akin to Gresham's Law applies in this field, with the weak material tending to drive out the strong. Eventually, I took Mark Twain's advice and cut about a quarter of what I had collected.

A crucial measure of the power of any opinion is its succinctness—what Mark Twain called the proper proportions of a maxim: "A minimum of sound to a maximum of sense." With this in mind, I have tried to keep individual quotes as concise as possible. Most entries are well under 100 words. If readers find some to be too concise, I can again only recommend the obvious—that they consult the original sources—which I hope they will do in any case.

Editorial notes following this introduction and bibliographical notes at the end of the book explain technical details of its construction. Here, I will merely emphasize that *The Quotable Mark Twain* presents Mark Twain's words with as little modification as possible. The quotes are taken from the most authoritative sources available to me; not a single sentence has been reworded or paraphrased; elisions are made only to save space and are always indicated by ellipses. The occasional words inserted to make sentences read more smoothly are always enclosed by brackets so that they cannot be confused with Mark Twain's own words. In the hope that readers will consult the original texts from which the quotes are taken, every entry is followed by a citation identifying its precise source.

Readers who pay attention to the sources of the quotes will make the happy discovery that Mark Twain's private letters are every bit as witty and profound as what he wrote for publication—and often they are even more interesting. Quotations from his correspondence account for nearly a fifth of the entries in *The Quotable Mark Twain*—despite the fact that the bulk of his letters remain to be published. As this book goes to press, the Mark Twain Project has completed only five of the over twenty volumes of letters that it plans to issue. In exhibiting a fraction of the riches to be found in Mark Twain's correspondence, I hope that this book will help call attention to the Project's continuing need for support so that it can complete its vital work. Only then will anything approximating a "definitive" edition of Mark Twain's quotations become possible.

Chronology

Highlights relating to Mark Twain's writing career

1835 Born Samuel Langhorne Clemens in Florida, Missouri (November 30)

1839–53 Lives in Hannibal, Missouri; spends many summers at uncle's Florida, Missouri, farm

1847 Father, John M. Clemens, dies (March 24)

1848–53 Apprentices as a printer and writes occasional newspaper sketches

1853–56 Works as a printer in St. Louis and eastern cities and writes occasional travel letters for his brother Orion's Keokuk, Iowa, newspaper

1857–61 Pilots steamboats on the Lower Mississippi

1861 Goes to Nevada with his brother, Orion Clemens

1861–62 Prospects in Nevada

1862–64 Holds reporting job in Virginia City, Nevada; begins his professional writing career

1863 Adopts the pen name "Mark Twain" (February)

1864–66 Lives in San Francisco

1864 Reports for the *San Francisco Morning Call*

1864–65 Prospects for gold in California's Tuolumne and Calaveras counties

1865 Widespread publication of the jumping frog story gives him a national reputation

1866 Writes travel letters from Hawaii; begins professional lecturing career on the West Coast

1867 Returns to East Coast (January); publishes *The Celebrated Jumping Frog of Calaveras County and Other Sketches*

1867 Visits Europe and the Holy Land on the *Quaker City*; builds national reputation with travel letters (June–November)

1868–69 Moves about and lectures in the East; buys interest in the *Buffalo Express*

1869 *The Innocents Abroad*

1870 Marries Olivia (Livy) Langdon (February 2)

1870–71 Lives in Buffalo, New York; writes for the *Express*, *Galaxy*, and other publications

1871–91 Lives in Hartford, Connecticut; spends most summers in Elmira, New York, where he does much of his writing

1872 *Roughing It*

1873 *The Gilded Age*

1875 *Sketches, New and Old*

1876 *The Adventures of Tom Sawyer*

1878–79 Travels in Europe

1880 *A Tramp Abroad*

1881 *The Prince and the Pauper*

1882 Revisits the Mississippi River (April–May)

1882 *The Stolen White Elephant, Etc.*

1883 *Life on the Mississippi*

1884 Launches own publishing firm, Charles Webster & Co. (May)

1884 *Adventures of Huckleberry Finn* (English edition)

1884–85 Lectures in Midwest with George Washington Cable

1885 *Adventures of Huckleberry Finn* (U.S. edition)

1889 *A Connecticut Yankee in King Arthur's Court*

1891–95 Lives in Europe with family

1892 *The American Claimant; Merry Tales*

1893 *The £1,000,000 Bank-note and Other New Stories*

1894 Charles Webster & Co. files for bankruptcy (April 18)

1894 *Tom Sawyer Abroad*; *Pudd'nhead Wilson*

1895–96 Lectures around the world

1896–1900 Lives in England and Europe

1896 *Personal Recollections of Joan of Arc*; *Tom Sawyer, Detective*

1896 Oldest daughter, Susy, dies in Hartford (August 18)

1897 *Following the Equator*; *How to Tell a Story and Other Essays*

c. 1897–1908 Works on "Mysterious Stranger" stories and other manuscripts that he never finishes

1900 Returns to the United States after five-year absence (October)

1900 *The Man That Corrupted Hadleyburg and Other Stories and Essays*

1902 *A Double-Barrelled Detective Story*

1903–04 Lives in Florence, Italy

1904 Wife, Livy, dies in Florence (June 5)

1904 *Extracts from Adam's Diary*; *A Dog's Tale*

1905 *King Leopold's Soliloquy*

1906 *Eve's Diary*; *What Is Man?*; *The $30,000 Bequest and Other Stories*

1906–07 Publishes "Chapters from My Autobiography" in *North American Review*

1907 Receives honorary degree from Oxford University (June 26)

1907 *Christian Science*; *A Horse's Tale*

1908–10 Lives in last home near Redding, Connecticut

1909 *Extract from Captain Stormfield's Visit to Heaven*; *Is Shakespeare Dead?*

1910 Dies in Redding, Connecticut (April 21); is buried in Elmira, New York

For a detailed chronology of Mark Twain's life, see the editor's *Mark Twain A to Z* (1995), pp. x–xxiv.

Editorial Notes

capitalization Upper- and lowercasing follows that of the original sources exactly, with the exception that the first word of every quote is capitalized.

character voices Quotes taken directly from dialogue are followed by the names of the speakers—e.g., "—Tom Sawyer."

dates Quotations are arranged chronologically under each headword, with the year of original publication, or composition, given in the left column; source citations give the most precise dates available for letters, speeches, and some other sources.

dates, approximated "c." (Latin *circa*, "about") preceding a date indicates an informed approximation; a question mark following a component of a date (e.g., "November 5?, 1906") indicates that that part of the date is an informed estimate.

dates, letters Dates cited for published letters are those given in the published sources' top matter; occasionally these dates differ from those assigned to postscripts in the same letters.

elisions Elisions (indicated by ellipses) have been kept to a minimum consistent with keeping quotations concise. The following example (see "Afterlife" in text) shows, in shaded type, the irrelevant text that is replaced by ellipses:

> I am sorry for you—very very sorry—but not for him nor for any body who is granted the privilege of prying behind the curtain to see if there is any contrivance there that is half so shabby & poor & foolish as the invention of mortal life.

ellipses [. . .] Ellipses replace elisions from middle or end portions of passages; with rare exceptions, elisions at the beginnings of passages are not indicated.

insertions [*italic*] Italicized insertions contain information that helps to identify references but that is not necessary to make the sentences readable; wherever possible inserted texts are taken from other parts of the passages in which the quotes originally appear.

insertions [roman] Textual insertions are limited to words necessary to make sentences read clearly. All such insertions are made within square brackets, in roman type; as with italic insertions, these added words are taken from Mark Twain's own text wherever possible.

n.d. No date available.

narrative voices Quotes other than dialogue taken from first-person narratives, such as *Huckleberry Finn*, are followed by their narrators' names in brackets—e.g., "—[Huck]."

page references The volume, chapter, and page references to books given in source citations may apply only to the editions listed in the bibliography to which the citations are keyed.

paragraph breaks Original paragraph breaks are usually retained; however, in rare instances in which short paragraphs are run together, ellipses indicate the elision of both text and paragraph breaks.

punctuation Just as Mark Twain Project editions scrupulously follow Mark Twain's eccentric original punctuation, the present book follows the punctuation in its sources.

punctuation, terminal Terminal punctuation follows that in the original texts, except in instances when ellipses replace elided text, or when a bracketed period ("[.]") replaces a question mark made irrelevant by the elision of an interrogative, or when a bracketed period is supplied where the original text lacks punctuation (as in many *N&J* entries).

quotation marks Quotation marks are used only for passages enclosed within quotation marks in the original sources.

source citations Each quote is followed by an abbreviated citation keyed to a book title and description listed in the bibliography at the end of this volume. (Full bibliographical details are given in the text citations for a few sources mentioned only once in this book.)

accident

1901 "Name the greatest of all the inventors. Accident."

(MTP, ts 44, p. 4; MTN, p. 374)

1906 A word which I constantly make use of when I am talking to myself about the chain of incidents which has constituted my life.

(Ibid., p. 387)

1906 I like that word "accident," although it is . . . absolutely destitute of meaning. I like it because it is short and handy and because it answers so well and so conveniently, and so briefly, in designating happenings which we should otherwise have to describe as odd, curious, interesting, and so on.

(Autob/MTIE, p. 386)

1907 "There ain't no such thing as an accident; there ain't nothing happens in the world but what's ordered just so by a wiser power than us, and it's always fur a good purpose . . . whenever a thing happens that you think is an accident you make up your mind it ain't no accident at all—it's a special providence."   —[Jim Blaine]

(Autob/MTIE, p. 221)

actors

1865 I have often wondered, myself, when reading critiques in the papers, what would become of an actor if he tried to follow all the fearfully conflicting advice they contained.

("Answers to Correspondents," ET&S-2, p. 215)

Adam (first man in the Bible)

1859 What a fool old Adam was. Had everything his own way; had succeeded in gaining the love of the best looking girl in the neighborhood, but yet unsatisfied with his conquest he had to eat a miserable little apple.

(Letter to John T. Moore, July 6, 1859, Ltrs-1, p. 91)

1883 Adam is the only solitary celebrity in our family, and the man that misuses him has got to walk over my dead body—or go around, that is all there is to that.

(Speech in Ottawa, May 23, 1883, MT Speaking, p. 179)

1883 To him we owe the two things which are most precious—life, and death.

(Ibid., p. 180)

1894 Adam was but human—this explains it all. He did not want the apple for the apple's sake, he wanted it only because it was forbidden. The mistake was in not forbidding the serpent; then he would have eaten the serpent.   —Pudd'nhead Wilson's Calendar

(Pudd. Wilson, ch. 2, PW&TET, p. 27)

1897 Let us be grateful to Adam our benefactor. He cut us out of the "blessing" of idleness and won for us the "curse" of labor.

—Pudd'nhead Wilson's New Calendar

(Foll. Equat., ch. 33, p. 305)

Adam and Eve

1894 Adam and Eve had many advantages, but the principal one was, that they escaped teething.

—Pudd'nhead Wilson's Calendar

(Pudd. Wilson, ch. 4, PW&TET, p. 52)

1905 I feel for Adam and Eve now, for I know how it was with them. I am existing, broken-hearted, in a Garden of Eden. . . . The Garden of Eden I now know was an unendurable solitude. I know that the advent of the serpent was a welcome change—anything for society.

(Autobiographical dictation, quoted in MT:Biog, ch. 247, p. 1315)

ADAM WAS BUT HUMAN

1910 What I cannot help wishing is, that Adam and Eve had been postponed, and Martin Luther and Joan of Arc put in their place—that splendid pair equipped with temperaments not made of butter, but of asbestos. By neither sugary persuasions nor by hellfire could Satan have beguiled *them* to eat the apple.

("The Turning-Point of My Life," WIM&OPW, *p. 464)*

adjectives

1894 As to the Adjective: when in doubt, strike it out.

—Pudd'nhead Wilson's Calendar

(Pudd. Wilson, ch. 11, PW&TET, *p. 130)*

adultery, Hawaiian

1866 The adultery law has been so amended that each party to the offense is now fined thirty dollars; and I would remark, in passing, that if the crime were invariably detected and the fines collected, the revenues of the Hawaiian Government would probably exceed those of the United States.

(Ltrs-Hawaii, Letter 24, p. 287)

adversity

1897 By trying we can easily learn to endure adversity. Another man's, I mean. —Pudd'nhead Wilson's New Calendar

(Foll. Equat., ch. 39, p. 357)

advertising

1889 Many a small thing has been made large by the right kind of advertising. —[Hank Morgan]

(Conn. Yankee, ch. 22, p. 210)

affection

1874 Affection and devotion are qualities that are able to adorn and render beautiful a character that is otherwise unattractive, and even repulsive.

(Gilded Age, ch. 33, p. 309)

affliction

1878 The only real thing about affliction is the affliction itself—the cause of it is not a thing to be considered; the loss of a king's crown and a young girl's trinket weigh just the same in the scales of the Angel of Calamity.

("The Lost Ear-ring," Fab. of Man, *p. 147)*

African Americans

1865 The "damned naygurs"—this is another descriptive title which has been conferred upon them by a class of our fellow-citizens who persist, in the most short-sighted manner, in being on bad terms with them in the face of the fact that they have got to sing with them in heaven or scorch with them in hell some day in the most familiar and sociable way, and on a footing of most perfect equality . . .

("Mark Twain on the Colored Man," ET&S-2, *p. 248)*

1885 We have ground the manhood out of them, & the shame is ours, not theirs, & we should pay for it.

(Letter to Francis Wayland, Dean, Yale University Law School, December 24, 1885; quoted in Shelley Fisher Fishkin, Lighting Out for the Territory *[New York: Oxford University Press, 1997], p. 101)*

afterlife

1894 I am sorry . . . but not for . . . any body who is granted the privilege of prying behind the curtain to see if there is any contrivance there that is half so shabby & poor & foolish as the invention of mortal life.

(Letter to Mary Fairbanks, July 16, 1894, Ltrs-Fairbanks, pp. 274–275)

age

1879 Age is not determined by years, but by trouble and infirmities of mind and body . . .

(Speech in Boston, December 3, 1879, MT Speaking, p. 136)

1891 Lord save us all from old age & broken health & a hope-tree that has lost the faculty of putting out blossoms.

(Letter to Joe T. Goodman, c. April 1891, Ltrs/Paine, 2:546)

1892 "Whatever a man's age may be, he can reduce it several years by putting a bright-colored flower in his button-hole."   —Sally Sellers

(Amer. Claim., ch. 20, p. 208)

1901 The whole scheme of things is turned wrong end to. Life should begin with age & its privileges and accumulations, & end with youth & its capacity to splendidly enjoy such advantages. As things are now, when in youth a dollar would bring a hundred pleasures, you can't have it. When you are old, you get it & there is nothing worth buying with it then. It's an epitome of life. The first half of it consists of the capacity to enjoy without the chance; the last half consists of the chance without the capacity.

(Letter to Edward L. Dimmitt, July 19, 1901, Ltrs/Paine, 2:709)

1905 I have achieved my seventy years in the usual way: by sticking strictly to a scheme of life which would kill anybody else. It sounds like an exaggeration, but that is really the common rule for attaining old age.

(70th birthday speech in New York City, December 5, 1905, Speeches/Paine, p. 256)

1905 We can't reach old age by another man's road. My habits protect my life, but they would assassinate you.

(Ibid., p. 260)

1906 Before seventy we are merely respected, at best, and we have to behave all the time, or we lose that asset; but after seventy we are respected, esteemed, admired, revered, and don't have to behave unless we want to. When I first knew you, Honored Sir, one of us was hardly even respected.

(Telegram to British prime minister Henry Campbell-Bannerman on the latter's seventieth birthday, August 27, 1906, quoted in MT:Biog, ch. 247, p. 1318)

1907 The fact that I am nearly seventy-two years old does not clearly indicate how old I am, because part of every day—it is with me as with you—you try to describe your age, and you cannot do it. Sometimes you are only

TROUBLE AND INFIRMITIES

5

fifteen. Sometimes you are twenty-five. It is very seldom in a day that I am seventy-two years old.

(Speech in London, July 6, 1907, Speeches/Paine, p. 355)

1908 There has never been an intelligent person of the age of sixty who would consent to live his life over again. His or anyone else's.

("Letters from the Earth," WIM&OPW, p. 428)

1909 "Neither a man nor a boy ever thinks the age he *has* is exactly the best one—he puts the *right* age a few years older or a few years younger than he is."
                                                                         —Sam Bartlett

(Stormfield, ch. 1, p. 53)

Albert, Prince (consort of Queen Victoria)

1872 A most excellent foreign gentleman who was a happy type of the Good, and the Kind, the Well-Meaning, the Mediocre, the Commonplace—and who did no more for his country than five hundred tradesmen did in his own time, whose works are forgotten.

("From an English Notebook," Lets. Earth, pp. 172–173)

Aldrich, Lilian (wife of Thomas Bailey Aldrich)

1908 A strange and vanity-devoured, detestable woman! I do not believe I could ever learn to like her except on a raft at sea with no other provisions in sight.

(Autob/MTIE, p. 293)

Aldrich, Thomas Bailey (writer and friend of Mark Twain)

1904 Aldrich was always witty, always brilliant, if there was anybody present capable of striking his flint at the right angle . . . Aldrich was as sure and prompt and unfailing as the red-hot iron on the blacksmith's anvil—you had only to hit it competently to make it deliver an explosion of sparks. . . .

(NAR, September 21, 1906; Autob/NAR, p. 19)

aliases

1883 Although Smith, Jones, and Johnson are easy names to remember when there is no occasion to remember them, it is next to impossible to recollect them when they are wanted. How do

IMPOSSIBLE TO
RECOLLECT

criminals manage to keep a brand-new *alias* in mind? This is a great mystery.

(Life on Miss., ch. 22, p. 247)

alphabet, English

1906 "The English alphabet is pure insanity. It can hardly spell any word in the language with any large degree of certainty. . . . That alphabet consists of nothing whatever except sillinesses." —Uncle Cadmus

("Simplified Spelling," Lets. Earth, pp. 162–163)

1907 There's not a vowel in it with a definite value, and not a consonant that you can hitch anything to.

(Speech in New York City, December 9, 1907, Speeches/Paine, p. 365)

1907 I ask you to pronounce s-o-w, and you ask me what kind of a one. If we had a sane, determinate alphabet, instead of a hospital of comminuted eunuchs, you would know whether one referred to the act of a man casting the seed over the ploughed land or whether one wished to recall the lady hog and the future ham.

(Ibid., p. 367)

7

altar cloths

1899 The altar-cloth of one aeon is the door-mat of the next.

(MTP, ts 42, p. 71; MTN, p. 346)

ambition

1865 I never had but two **powerful** ambitions in my life. One was to be a pilot, & the other a preacher of the gospel. I accomplished the one & failed in the other, **because** I could not supply myself with the necessary stock in trade—i.e. religion. I have given it up forever. I never had a "call" in that direction, anyhow, & my aspirations were the very ecstasy of presumption.

(Letter to Orion and Mollie Clemens, October 19–20, 1865, Ltrs-1, p. 322)

1906 What is ambition? It is only the desire to be conspicuous. The desire for fame is only the desire to be continuously conspicuous and attract attention and be talked about.

(NAR, April 5, 1907; Autob/NAR, p. 136)

America

1894 It was wonderful to find America, but it would have been more wonderful to miss it.
—Pudd'nhead Wilson's Calendar
*(Pudd. Wilson, **Conclusion**, PW&TET, p. 300)*

American

1879 There is not any name among the world's nationalities that can oversize that one.

(Letter to D. D. Poltier, October 14, 1879, MTSFH, p. 123)

American Publishing Company
(early publisher of Mark Twain's books)

1883 They swindled me out of huge sums of money in the old days, but they do know how to push a book; and besides, I think they are honest people now. I think there was only one thief [*Elisha Bliss*] in the concern, and he is shoveling brimstone now.

(Letter to G. W. Cable, June 4, 1883, Ltrs-Cable, p. 95)

Americans

1895 There isn't a single human characteristic that can be safely labeled "American." There isn't a single human ambition, or religious trend, or drift of thought, or peculiarity of education, or code of principles, or breed of folly, or style of conversation, or preference for a particular subject for discussion, or form of legs or trunk or head or face or expression or complexion, or gait, or dress, or manners, or disposition, or any other human detail, inside or outside, that can rationally be generalized as "American."

("What Paul Bourget Thinks of Us," CT-2, pp. 168–169)

1895 I think that there is but a single specialty with us, only one thing that can be called by the wide name "American." That is the national devotion to ice-water.

(Ibid., p. 172)

1896 *The* American characteristic is Uncourteousness. We are the Impolite Nation. In this detail we stand miles & miles above or below or beyond any other nation, savage or civilized.

(MTP, ts 38, p. 52; MTN, *p. 298)*

1906 We are by long odds the most ill-mannered nation, civilized or savage, that exists on the planet today.

(Autob/MTIE, p. 33)

ancestors

1881 My first American ancestor . . . was an Indian—an early Indian. Your ancestors skinned him alive, and I am an orphan. . . . All those Salem witches were ancestors of mine. Your people made it tropical for them. . . .

The first slave brought into New England out of Africa by your progenitors was an ancestor of mine—for I am of a mixed breed, an infinitely shaded and exquisite Mongrel.

(Speech in Philadelphia, December 22, 1881, Speeches/Paine, *pp. 88–90)*

1890 I used to almost wish I hadn't any ancestors, they were so much trouble to me.

("Jane Lampton Clemens," HF&TS, *p. 87)*

angels

1889 They are always on deck when there is a miracle to the fore—so as to get put in the picture, perhaps. Angels are as fond of that as a fire company; look at the old masters. —[Hank Morgan]

(Conn. Yankee, ch. 22, p. 209)

1900 Their ways are not like our ways; and, besides, human beings are nothing to them; they think they are only freaks.

("The Chronicle of Young Satan," ch. 6, Mys. Stranger Mss., *p. 119)*

1909 "Angels have to go to the earth every day—millions of them—to appear in visions to dying children and good people . . . it's the heft of their business." —Sandy McWilliams

(Stormfield, ch. 2, p. 66)

9

WHEN ANGRY, COUNT . . .

anger

1894 When angry, count four; when very angry, swear.

—Pudd'nhead Wilson's Calendar
(Pudd. Wilson, ch. 10, PW&TET, p. 121)

anniversaries

1896 What ought to be done to the man who invented the celebrating of anniversaries? Mere killing would be too light.

(MTP, ts 38, p. 67; MTN, p. 300)

ants

1880 In the matter of intellect the ant must be a strangely overrated bird. During many summers, now, I have watched him, when I ought to have been in better business, and I have not yet come across a living ant that seemed to have any more sense than a dead one. I refer to the ordinary ant, of course; I have had no experience of those wonderful Swiss and African ones which vote, keep drilled armies, hold slaves, and dispute about religion. Those particular ants may be all that the naturalist paints them, but I am persuaded that the average ant is a sham.

(Tramp Abroad, ch. 22, p. 215)

1906 As a thinker and planner the ant is the equal of any savage race of men; as a self-educated specialist in several arts she is the superior of any savage race of men; and in one or two high mental qualities she is above the reach of any man, savage or civilized!   —Old Man

("What Is Man?," ch. 6, WIM&OPW, p. 193)

apprentice work

1878 Every man must *learn* his trade—not pick it up. God requires that he learn it by slow & painful processes. The apprentice-hand, in blacksmithing, in medicine, in literature, in everything, is a thing that can't be hidden. It always shows.

But happily there is a market for apprentice work, else the "Innocents Abroad" would have had no sale.

(Letter to Orion Clemens, March 23, 1878, Ltrs/Paine, 1:322)

approval

1880 . . . is approval the proper word? I find it is the one I most value here in the household, & seldomest get.

(Letter to W. D. Howells, May 6–7, 1880, Ltrs-Howells, 1:307)

1897 We can secure other people's approval, if we do right and try hard; but our own is worth a hundred of it, and no way has been found out of securing that.   —Pudd'nhead Wilson's New Calendar

(Foll. Equat., ch. 14, p. 151)

1901 Each man is afraid of his neighbor's disapproval—a thing which, to the general run of the human race, is more dreaded than wounds and death.

("The United States of Lyncherdom," E&E, pp. 244–245)

April First

1894 This is the day upon which we are reminded of what we are on the other three hundred and sixty-four.

—Pudd'nhead Wilson's Calendar

(Pudd. Wilson, ch. 21, PW&TET, p. 278)

architects

1874 Architects cannot teach nature anything.

("A Memorable Midnight Experience," E&E, p. 4)

argument

1889 Arguments have no chance against petrified training; they wear it as little as the waves wear a cliff.   —[Hank Morgan]

(Conn. Yankee, ch. 17, p. 155)

aristocracy

1889 *Any* kind of royalty, howsoever modified, *any* kind of aristocracy, however pruned, is rightly an insult; but if you are born and brought up

under that sort of arrangement you probably never find it out for yourself, and don't believe it when somebody else tells you.

—[Hank Morgan]

(Conn. Yankee, ch. 8, p. 64)

1889 A privileged class, an aristocracy, is but a band of slaveholders
under another name.

(Ibid., ch. 25, p. 239)

1906 We have to be despised by somebody whom we regard as above
us, or we are not happy; we have to have somebody to worship and envy,
or we cannot be content. In America we manifest this in all the ancient
and customary ways. In public we scoff at titles and hereditary privilege, but privately we hanker after them, and when we get a chance we
buy them for cash and a daughter.

(NAR, January 4, 1907; Autob/NAR, p. 80)

armor

1889 A man that is packed away like that, is a nut that isn't worth the
cracking, there is so little of the meat, when you get down to it, by comparison with the shell.

(Conn. Yankee, ch. 11, p. 95)

Arno River, Italy

1869 It is popular to admire the Arno. It is a great historical creek with
four feet in the channel and some scows floating around. It would be a
very plausible river if they would pump some water into it.

(Inn. Abroad, ch. 24, p. 247)

art

1867 The very point in a picture that fascinates me with its beauty, is
to the cultured artist a monstrous crime against the laws of coloring; and
the very flush that charms me in a lovely face, is, to the critical surgeon,
nothing but a sign hung out to advertise a decaying lung. Accursed be
all such knowledge. I want none of it.

(Letter to Alta, May 28, 1867; MTTB, p. 238)

1869 It vexes me to hear people talk so glibly of "feeling," "expression," "tone," and those other easily acquired and inexpensive technicalities of art that make such a fine show in conversations concerning pictures. There is not one man in seventy-five hundred that can tell *what* a pictured face is intended to express.

(*Inn. Abroad, ch. 19, p. 193*)

1878 I understand good art to be, that way of representing a thing on canvas wh[ich] shall be farthest from resembling anything in heaven or on earth or in the waters under the earth.

In good art, a correct complexion is the color of a lobster, or of a bleached tripe or of a chimney sweep—there are no intermediates or modifications.

(*N&J-2, p. 241*)

UNDERSTANDING GOOD ART

1891 Whenever I enjoy anything in art it means that it is mighty poor. The private knowledge of this fact has saved me from going to pieces with enthusiasm in front of many and many a chromo.

(*"At the Shrine of St. Wagner," WIM&OE, p. 227*)

Arthur, King (legendary sixth-century king of England)

1889 He wasn't a very heavy weight, intellectually. His head was an hour-glass; it could stow an idea, but it had to do it a grain at a time, not the whole idea at once. —[Hank Morgan]

(*Conn. Yankee, ch. 28, p. 276*)

artists

1893 "The merit of many a great artist has never been acknowledged until after he was starved and dead. This has happened so often that I make bold to found a law upon it. This law: that the merit of *every* great

13

unknown and neglected artist must and will be recognized, and his pictures climb to high prices after his death." —Carl

("Is He Living or Is He Dead?," CT-2, *p. 113)*

assassination

1890 Assassination of a crowned head whenever & wherever opportunity offers, should be the first article of all subjects' religion.

(N&J-3, p. 540)

asses

1894 There is no character, howsoever good and fine, but it can be destroyed by ridicule, howsoever poor and witless. Observe the ass, for instance: his character is about perfect, he is the choicest spirit among all the humbler animals, yet see what ridicule has brought him to. Instead of feeling complimented when we are called an ass, we are left in doubt.

(Pudd. Wilson, "A Whisper to the Reader," p. 15)

1896 It is no harm to be an ass, if one is content to bray and not kick.

(Joan of Arc, bk. 2, ch. 3, PW&TET, p. 83)

1899 Mrs. Pilgrim was a kind-hearted creature who didn't know anything, but didn't know she didn't know anything, and this protected her from embarrassment. . . . She had good instincts and was an ass, and this made her welcome everywhere.

("Indiantown," WWD&OSW, p. 162)

1902 None but an ass pays a compliment & asks a favor at the same time. There are many asses.

(MTP, ts 45, p. 43)

Associated Press

1906 There are only two forces that can carry light to all corners of the globe—only two—the sun in the heavens and the Associated Press down here.

(Speech in New York City, September 19, 1906, Speeches/Paine, p. 315)

asteroids

1888 At bottom I don't really mind comets so much, but somehow I have always been down on asteroids. There is nothing mature about them; I wouldn't sit up nights, the way that man does, if I could get a basketful of them.

(Speech about Yale, c. late 1888, Speeches/Paine, *p. 144)*

Athens, Greece

1867 Athens by moonlight! When I forget it I shall be dead—not before.

(N&J-1, p. 391)

Atlantic Monthly (literary journal)

1906 A place which would make any novel respectable and any author noteworthy.

(NAR, December 1907; Autob/NAR, p. 235)

audiences

1883 When an audience do not complain, it is a compliment, & when they *do* it is a compliment, too, if unaccompanied by violence.

(Letter to G. W. Cable, January 15, 1883, Ltrs-Cable, *p. 89)*

1900 I knew the audiences would come forward & shake hands with you—that one infallible sign of sincere approval. In all my life, wherever it failed me I left the hall sick & ashamed, knowing what it meant.

(Letter to W. D. Howells, January 25, 1900,
Ltrs-Howells, *2:715)*

1906 I know all about audiences. They believe everything you say—except when you are telling the truth.

(Letter to New York Times, April 15, 1906,
MTSFH, *p. 215)*

SINCERE APPROVAL

15

1908 You ought never to have any part of the audience behind you; you never can tell what they are going to do.

(Speech in New York City, April 18, 1908, Speeches/Paine, *p. 386)*

Austen, Jane (English novelist)

1897 Jane Austen's books, too, are absent from this [*ship's*] library. Just that one omission alone would make a fairly good library out of a library that hadn't a book in it.

(Foll. Equat., ch. 62, p. 615)

1909 I could read his [*Poe's*] prose on salary, but not Jane's. Jane is entirely impossible. It seems a great pity that they allowed her to die a natural death.

(Letter to W. D. Howells, January 18, 1909, Ltrs-Howells, *2:841)*

Australia

1897 Australian history is almost always picturesque; indeed, it is so curious and strange, that it is itself the chiefest novelty the country has to offer, and so it pushes the other novelties into second and third place. It does not read like history, but like the most beautiful lies. And all of a fresh new sort, no mouldy old ones.

(Foll. Equat., ch. 16, p. 169)

Austria

1898 The [*Austrian*] empire is made up of health resorts; it distributes health to the whole world. Its waters are all medicinal. They are bottled and sent throughout the earth; the natives themselves drink beer. This is self-sacrifice, apparently.

("At the Appetite Cure," MTCH&c, *p. 147)*

authenticity

1868 There is nothing that makes me prouder than to be regarded by intelligent people as "authentic." A name I have coveted so long—& secured at last! *I* don't care anything about being humorous, or poetical, or eloquent, or anything of that kind—the end & aim of my ambition is to be authentic—is to be considered authentic.

(Letter to Mary Fairbanks, February 20, 1868, Ltrs-2, *p. 189)*

authority

1896 A thing that is backed by the cumulative experience of centuries naturally gets nearer and nearer to being proof all the time; and if this continue and continue, it will some day become authority—and authority is a bedded rock, and will abide.

(Joan of Arc, bk. 1, ch. 2, pp. 11–12)

authors

1867 [New authors] always think they know more than anybody else when they are getting out their first book. Nobody can tell *them* anything.

("The Facts Concerning the Recent Resignation," CT-1, p. 242)

1894 There are three infallible ways of pleasing an author, and the three form a rising scale of compliment: 1, to tell him you have read one of his books; 2, to tell him you have read all of his books; 3, to ask him to let you read the manuscript of his forthcoming book. No. 1 admits you to his respect; No. 2 admits you to his admiration; No. 3 carries you clear into his heart.   —Pudd'nhead Wilson's Calendar

(Pudd. Wilson, ch. 11, PW&TET, p. 130)

1906 An author values a compliment even when it comes from a source of doubtful competency.

(Autob/MTIE, p. 183)

authorship

1887 Authorship is not a Trade, it is an inspiration; Authorship does not keep an Office, its habitation is all out under the sky, and everywhere the winds are blowing and the sun is shining and the creatures of God are free. Now then, since I have no Trade and keep no Office, I am not taxable . . .

("A Petition to the Queen of England," How to Tell a Story, p. 238)

autobiography

1887 Apparently no narrative that tells the facts of a man's life in the man's own words, can be uninteresting.

(Letter to Olivia Clemens, July 26, 1887, Ltrs-Love, p. 249)

17

1904 The truest of all books; for while it inevitably consists mainly of extinctions of the truth, shirkings of the truth, partial revealments of the truth, with hardly an instance of plain straight truth, the remorseless truth *is* there, between the lines, where the author-cat is raking dust upon it which hides from the disinterested spectator neither it nor its smell.

(Letter to W. D. Howells, March 14, 1904, Ltrs-Howells, 2:782)

1907 An autobiography is the most treacherous thing there is. It lets out every secret its author is trying to keep; it lets the truth shine unobstructed through every harmless little deception he tries to play; it pitilessly exposes him as a tin hero worshipping himself as Big Metal every time he tries to do the modest-unconsciousness act before the reader.

("Christian Science," bk. 2, ch. 1, WIM&OPW, p. 266)

autobiography, Mark Twain's

1885 My Autobiography is pretty freely dictated, but my idea is to jack-plane it a little before I die, some day or other; I mean the rude construction and rotten grammar.

(Letter to Henry Ward Beecher, September 11, 1885, Ltrs/Paine, 2:462)

1886 If one's autobiography may be called a book—in fact mine will be nearer a library.

(Letter to Mary Fairbanks, November 16, 1886, Ltrs-Fairbanks, p. 258)

1906 I intend that this autobiography shall become a model for all future autobiographies when it is published, after my death, and I also intend that it shall be read and admired a good many centuries because of its form and method—a form and method whereby the past and the present are constantly brought face to face, resulting in contrasts which newly fire up the interest of all along, like contact of flint with steel.

(NAR, September 7, 1906; Autob/NAR, p. 3)

1906 It is a system which follows no charted course and is not going to follow any such course. It is a system which is a complete and purposed jumble—a course which begins nowhere, follows no specified route, and can never reach an end while I am alive, for the reason that, if I should talk to the stenographer two hours a day for a hundred years, I should still never be able to set down a tenth part of the things which have interested me in my lifetime.

(Ibid., p. 4)

1906 I don't care for my other books, now, but I dote on this one as Adam used to dote on a fresh new deformed child after he was 900 years old & wasn't expecting any more surprises.

(Letter to W. D. Howells, June 17, 1906, Ltrs-Howells, *2:811)*

1907 In this Autobiography I shall keep in mind the fact that I am speaking from the grave. I am literally speaking from the grave, because I shall be dead when the book issues from the press. I speak from the grave rather than with my living tongue, for a good reason: I can speak thence freely.

(Autob/MTA, Preface, 1:xv)

1907 Now, then, that is the tale. Some of it is true.

(NAR, December 1907; Autob/NAR, p. 242)

autographs

1879 It is wonderful how that little "per" does take the stuffing out of an autograph.

(Letter to W. D. Howells, October 27, 1879, Ltrs-Howells, *1:277)*

babies

1865 And so you think a baby is a thing of beauty and a joy forever? Well, the idea is pleasing, but not original—every cow thinks the same of its own calf. . . . But really . . . I find that the correctness of your assertion does not manifest itself in all cases. A sore-faced baby with a neglected nose cannot be conscientiously regarded as a thing of beauty, and inasmuch as babyhood spans but three short years, no baby is competent to be a joy "forever."

("Answers to Correspondents," ET&S-2, *p. 204)*

1879 We haven't all had the good fortune to be ladies; we haven't all been generals, or poets, or statesmen; but when the toast works down to the babies, we stand on common ground, for we've all been babies.

(Speech in Chicago, November 13, 1879, MT Speaking, *p. 131)*

1879 The idea that a *baby* doesn't amount to anything! Why, *one* baby is just a house and a front yard full by itself. *One* baby can furnish more business than you and your whole Interior Department can attend to. He is enterprising, irrepressible, brimful of lawless activities. Do what you please, you can't make him stay on the reservation. Sufficient unto the day is one baby—as long as you are in your right mind don't you ever pray for twins. Twins amount to a permanent riot; and there ain't any real difference between triplets and an insurrection.

(Ibid., pp. 132–133)

baggage

1889 None but a lunatic would separate himself from his baggage.
(Letter to Pamela A. Moffett, October 9, 1889, Ltrs/Paine, *2:519)*

Balboa, Vasco Nuñez de (Spanish explorer)

1866 That infatuated old ass . . . named his great discovery "Pacific"— thus uttering a lie which will go on deceiving generation after generation of students while the old ocean lasts.

(Ltrs-Hawaii, Letter 2, p. 10)

banquets

1907 Probably the most fatiguing thing in the world except ditchdigging. It is the insanest of all recreations. The inventor of it overlooked no detail that could furnish weariness, distress, harassment, and acute and long-sustained misery of mind and body.

(Autob/MTIE, p. 320)

barbers

1867 I think they have sent agents far and near and drummed up all the worthless barbers in the world and set them up in New York. I believe they sharpen their razors on the curbstone. They snatch all the beard out of your face in about two minutes, swab your jaws a little with a damp rag, put a microscopic drop of oil on your hair, give it one rub forward, another backward, and a third sideways, stack it up in a ragged pile on top of your head like a Street Commissioner's monument, and let you go. And you go, hoping your beard will never grow again.

(Letter to Alta, *February 23, 1867;* MTTB, *p. 109)*

1871 All things change except barbers, the ways of barbers, and the surroundings of barbers. These never change. What one experiences in a barber's shop the first time he enters one is what he always experiences in barbers' shops afterward till the end of his days.

("About Barbers," CT-1, *p. 524)*

UNCHANGING BARBERS

21

barkeepers

1872 In Nevada, for a time, the lawyer, the editor, the banker, the chief desperado, the chief gambler, and the saloon-keeper, occupied the same level in society, and it was the highest. The cheapest and easiest way to become an influential man and be looked up to by the community at large, was to stand behind a bar, wear a cluster-diamond pin, and sell whisky. I am not sure but that the saloon-keeper held a shade higher rank than any other member of society. His opinion had weight.

(Rough. It, ch. 48, p. 318)

1909 "I've always noticed this peculiarity about a dead barkeeper—he not only expects all hands to turn out when he arrives [in heaven], but he expects to be received with a torchlight procession."

—Sandy McWilliams

(Stormfield, ch. 2, p. 69)

baseball

1889 The very symbol, the outward and visible expression of the drive, and push, and rush and struggle of the raging, tearing, booming nineteenth century!

(Speech in New York City, April 5, 1889, MT Speaking, *p. 244)*

baths, curative

1891 It is a mistake that there is no bath that will cure people's manners. But drowning would help.

("Marienbad—A Health Factory," E&E, *p. 126)*

bats

1897–98 I think a bat is as friendly a bird as there is. . . . A bat is beautifully soft and silky; I do not know any creature that is pleasanter to the touch, or is more grateful for caressings, if offered in the right spirit.

(NAR, March 1, 1907; Autob/NAR, *p. 117)*

Bayreuth, Germany

1891 Photographs fade, bric-à-brac gets lost, busts of Wagner get broken, but once you absorb a Bayreuth-restaurant meal, it is your possession and your property until the time comes to embalm the rest of you.

("At the Shrine of St. Wagner," WIM&OE, *p. 223)*

beard

1909 It performs no useful function; it is a nuisance and a discomfort; all nations hate it; all nations persecute it with the razor.

("The Lowest Animal," Lets. Earth, *p. 231)*

No useful function

beauty

1869 One frequently only finds out how really beautiful a really beautiful woman is after considerable acquaintance with her; and the rule applies to Niagara Falls, to majestic mountains and to mosques—especially to mosques.

(Inn. Abroad, ch. 54, pp. 578-579)

1892 In true beauty, more depends upon right location and judicious distribution of feature than upon multiplicity of them.

(Amer. Claim., ch. 5, p. 62)

beds

1897 Many ships have good beds, but no ship has *very* good ones. In the matter of beds all ships have been badly edited, ignorantly edited, from the beginning. The selection of beds is given to some hearty, strong-backed, self-made man, when it ought to be given to a frail woman accustomed from girlhood to backaches and insomnia. Nothing is so rare, on either side of the ocean, as a perfect bed; nothing is so difficult to make. Some of the hotels on both sides provide it, but no ship ever does or ever did. In Noah's Ark the beds were simply scandalous. Noah set the fashion, and it will endure in one degree of modification or another till the next flood.

(Foll. Equat., ch. 64, p. 630)

Beecher, Thomas K.
(Protestant minister and friend of Mark Twain)

1870 A man who abhors the lauding of people, either dead or alive, except in dignified and simple language, and then only for merits which they actually possessed or possess, not merits which they merely ought to have possessed.

("Post-Mortem Poetry," $30k Bequest, p. 251)

bells

1878 Church bells are usually hateful things . . .

(N&J-2, p. 80)

1880 Most church-bells in the world are of poor quality, and have a harsh and rasping sound which upsets the temper and produces much sin . . . There is much more profanity in America on Sunday than in all the other six days of the week put together, and it is of a more bitter and malignant character than the week-day profanity, too. It is produced by the cracked-pot clangor of the cheap church bells.

(Tramp Abroad, ch. 36, p. 401)

Benares, India (religious center)

1897 The city of Benares is in effect just a big church, a religious hive, whose every cell is a temple, a shrine or a mosque, and whose every conceivable earthly and heavenly good is procurable under one roof, so to speak—a sort of Army and Navy Stores, theologically stocked.

(Ibid., ch. 51, p. 484)

benefit of clergy

n.d. Half-rate on the railroad.

(More Max., p. 6)

Berlin, Germany

1892 It is a new city; the newest I have ever seen. Chicago would seem venerable beside it; for there are many old-looking districts in Chicago, but not many in Berlin. The main mass of the city looks as if it had been built last week, the rest of it has a just perceptibly graver tone, and looks as if it might be six or even eight months old.

("The German Chicago," £1m Bank-note, pp. 210–211)

1892 Berlin is the European Chicago.

(Ibid., p. 246)

Bermuda

1907 In the sweet and unvexed spiritual atmosphere of the Bermudas one does not achieve gray hairs at forty-eight.

(NAR, August 2, 1907; Autob/NAR, p. 196)

1910 There are no newspapers, no telegrams, no mobiles, no trolleys, no trams, no tramps, no railways, no theatres, no noise, no lectures, no riots, no murders, no fires, no burglaries, no politics, no offences of any kind, no follies but church, & I don't go there.

(Letter to Elizabeth Wallace, March 12, 1910, quoted in Ltrs-Howells, 2:853)

Bernhardt, Sarah (French actress)

1905 Madame Bernhardt is so marvelously young. Why, she is the youngest person I ever saw, except myself.

(Speech in New York City, December 18, 1905, MT Speaking, *p. 468)*

Bible, the

1869 It is hard to make a choice of the most beautiful passage in a book which is so gemmed with beautiful passages as the Bible . . .

(Inn. Abroad, ch. 47, p. 492)

1890 The Christian's Bible is a drug store. Its contents remain the same; but the medical practice changes.

("Bible Teaching and Religious Practice," WIM&OPW, *p. 71)*

1890 The world has corrected the Bible. The Church never corrects it; and also never fails to drop in at the tail of the procession—and take the credit of the correction.

(Ibid., p. 73)

25

1903 When one reads Bibles one is less surprised at what the Deity knows than at what He doesn't know.

(MTP, ts 46, p. 34; MTN, *p. 385)*

1908 It is full of interest. It has noble poetry in it; and some clever fables; and some blood-drenched history; and some good morals; and a wealth of obscenity; and upwards of a thousand lies.

("Letters from the Earth," WIM&OPW, *p. 412)*

bigamists

n.d. Some of us cannot be optimists, but all of us can be bigamists.

(More Max., p. 12)

FULL OF INTEREST

bilgewater

1893 Where bilge-water is, only the dead can enjoy life. This is on account of the smell. In the presence of bilge-water, Limburger cheese becomes odorless and ashamed.

("About All Kinds of Ships," CT-2, p. 92)

billiards

1906 The game of billiards has destroyed my naturally sweet disposition.

(Speech in New York City, April 24, 1906, Speeches/Paine, p. 302)

1906 The billiard table, as a Sabbath-breaker can beat any coal-breaker in Pennsylvania and give it 30 in the game.

(Letter to Emilie Rogers, November 5?, 1906, Ltrs-Rogers, p. 620)

1906 I wonder why a man should prefer a good billiard-table to a poor one; and why he should prefer straight cues to crooked ones; and why he should prefer round balls to chipped ones; and why he should prefer a level table to one that slants; and why he should prefer responsive cushions to the dull and unresponsive kind. I wonder at these things, because when we examine the matter we find that the essentials involved in billiards are as competently and exhaustively furnished by a bad billiard outfit as they are by the best one. One of the essentials is amusement. Very well, if there is any more amusement to be gotten out of the one outfit than out of the other, the facts are in favor of the bad outfit.

(NAR, November 1907; Autob/NAR, pp. 225–226)

biography

1886 What is biography? Unadorned romance. What is romance? Adorned biography. Adorn it less & it will be better than it is.

(N&J-3, p. 239)

c. 1907 Biographies are but the clothes and buttons of the man—the biography of the man himself cannot be written.

(Autob/MTA, 1:2)

birds

1866 Wisdom teaches us that none but birds should go out early, and that not even birds should do it unless they are out of worms.

(Letter to Territorial Enterprise, *January 1866,* MTSF, *p. 186)*

birth, Mark Twain's

1897–98 I do not remember anything about it. I was postponed— postponed to Missouri. Missouri was an unknown new State and needed attractions.

(NAR, September 7, 1906; Autob/NAR, *p. 7)*

1897–98 My parents removed to Missouri in the early thirties; I do not remember just when, for I was not born then, and cared nothing for such things. . . . The home was made in the wee village of Florida, in Monroe County, and I was born there in 1835. The village contained a hundred people and I increased the population by one per cent. It is more than the best man in history ever did for any other town. It may not be modest in me to refer to this, but it is true. There is no record of a person doing as much—not even Shakespeare. But I did it for Florida, and it shows that I could have done it for any place—even London, I suppose.

(NAR, March 1, 1907; Autob/NAR, *p. 112)*

blackbirds

1897 The blackbird is a perfect gentleman, in deportment and attire, and is not noisy, I believe, except when holding religious services and political conventions in a tree . . .

(Foll. Equat., ch. 38, p. 354)

Blaine, Jim (character in *Roughing It*)

1872 His situation was such that even the most fastidious could find no fault with it—he was tranquilly, serenely, symmetrically drunk—not a hiccup to mar his voice, not a cloud upon his brain thick enough to obscure his memory.

(Rough. It, ch. 53, p. 361)

IGNORANT, UNWASHED,
INSUFFICIENTLY FED

Blankenship, Tom
(boyhood friend of Mark Twain)

1906 In "Huckleberry Finn" I have drawn Frank [i.e., *Tom Blankenship*] exactly as he was. He was ignorant, unwashed, insufficiently fed; but he had as good a heart as ever any boy had. His liberties were totally unrestricted. He was the only really independent person—boy or man—in the community, and by consequence he was tranquilly and continuously happy, and was envied by all the rest of us. We liked him; we enjoyed his society. And as his society was forbidden us by our parents, the prohibition trebled and quadrupled its value, and there fore we sought and got more of his society than of any other boy's.

("Chapters from My Autobiography," NAR, *August 2, 1907; Autob/NAR, p. 191; Mark Twain evidently forgot Blankenship's name when he dictated this passage.)*

blessing

c. 1905 If you would beseech a blessing upon yourself, beware! lest without intent you invoke a curse upon a neighbor at the same time.
—The Stranger
("The War Prayer," Pen Warmed Up, *p. 110)*

bliss

1878 That exquisite and indescribable tingling of the scalp which has no name, but might fairly be called bliss, and which gives one the sense of being under a spell while it lasts—a spell which one longs to remain under, and dreads to see broken.

("Simon Wheeler, Detective," ch. 4, S&B, *p. 345)*

Bliss, Elisha (officer of the American Publishing Company)

1870 He is wise. He is one of the smartest business men in America . . .
(Letter to Orion Clemens, November 5, 1870, Ltrs-4, p. 220)

1906 A tall, lean, skinny, yellow, toothless bald-headed, rat-eyed professional liar and scoundrel. . . . He was a most repulsive creature. . . .

It is my belief that Bliss never did an honest thing in his life, when he had a chance to do a dishonest one.

(Autobiographical dictation, February 21, 1906, quoted in Ltrs-Publs, *p. 1)*

1906 He has been dead a quarter of a century now. My bitterness against him has faded away and disappeared. I feel only compassion for him and if I could send him a fan I would.

(Autob/MTIE, p. 155)

Bliss, Frank E.
(son of Elisha Bliss and one of Mark Twain's publishers)

1897 He is the most *indefinite* man that ever was. He is intangible. He is a gas, and nothing but a pressure of 250,000 atmospheres can solidify him.

(Letter to H. H. Rogers, June 3, 1897, Ltrs-Rogers, *p. 277)*

bloodhounds

1896 There ain't any dog that's got a lovelier disposition than a bloodhound . . .   —[Huck Finn]

(Tom Sawyer Det., ch. 9, p. 152)

29

"blow"

1864 A blow at sea may be a breeze, a gale or a tempest, but a blow on land is very likely to be an assault and battery.

(Article in Call, *August 3, 1864;* Cl. of Call, *p. 157)*

bluejays

1880 "There's more *to* a bluejay than any other creature. He has got more moods, and more different kinds of feelings . . .

You may call a jay a bird. Well, so he is, in a measure—because he's got feathers on him, and don't belong to no church, perhaps; but otherwise he is just as much a human as you be. . . . A jay's gifts, and instincts, and feelings, and interests, cover the whole ground. A jay hasn't got any more principle than a Congressman. A jay will lie, a jay will steal, a jay will deceive, a jay will betray; and four times out of five, a jay will go back on his solemnest promise."   —Jim Baker

(Tramp Abroad, ch. 2, pp. 36–37)

blush

1891 A thing that does not commend a person to a policeman.

("Down the Rhône," E&E, p. 153)

1897 Man is the Only Animal that Blushes. Or needs to.

—Pudd'nhead Wilson's New Calendar

(Foll. Equat., ch. 27, p. 256)

Boer War

1900 A sordid & criminal war, & in every way shameful & excuseless. Every day I write (in my head) bitter magazine articles about it, but I have to stop with that. For England must not fall: it would mean an inundation of Russian & German political degradations which would envelop the globe & steep it in a sort of Middle-Age night & slavery which would last till Christ comes again—which I hope he will not do; he made trouble enough before. Even wrong—& she is wrong—England must be upheld.

(Letter to W. D. Howells, January 25, 1900, Ltrs-Howells, 2:715-716)

1900 I notice that God is on both sides in this war; thus history repeats itself.

(Ibid., p. 347)

Boers (South Africans of Dutch descent)

1897 First catch your Boer, then kick him.

—Pudd'nhead Wilson's New Calendar

(Foll. Equat., ch. 67, p. 667)

Book of Mormon

1872 The book is a curiosity to me, it is such a pretentious affair, and yet so "slow," so sleepy; such an insipid mess of inspiration. It is chloroform in print. If Joseph Smith composed this book, the act was a miracle—keeping awake while he did it was, at any rate. . . .

The book seems to be merely a prosy detail of imaginary history, with the Old Testament for a model; followed by a tedious plagiarism of the New Testament.

(Rough. It, ch. 16, p. 107)

books

1853 If books are not good company, where will I find it?

(Letter to mother, August 31, 1853, Ltrs-1, p. 10)

1887 Great books are weighed and measured by their style and matter, and not by the trimmings and shadings of their grammar.

("General Grant's Grammar," MT:Biog, p. 1652)

1897 A successful book is not made of what is *in* it, but of what is left *out* of it.

(Letter to H. H. Rogers, April 26–28, 1897, Ltrs-Rogers, p. 274)

1906 In a century we have produced two hundred and twenty thousand books; not a bathtub-full of them are still alive and marketable.

(Autob/MTIE, p. 376)

books, Mark Twain's own

1870 My book [*Roughing It*] is not named yet. Have to write it first— you wouldn't make a garment for an animal till you have seen the animal, would you?

(Letter to Mary Fairbanks, October 13, 1870, Ltrs-4, p. 208)

1886 My books are water; those of the great geniuses is wine. Everybody drinks water.

(N&J-3, p. 238; for another version, see letter to W. D. Howells, February 15, 1887, Ltrs-Howells, 2:587)

c. 1890 I have never tried in even one single little instance, to help cultivate the cultivated classes. I was not equipped for it, either by native gifts or training. And I never had any ambition in that direction, but always hunted for bigger game—the masses. I have seldom deliberately tried to instruct them, but have done my best to entertain them.

(Letter to Andrew Lang, c. 1890, Ltrs/Paine, 2:527)

1893 I think it [*Pudd'nhead Wilson*] is good, and I thought the [American] Claimant bad, when I saw it in print; but as for any real judgment, I think I am destitute of it.

(Letter to Fred J. Hall, February 3, 1893, Ltrs-Publs, p. 337)

1908 My favorites are: Joan of Arc; Prince and Pauper; Huck Finn; Tom Sawyer.

(Letter to Margaret Blackmer, September 18, 1908, Ltrs-Angelfish, p. 205)

Borgia, Lucrezia
(member of powerful Italian family during Renaissance period)

1869 A lady for whom I have always entertained the highest respect, on account of her rare histrionic capabilities, her opulence in solid gold goblets made of gilded wood, her high distinction as an operatic screamer, and the facility with which she could order a sextuple funeral and get the corpses ready for it.

(Inn. Abroad, ch. 19, p. 185)

Boston, Massachusetts

1871 There is no section in America half so good to live in as splendid old New England—& there is no city on this continent so lovely & lovable as Boston . . .

(Letter to Mollie Clemens, January 5?, 1871, Ltrs-4, p. 298)

boys

1889 In my experience, boys are the same in all ages. They don't respect anything, they don't care for anything or anybody.   —[Hank Morgan]

(Conn. Yankee, ch. 11, p. 96)

1897–98 We think boys are rude, unsensitive animals but it is not so in all cases. Each boy has one or two sensitive spots, and if you can find out where they are located you have only to touch them and you can scorch him as with fire.

(NAR, September 21, 1906; Autob/NAR, p. 17)

brains

1863 Doesn't it strike you that there are more brains and fewer oysters in my head than a casual acquaintance with me would lead one to suppose?

("Mark Twain—More of Him," ET&S-1, p. 311)

1865 I know a good deal more than a boiled carrot, though I may not appear to.

(Letter to Bishop Francis Lister Hawks, March 1865, ET&S-2, *p. 151)*

1879 A certain amount of pride always goes along with a teaspoonful of brains, and . . . this pride protects a man from deliberately stealing other people's ideas. That is what a teaspoonful of brains will do for a man—and admirers had often told me I had nearly a basketful—though they were rather reserved as to the size of the basket.

(Speech in Boston, December 3, 1879, MT Speaking, *p. 135)*

1898 A man's brain (intellect) is stored powder; it cannot touch itself off; the fire must come from outside.

(MTP, ts 40, p. 29; MTN, *p. 365)*

bravery

1882 Is anybody brave when he has no *audience*?

(N&J-2, p. 497)

1896 "When a person in Joan of Arc's position tells a man he is brave, he *believes* it; and *believing* it is enough; in fact, to believe yourself brave is to *be* brave; it is the one only essential thing."

—*Sieur Louis de Conte (*Joan of Arc, *bk. 2, ch. 11, p. 140)*

1906 A brave man does not *create* his bravery. He is entitled to no personal credit for possessing it. It is born to him.   —Old Man

("What Is Man?," ch. 1, WIM&OPW, *p. 131)*

breath

1897 Each person is born to one possession which outvalues all his others—his last breath.   —Pudd'nhead Wilson's New Calendar

(Foll. Equat., ch. 42, p. 386)

breeding

1889 There isn't anything you can't stand, if you are only born and bred to it.   —[Hank Morgan]

(Conn. Yankee, ch. 8, p. 67)

1899 Good breeding consists in concealing how much we think of ourselves & how little we think of the other person.

(MTP, ts 42, p. 65; MTN, p. 345)

brokers

1864 I consider that a broker goes according to the instincts that are in him, and means no harm, and fulfils his mission according to his lights, and has a right to live, and be happy in a general way, and be protected by the law to some extent, just the same as a better man. I consider that brokers come into the world with souls—I am satisfied they do; and if they wear them out in the course of a longer career of stock-jobbing, have they not a right to come in at the eleventh hour and get themselves half-soled, like old boots, and be saved at last?

("Daniel in the Lion's Den—and Out Again All Right," ET&S-2, *p. 101)*

1864 I have been told by a friend, whose judgment I respect, that they are not any more unprincipled than they look.

(Ibid., p. 107)

No proper pet

brontosaurus

1906 "I said a pet twenty-one feet high and eighty-four feet long would be no proper thing to have about the place, because, even with the best intentions and without meaning any harm, it could sit down on the house and mash it, for any one could see by the look of its eye that it was absent-minded." —Adam

(Eve's Diary, pp. 73-75)

Brooks, Noah (editor of the *Alta California*, for which Mark Twain wrote travel letters during the 1860s)

1904 Noah Brooks was . . . a man of sterling character and equipped with a right heart, also a good historian where facts were not essential.

(NAR, *July 5, 1907; Autob/NAR, p. 184*)

brotherhood

1897 The universal brotherhood of man is our most precious possession, what there is of it.   —Pudd'nhead Wilson's New Calendar

(Foll. Equat., *ch. 27, p. 256*)

Buffalo, New York

1870 Our [*Buffalo*] home . . . is the daintiest, & the most exquisite & enchanting that can be found in all America—& the longer we know it the more fascinating it grows & the firmer the hold it fastens upon each fettered sense. It is perfect. Perfect in all its dimensions, proportions & appointments.

(Letter to his mother-in-law, February 20, 1870, Ltrs-4, *p. 75*)

1871 Leave Buffalo *out* . . . I think they hate me there, for hating their town.

(Letter to James Redpath, June 28, 1871, Ltrs-4, *p. 420*)

burglars

1908 It is only circumstances & environment that make burglars, therefore anybody is liable to be one. I don't quite know how I have managed to escape myself.

(Letter to Marjorie Breckenridge, December 1, 1908, Ltrs-Angelfish, *p. 238*)

burlesque

1870 To write a burlesque so wild that its pretended facts will not be accepted in perfect good faith by somebody, is very nearly an impossible thing to do.

("A Couple of Sad Experiences," CT-1, *pp. 388–389*)

AN INTERESTING PERSON

36

burning at the stake

1898 To my mind there is nothing that makes a person interesting like his being about to get burnt up. —[August Feldner]

(No. 44, ch. 14, p. 79)

business

1893 I am terribly tired of business. I am by nature and disposition unfitted for it and I want to get out of it.

(Letter to Fred J. Hall, June 2, 1893, Ltrs-Publs, p. 343)

1901 My axiom is, to succeed in business: avoid my example.

(Speech in New York City, March 30, 1901, Speeches/Paine, p. 238)

busyness

1868 To be *busy* is a man's only happiness—& I *am*—otherwise I should die.

(Letter to Orion Clemens, February 21, 1868, Ltrs-2, p. 198)

Byron, Lord (early-19th-century English poet)

n.d. What a man sees in the human race is merely himself in the deep and honest privacy of his own heart. Byron despised the race because he despised himself. I feel as Byron did, and for the same reason.

(Marginal note in book, quoted in MT:Biog, ch. 287, p. 1539)

cabinet officers

1868 In cases where a Cabinet officer refuses to resign and will not be removed; may we not put a barrel of powder under him and blast him from his position? The thing looks feasible to me. It is expeditious, unostentatious, and singularly effective.

(Article in Washington Star, *c. January 1868;* MTSFH, *p. 51)*

Cable, George Washington
(writer with whom Mark Twain went on lecture tour in 1884–85)

1882 When it comes down to moral honesty, limpid innocence, and utterly blemishless piety, the apostles were mere policemen to Cable . . .

(Letter to W. D. Howells, November 4, 1882, Ltrs-Howells, *1:419)*

1883 The South's finest literary genius . . . In him the South has found a masterly delineator of its interior life and its history.

(Life on Miss., ch. 44, p. 442)

1885 His body is small, but it is much too large for his soul. He is the pitifulest human louse I have ever known.

(Letter to Olivia Clemens, February 17, 1885, Ltrs-Love, *p. 237)*

1885 In him & his person I have learned to hate all religions. He has taught me to abhor & detest the Sabbath-day & hunt up new & troublesome ways to dishonor it.

(Letter to W. D. Howells, February 27, 1885, Ltrs-Howells, *2:520)*

1895 I liked you in spite of your religion; & I always said to myself that a man that could be good & kindly with that kind of a load on him was entitled to homage—& I *paid* it. And I have always said, & still maintain, that as a railroad-comrade you were perfect—the only railroad-comrade in the world that a man of moods & frets & uncertainties of disposition could travel with, a third of a year, and never weary of his company.

(Letter to G. W. Cable, June 25, 1895, Ltrs-Cable, *p. 111)*

Caesar, Julius (ancient Roman general and statesman)

1864 A feeling of regret has often come over me that I was not reporting in Rome when Caesar was killed—reporting on an evening paper and the only one in the city, and getting at least twelve hours ahead of the morning paper boys with this most magnificent "item" that ever fell to the lot of the craft.

("The Killing of Julius Caesar 'Localized,'" ET&S-2, p. 110)

Cain (Genesis figure who murdered his brother, Abel)

1871   *To the Late Cain.*
This Book is Dedicated:
Not on account of respect for his memory, for it merits little
respect; not on account of sympathy with him, for his bloody
deed placed him without the pale of sympathy, strictly
speaking: but out of a mere human commiseration for him
that it was his misfortune to live in a dark age that knew not
the beneficent Insanity Plea.

(Unused dedication for Roughing It, *quoted in letter to Elisha Bliss,*
May 15, 1871, Ltrs-4, pp. 391–392)

California

1862 Hell is peopled with honester men than California.
(Letter to Orion and Mollie Clemens, October 21, 1862, Ltrs-1, p. 241)

1863 How I *hate* everything that looks, or tastes, or smells like California!—and how I hate everybody that loves the cursed State! Californians hate Missourians,—consequently I take great pains to let the public know that "Mark Twain" hails from there.
(Letter to mother and sister, April 11–12, 1863, Ltrs-1, p. 248)

1872 No land with an unvarying climate can be very beautiful.
(Rough. It, ch. 56, p. 386)

camels

1869 When he is down on all his knees, flat on his breast to receive his load, he looks something like a goose swimming; and when he is upright he looks like an ostrich with an extra set of legs. Camels are not beautiful, and their long under lip gives them an exceedingly "gallus" expression. . . . They are not particular about their diet. They would eat a tombstone if they could bite it.

(*Inn. Abroad, ch. 42, p. 439*)

1869 I can not think of any thing, now, more certain to make one shudder, than to have a soft-footed camel sneak up behind him and touch him on the ear with its cold, flabby under-lip.

(*Ibid., ch. 50, p. 526*)

Canadian publishers

1878 I suppose they are all born pirates.

(*Letter to W. D. Howells, June 27, 1878, Ltrs-Howells, 1:236*)

1881 Those sons of up there will steal anything they can get their hands on—possible suits for damages and felony would be no more restraint upon them, I think, than would the presence of a young lady be upon a stud-horse who had just found a mare unprotected by international copyright. In the one case, theft and piracy is the fateful doom; in the other, copulation and adultery.

(*Letter to James R. Osgood, October 28, 1881, Ltrs-Publs, p. 144*)

Canty, Tom (pauper boy of *The Prince and the Pauper*)

1881 Tom's reading and dreaming about princely life wrought such a strong effect upon him that he began to *act* the prince, unconsciously. His speech and manners became curiously ceremonious and courtly, to the vast admiration and amusement of his intimates. But Tom's influence among these young people began to grow, now, day by day; and in time he came to be looked up to, by them, with a sort of wondering awe, as a superior being. He seemed to know so much! and he could do such marvelous things! and withal, he was so deep and wise! Tom's remarks, and Tom's performances, were reported by the boys to their elders, and these also presently began to discuss Tom Canty, and to regard him as a most gifted and extraordinary creature. Full grown people brought

A tough statement.

Not particular about diet

39

their perplexities to Tom for solution, and were often astonished at the wit and wisdom of his decisions. In fact, he was become a hero to all who knew him except his own family—these, only, saw nothing in him.

(Prince & Pauper, ch. 2, p. 8)

capital

1899 Spending one's capital is feeding a dog on his own tail.

(MTP, ts 42, p. 65; MTN, p. 345)

capital punishment

1879 I disfavor capital punishment.

(N&J-2, p. 300)

1887 All crimes should be punished with humiliations—life-long public exposure in ridiculous & grotesque situations—& never in any other way. Death/Gallows makes a hero of the villain, & he is envied by some spectators & by & by imitated.

(N&J-3, p. 346)

1888 Hanging is not based on knowledge of human nature. When death penalty was instituted, revenge was the object, & passionate quick revenge. But now when our object is deterrent, *not* punitive, the death pen[alty] is an anachronism & is irrational & ridiculous. It is the opposite of a deterrent, often.

(Ibid., p. 347)

Carlyle, Thomas (English historian)

1877 [Carlyle's *History of the French Revolution*:] One of the greatest creations that ever flowed from a pen.

(Letter to Mollie Fairbanks, August 6, 1877, Ltrs-Fairbanks, p. 207)

1885 Carlyle, whose life was one long stomach-ache & one ceaseless wail over it.

(N&J-3, p. 114)

1906 Carlyle said "a lie cannot live." It shows that he did not know how to tell them.

(NAR, January 5, 1907; Autob/NAR, p. 89)

Carnegie, Andrew

(Scottish-American industrialist and philanthropist)

1907 If I were going to describe him in a phrase, I think I should call him the Human Being Unconcealed. He is just like the rest of the human race but with this difference, that the rest of the race try to conceal what they are and succeed, whereas Andrew tries to conceal what he is but doesn't succeed.

(Autob/MTIE, p. 36)

1907 He is an astonishing man in his genuine modesty as regards the large things he has done, and in his juvenile delight in trivialities that feed his vanity.

(Ibid., p. 42)

Carroll, Lewis (author of *Alice in Wonderland*)

1906 He was only interesting to look at, for he was the stillest and shyest full-grown man I have ever met except "Uncle Remus."

(NAR, November 16, 1906; Autob/NAR, p. 64)

Carson City, Nevada

1864 What Carson needs is a few more undertakers—there is vacant land enough here for a thousand cemeteries.

(Letter to Territorial Enterprise, February 5, 1864, MTOE, p. 152)

Casanova (18th-century Italian adventurer and writer)

1880 The supremest charm in Casanova's Memoires . . . is, that he frankly, flowingly, & felicitously tells the dirtiest & vilest & most contemptible things on himself, without ever suspecting that they are other than things which the reader will admire & applaud.

(Letter to Orion Clemens, February 26, 1880, MT:Bus. Man, pp. 143-144)

caste

1905 Each commonality-caste is a little aristocracy by itself, and each has a caste to look down upon, plum all the way down to the bottom, where you find the burglar looking down upon the house-renting landlord, and the landlord looking down upon his oily-brown-wigged pal the real estate agent—which is the bottom, so far as ascertained.

("Three Thousand Years among the Microbes," ch. 15,
WWD&OSW, p. 528)

cats

1873 Next to a wife whom I idolise, give me a cat—an *old* cat, with kittens.

(Letter to Olivia Clemens, April 26, 1873, Ltrs-5, p. 358)

1890 We had nineteen cats at one time, in 1845. And there wasn't one in the lot that had any character; not one that had a merit, except the cheap and tawdry merit of being unfortunate.

("Jane Lampton Clemens," HF&TS, p. 85)

1894 One of the most striking differences between a cat and a lie is that a cat has only nine lives.

—Pudd'nhead Wilson's Calendar
(Pudd. Wilson, ch. 7, PW&TET, p. 86)

c. 1894 Of all God's creatures there is only one that cannot be made the slave of the lash. That one is the cat. If man could be crossed with the cat it would improve man, but it would deteriorate the cat.

(MTP, ts 33, pp. 54–55; MTN, p. 236)

NO SLAVE TO THE LASH

cauliflower

1894 Training is everything. The peach was once a bitter almond; cauliflower is nothing but cabbage with a college education.

—Pudd'nhead Wilson's Calendar
(Pudd. Wilson, ch. 5, PW&TET, p. 67)

Celebrated Jumping Frog and Other Sketches, The
(Mark Twain's first published book)

1867 It will have a truly gorgeous gold frog on the back of it, and that frog alone will be worth the money. I don't know but what it would be well to publish the frog and leave the book out.

(Letter to Alta, April 19, 1867; MTTB, p. 158)

1867 The book is out, & is handsome. It is full of damnable errors of grammar & deadly inconsistencies of spelling in the Frog sketch because I was away & did not read the proofs—but be a friend & say nothing about these things.

(Letter to Bret Harte, May 1, 1867, Ltrs-2, p. 39)

celebrity

1906 What a boy or a youth longs for more than for any other thing. He would be a clown in a circus, he would be a pirate, he would sell himself to Satan, in order to attract attention and be talked about and envied. True, it is the same with every grown-up person.

(Autob/MTIE, p. 233)

chameleons

1897 His eyes are his exhibition feature. A couple of skinny cones project from the sides of his head, with a wee shiny bead of an eye set in the apex of each; and these cones turn bodily like pivot-guns and point every-which-way, and they are independent of each other; each has its own exclusive machinery. When I am behind him and C. in front of him, he whirls one eye rearwards and the other forwards—which gives him a most Congressional expression (one eye on the constituency and one on the swag).

(Foll. Equat., ch. 65, p. 645)

change

1882 A change of air and scene invigorates infallibly all but the dead, and 'livens them up, too, I suppose, if they land in the wrong end of the here-after.

(Letter to Pamela A. Moffett, December 2, 1882, MT:Bus. Man, p. 206)

1906 It is the *sudden* changes—in principles, morals, religions, fashions, and tastes—that have the best chance of winning in our day.

(Article in Harper's Weekly, *April 7, 1906; MTSFH, p. 209)*

character

1902 "There must be something fearfully disintegrating to character in the loss of money. Men suffer other bereavements and keep up; but when they lose their money, straightway the structure which we call character, and are so proud of, and have such placid confidence in, and think is granite, begins to crumble and waste away, and then . . . the granite that had been sand once is sand again!"   —Andrew Harrison

("Which Was It?," ch. 1, WWD&OSW, p. 195.
Ellipsis is in original text.)

1907 One must keep up one's character. Earn a character first if you can, and if you can't, then assume one.

(Speech in New York City, December 22, 1907, MT Speaking, p. 600)

characters, fictional

after 1874 If Byron—if any man—draws 50 characters, they are all himself—50 shades, 50 moods, of his own character. And when the man draws them well why do they stir my admiration? Because they are me—I recognize myself.

(Marginal note in book, quoted in MT:Biog, ch. 287, p. 1540)

1883 When I find a well-drawn character in fiction or biography, I generally take a warm personal interest in him, for the reason that I have known him before—met him on the river.

(Life on Miss., ch. 18, p. 217)

charity

1873 A dignified and respectworthy thing, and there is small merit about it and less grace when it don't cost anything.

(Letter to Hartford Courant, January 29, 1873, MTSFH, p. 73)

1905 In all the ages, three-fourths of the support of the great charities has been conscience-money.

("A Humane Word from Satan," CT-2, p. 656)

chauffeur

1905 A good enough word when strictly confined to its modest and rightful place . . . but when we come to apply it to the admiral of the thunderous 'mobile or of the mighty elephant, we realize that it is inadequate. No . . . chauffeur is not the thing, mahout is the thing—mahout is the word we need. Besides, there is only one way of saying mahout, whereas there are nine ways of saying chauffeur, and none of them right.

(Letter to Harper's Weekly, December 24, 1905, MTSFH, pp. 206–207)

cheerfulness

1870 A healthy and wholesome cheerfulness is not necessarily impossible to *any* occupation.

("The Undertaker's Chat," SN&O, p. 249)

1896 The best way to cheer yourself up is to try to cheer somebody else up.

(MTP, ts 39, p. 27; MTN, p. 310)

chestnut

n.d. The ordinary chestnut can beget a sickly and reluctant laugh, but it takes a horse chestnut to fetch the gorgeous big horse-laugh.

(More Max., p. 11)

Chicago, Illinois

1883 A city where they are always rubbing the lamp, and fetching up the genii, and contriving and achieving new impossibilities. It is hopeless for the occasional visitor to try to keep up with Chicago—she outgrows his prophecies faster than he can make them. She is always a novelty, for she is never the Chicago you saw when you passed through the last time.

(Life on Miss., ch. 60, p. 593)

1897 SATAN (impatiently) to NEW-COMER. The trouble with you Chicago people is, that you think you are the best people down here; whereas you are merely the most numerous.

—Pudd'nhead Wilson's New Calendar
(Foll. Equat., ch. 60, p. 582)

chicken, fried

1897 The North seldom tries to fry chicken, and this is well; the art cannot be learned north of the line of Mason and Dixon, nor anywhere in Europe. This is not hearsay; it is experience that is speaking.

(Autob/MTA, 1:97)

children

n.d. The burnt child shuns the fire. Until next day.

(More Max., p. 6)

45

n.d. It is a wise child that knows its own father, and an unusual one that unreservedly approves of him.

(Ibid., p. 9)

Chinese, the

1872 They are a harmless race when white men either let them alone or treat them no worse than dogs; in fact they are almost entirely harmless anyhow, for they seldom think of resenting the vilest insults or the cruelest injuries. They are quiet, peaceable, tractable, free from drunkenness, and they are as industrious as the day is long. A disorderly Chinaman is rare, and a lazy one does not exist.

*(*Rough. It*, ch. 54, p. 369)*

choirs, church

1876 There was once a church choir that was not ill-bred, but I have forgotten where it was, now. It was a great many years ago, and I can scarcely remember anything about it, but I think it was in some foreign country.

*(*Tom Sawyer*, ch. 5, p. 38)*

Christ

1878 Neither Howells nor I believe in hell or the divinity of the Savior—but no matter, the Savior is none the less a sacred Personage and a man should have no desire or disposition to refer to him lightly, profanely or otherwise than with the profoundest reverence.

(Letter to Orion Clemens, March 23, 1878, Ltrs/Paine, *1:323)*

AN ILL-BRED CHOIR

1896 If Christ was God, then the crucifixion is without dignity, it is merely ridiculous. For to endure several hours' pain is nothing heroic in a God in any case . . .

(MTP, ts 37, p. 49; MTN, *p. 290)*

1897 If Christ were here now, there is one thing he would *not* be—A Christian.

(MTP, ts 41, p. 43; MTN, *p. 328)*

1898–99 There has been only one [Christia]n. They caught him & crucified him—early.

(MTP, ts 42, p. 63; MTN, p. 344)

Christian Science

1907 From end to end of the Christian Science literature not a single (material) thing in the world is conceded to be real, except the Dollar.

("Christian Science," bk. 1, ch. 7, WIM&OPW, p. 249)

1907 It is a reasonably safe guess that in America in 1920 there will be 10,000,000 Christian Scientists, and 3,000,000 in Great Britain; that these figures will be trebled in 1930; that in America in 1920 the Christian Scientists will be a political force, in 1930 politically formidable, and in 1940 the governing power in the Republic—to remain that, permanently. And I think it a reasonable guess that the Trust . . . will then be the most insolent and unscrupulous and tyrannical politico-religious master that has dominated a people since the palmy days of the Inquisition.

(Ibid., p. 251)

47

1909 My view of the matter has not changed. To-wit, that Christian Science is valuable; that it has just the same value now that it had when Mrs. Eddy stole it from [*Phineas Parkhurst*] Quimby; that its healing principle (its most valuable asset) possesses the same force now that it possessed a million years before Quimby was born.

(Letter to J. Wylie Smith, August 7, 1909, Ltrs/Paine, 2:832)

Christianity

1899 Christianity will doubtless still survive in the earth ten centuries hence—stuffed & in a museum.

(MTP, ts 42, p. 69; MTN, p. 346)

Christmas

1907 The xmas holidays have this high value: that they remind Forgetters of the Forgotten, & repair damaged relationships.

(Letter to Carlotta Welles, December 30, 1907, Ltrs-Angelfish, p. 89)

ENEMY TO HUMAN LIBERTY

church

1889 A united Church . . . makes a mighty power, the mightiest conceivable, and then when it by and by gets into selfish hands, as it is always bound to do, it means death to human liberty, and paralysis to human thought.

—[Hank Morgan]
(Conn. Yankee, ch. 10, p. 81)

1889 Any Established Church is an established crime, an established slave-pen . . . —[Hank Morgan]
(Ibid., ch. 16, p. 139)

1889 An Established Church is only a political machine; it was invented for that, it is nursed, coddled, preserved for that; it is an enemy to human liberty, & does no good which it could not better do in a split-up & scattered condition. —[Hank Morgan]
(Ibid., ch. 18, p. 161)

cigars

1893 No one can tell me what is a good cigar—for me. I am the only judge. . . . To me, almost any cigar is good that nobody else will smoke, and to me almost all cigars are bad that other people consider good.
("Concerning Tobacco," WIM&OE, pp. 275, 277)

1905 I know a bad cigar better than anybody else; I judge by the price only; if it costs above five cents I know it to be either foreign or half foreign, and unsmokeable. By me.
(Letter to L. M. Powers, November 9, 1905, Ltrs/Paine, 2:784)

1905 I have made it a rule never to smoke more than one cigar at a time. I have no other restriction as regards smoking.
(Speech in New York City, December 5, 1905, Speeches/Paine, p. 258)

circumstance

1865 There is no use in a man trying to maintain a particular tone of feeling—a certain mood—when circumstances and surroundings are against him. He may hold out for a while, but in the end he is bound to succumb to those circumstances and surroundings . . . There is no use in a man trying to be a cynical, stoical humbug in the society of a lovely girl; and there is no use in his hoping to keep up a boisterous flow of spirits all through a Quaker meeting; and there is no use in his trying to remain cheerful and wide awake in a chloroform factory.

(Article in Dramatic Chronicle, *November 3, 1865; ET&S-2, p. 486)*

1902 Circumstances make men, not men circumstances.

(MTP, ts 45, p. 43; MTN, p. 379)

1905 We are mere creatures of Circumstance. Circumstance is master, we are his slaves. We cannot do as we desire, we have to be humbly obedient and do as Circumstances command. Command—that is the word; Circumstance never requests, he always commands: then we do the thing, and think *we* have planned it. When our circumstances change, we have to change with them, we cannot help it.

("Three Thousand Years among the Microbes," ch. 8, WWD&OSW, p. 470)

1906 That stupendous power—*Circumstance*—which moves by laws of its own, regardless of parties and policies, and whose decrees are final, and must be obeyed by all—and will be.

(NAR, January 4, 1907; Autob/NAR, p. 79)

1910 Necessity is a *Circumstance*; Circumstance is man's master—and when Circumstance commands, he must obey . . .

("The Turning-Point of My Life," WIM&OPW, p. 459)

circumstantial evidence

1894 Even the clearest and most perfect circumstantial evidence is likely to be at fault, after all, and therefore ought to be received with great caution. Take the case of any pencil, sharpened by any woman: if you have witnesses, you will find she did it with a knife; but if you take simply the aspect of the pencil, you will say she did it with her teeth.

—Pudd'nhead Wilson's Calendar

(Pudd. Wilson, ch. 20, PW&TET, p. 263)

citizenship

1906 Citizenship is what makes a republic; monarchies can get along without it.

(Speech in New York City, March 4, 1906, Speeches/Paine, p. 281)

civil war

1897 *"Civil* war! Dey ain' no sich war. De idear!—people dat's good en kind en polite en b'long to de church a-marchin' out en slashin' en choppin' en cussin' en shootin' one another—lan', *I* knowed dey warn't no sich thing." —Jim

("Tom Sawyer's Conspiracy," HF&TS, *ch. 1, pp. 136–137)*

Civil War, U.S.

1883 In the South, the war is what A.D. is elsewhere: they date from it. All day long you hear things "placed" as having happened since the waw; or du'in' the waw; or right aftah the waw; or 'bout two yeahs or five yeahs or ten yeahs befo' the waw or aftah the waw.

(Life on Miss., ch. 45, p. 454)

1897 It don't seem right and fair that Harriet Beacher Stow [*Harriet Beecher Stowe*] and all them other second-handers gets all the credit of starting that war and you never hear Tom Sawyer mentioned in the histories ransack them how you will, and yet he was the first one that thought of it. —[Huck Finn]

("Tom Sawyer's Conspiracy," HF&TS, *ch. 1, p. 138)*

DISCUSSING THE "WAW"

civilization

n.d. Civilization is a limitless multiplication of unnecessary necessaries.

(More Max., p. 6)

1878 The *one* evidence of high civilization must surely be to *not lie.*

(N&J-2, p. 176)

1890 What is a "real" civilization? . . . any system which has in it any one of these things, to wit, human slavery, despotic government, inequality, numerous and brutal punishments for crimes, superstition almost universal, ignorance almost universal, and dirt and poverty almost universal—is not a real civilization, and any system which has none of them, is.

. . . How old is real civilization? The answer is easy and unassailable. . . . since civilization must surely mean the humanizing of a people, not a class—there is today but one real civilization in the world, and it is not yet thirty years old. We made the trip and hoisted the flag when we disposed of our slavery.

(Speech in Boston, April 27, 1890, MT Speaking, p. 258)

1900 My idea of our civilization is that it is a shabby poor thing & full of cruelties, vanities, arrogancies, meannesses, & hypocrisies. As for the word, I hate the sound of it, for it conveys a lie; & as for the thing itself, I wish it was in hell, where it belongs.

(Letter to J. H. Twichell, January 27, 1900, Ltrs/Paine, 2:695)

1901 Is it, perhaps, possible that there are two kinds of Civilization— one for home consumption and one for the heathen market?

("To the Person Sitting in Darkness," E&E, p. 257)

Civita Vecchia, Italy

1869 This is the first Italian town I have seen which does not appear to have a patron saint. I suppose no saint but the one that went up in the chariot of fire could stand the climate.

(Inn. Abroad, ch. 25, p. 265)

claimants

1909 There was never a Claimant that couldn't get a hearing, nor one that couldn't accumulate a rapturous following, no matter how flimsy and apparently unauthentic his claim might be.

(ISD, ch. 1, p. 2)

clarity

1900 Plain clarity is better than ornate obscurity.

(Draft letter to unnamed editor, quoted in MT:Biog, ch. 207, p. 1092)

class

1889 The master minds of all nations, in all ages, have sprung, in afflu- ent multitude, from the mass of the nation, and from the mass of the nation only—not from its privileged classes; and so, no matter what the nation's intellectual grade was, whether high or low, the bulk of its abil- ity was in the long ranks of its nameless and its poor . . .

—[Hank Morgan]

(Conn. Yankee, ch. 25, p. 242)

classic

1897 A book which people praise and don't read.

—Pudd'nhead Wilson's New Calendar
(Foll. Equat., ch. 25, p. 241)

Clemens, Henry (Mark Twain's younger brother)

1906 I never knew Henry to do a vicious thing toward me, or toward anyone else—but he frequently did righteous ones that cost me as heavily. It was his duty to report me, when I needed reporting and neglected to do it myself, and he was very faithful in discharging that duty. He is "Sid" in "Tom Sawyer." But Sid was not Henry. Henry was a very much finer and better boy than ever Sid was.

(NAR, November 2, 1906; Autob/NAR, p. 51)

Clemens, Jane Lampton (Mark Twain's mother)

1869 My most patient reader and most charitable critic.

(Inn. Abroad, Dedication, p. iii)

1871 Ma is a wonderfully winning woman, with her gentle simplicity & her never-failing goodness of heart & yearning interest in all creatures & their smallest joys & sorrows. It is why she is such a good letter-writer—this warm personal interest of hers in every thing that others have at heart. Whatever is important to another is important to her.

(Letter to Olivia L. Clemens, August 10, 1871, Ltrs-4, pp. 443-444)

1885 The unconsciously pathetic is her talent—& how richly she is endowed with it—& how naturally eloquent she is when it is to the fore! What books she could have written!—& now the world has lost them.

(Letter to Olivia Clemens, January 14, 1885, Ltrs-Love, p. 229)

1890 Technically speaking, she had no career; but she had a character, and it was of a fine and striking and lovable sort. . . .

The greatest difference which I find between her and the rest of the people whom I have known, is this, and it is a remarkable one: those others felt a strong interest in a few things, whereas to the very day of her death she felt a strong interest in the whole world and everything and everybody in it.

("Jane Lampton Clemens," HF&TS, pp. 82–83)

Clemens, Olivia Langdon (Mark Twain's wife)

1868 That girl is one in a million. She is fearfully & wonderfully made.

(Letter to Mary Fairbanks, December 24, 1868, Ltrs-2, p. 349)

1870 She is much the most beautiful girl I ever saw (I said that before she was anything to me, & so it is worthy of all belief) & she is the *best* girl, & the sweetest, & the gentlest, & the daintiest, & the most modest & unpretentious, & the wisest in all things she should be wise in & the most ignorant in all matters it would not grace her to know, & she is sensible & quick, & loving & faithful, forgiving, full of charity—& her beautiful life is ordered by a religion that is all kindliness & unselfishness. . . .

She is the very most perfect gem of womankind that ever I saw in my life—& I will stand by that remark till I die.

(Letter to William Bowen, February 6, 1870, Ltrs-4, pp. 51–52)

1893 I am notorious, but you are great—that is the difference between *us.*

(Letter to Olivia Clemens, September 13, 1893, Ltrs-Love, p. 268)

1902 She has been the best friend I have ever had, and that is saying a good deal.

(Speech in New York City, November 28, 1902, Speeches/Paine, p. 252)

1906 I have compared and contrasted her with hundreds of persons, and my conviction remains that hers was the most perfect character I have ever met.

(NAR, October 5, 1906; Autob/NAR, p. 23)

Clemens, Olivia L., death of (June 5, 1904)

1904 She was all our riches and she is gone; she was our breath, she was our life, and now we are nothing.

(Letter to Gilder family, June 7, 1904, MT:Biog, ch. 232, p. 1221)

1904 I am a man without a country. Wherever Livy was, that was my country. And now she is gone.

(Letter to Charles Langdon, June 19, 1904, WWD&OSW, p. 23)

1904 In my life there have been 68 Junes—but how vague and colorless 67 of them are contrasted with the deep blackness of this one.

(MTN, p. 388)

Clemens, Orion (Mark Twain's older brother)

1862 I wish he had been endowed with some conception of music—for, with his diabolical notions of time and tune he is worse than the itch when he begins to whistle.

(Letter to mother, April 2, 1862, Ltrs-1, p. 180)

1870 There isn't money enough in America to get him to do a dishonest act—whereas I am different.

(Letter to Elisha Bliss, November 5, 1870, Ltrs-4, p. 223)

1879 I don't believe that that character exists in literature in so well developed a condition as it exists in Orion's person. . . . Orion is as good & ridiculous a soul as ever was.

(Letter to W. D. Howells, January 21, 1879, Ltrs-Howells, 1:246)

1880 Orion's head is as full of projects as ever, but there is one merciful provision—he will never stick to one of them long enough to injure himself.

(Letter to mother and sister, 1880, MT:Bus. Man, p. 146)

1906 One of his characteristics was eagerness. He woke with an eagerness about some matter or other every morning; it consumed him all day; it perished in the night and he was on fire with a fresh new interest next morning before he could get his clothes on. He exploited in this way three hundred and sixty-five red-hot new eagernesses every year of his life.

(NAR, January 18, 1907; Autob/NAR, p. 90)

1906 He was correspondingly erratic in his politics—Whig to-day, Democrat next week, and anything fresh that he could find in the political market the week after. I may remark here that throughout his long life he was always trading religions and enjoying the change of scenery. I will also remark that his sincerity was never doubted; his truthfulness was never doubted; and in matters of business and money his honesty was never questioned. Notwithstanding his forever-recurring caprices and changes, his principles were high, always high, and absolutely unshakable. He was the strangest compound that ever got mixed in a human mould.

(Ibid., p. 91)

1906 I think he was the only person I have ever known in whom pessimism and optimism were lodged in exactly equal proportions. Except in the matter of grounded principle, he was as unstable as water. You could dash his spirits with a single word; you could raise them into the sky again with another one. . . .

He was so eager to be approved, so girlishly anxious to be approved by anybody and everybody, without discrimination, that he was commonly ready to forsake his notions opinions, and convictions at a moment's notice in order to get the approval of any person who disagreed with them. . . . He was always truthful; he was always sincere; he was always honest and honorable. But in light matters—matters of small consequence, like religion and politics and such things—he never acquired a conviction that could survive a disapproving remark from a cat.

(Ibid., pp. 91-92)

1906 He was treasurer of all the benevolent institutions; he took care of the money and other property of widows and orphans; he never lost a cent for anybody, and never made one for himself.

(NAR, February 15, 1907; Autob/NAR, p. 108)

Clemens, Samuel L. (Mark Twain himself)

1863 I lead an easy life, though, & I don't care a cent whether school keeps or not. Everybody knows me, & I fare like a prince wherever I go, be it on this side of the mountains [*Nevada*] or the other [*California*]. And I am proud to say that I am the most conceited ass in the Territory.

(Letter to mother and sister, April 16, 1863, Ltrs-1, p. 264)

1877 Ah, well, I am a great & sublime fool. But then I am God's fool, & all His works must be contemplated with respect.

(Letter to W. D. Howells, December 28?, 1877, Ltrs-Howells, 1:215)

1881 I am a border-ruffian from the State of Missouri. I am a Connecticut Yankee by adoption. In me, you have Missouri morals, Connecticut culture; this, gentlemen, is the combination which makes the perfect man.

(Speech in Philadelphia, December 22, 1881, Speeches/Paine, p. 88)

1886 I am . . . made merely in the image of God, but not otherwise resembling him enough to be mistaken for him by anybody but a very near-sighted person.

(Letter to Pamela A. Moffett, c. mid-July 1886, MT:Bus. Man, p. 362)

1887 Twenty-four years ago, I was strangely handsome. The remains of it are still visible through the rifts of time. I was so handsome that human activities ceased as if spellbound when I came in view, & even inanimate things stopped to look—like locomotives & district messenger boys & so-on.

(Unmailed letter to W. R. Ward, September 8, 1887, Ltrs/Paine, 2:477)

1890 I have never seen an opinion of me in print which was as low down as my private opinion of myself.

(Letter to Charles Fairbanks, June 25, 1890, Ltrs-Fairbanks, p. 265)

1891 I have been an author for 20 years & an ass for 55.

(Fragment of letter to unnamed correspondent,
after February 1891, Ltrs/Paine, 2:543)

1902 Yes, you are right—I am a moralist in disguise; it gets me into heaps of trouble when I go thrashing around in political questions.

(Letter to Helene Picard, February 22, 1902, Ltrs/Paine, 2:719)

1907 I am the human race compacted and crammed into a single suit of clothes but quite able to represent its entire massed multitude in all its moods and inspirations.

(Ibid., p. 95)

Clemens, Susy

(Mark Twain's oldest daughter, who died at twenty-four)

1896 She was a poet—a poet who[se] song died unsung.

(MTP, ts 39, p. 45; MTN, p. 315)

1896 It kills me to think of the books that Susy would have written, and that I shall never read now. This family has lost its prodigy. . . . only we have seen the flash and play of that imperial intellect at its best.

(Letter to H. H. Rogers, September 10, 1896, Ltrs-Rogers, p. 235)

1896 A rare creature; the rarest that has been reared in Hartford in this generation. And Livy knew it, and you knew it . . . And I also was of the number, but not in the same degree—for she was above my duller comprehension. I merely knew that she was my superior in fineness of mind, in the delicacy and subtlety of her intellect, but to fully measure her I was not competent.

(Letter to J. H. Twichell, September 27, 1896, Ltrs/Paine, 2:635)

Clemens, Susy, news of her death (August 18, 1896)

1906 It is one of the mysteries of our nature that a man, all unprepared, can receive a thunder-stroke like that and live. There is but one reasonable explanation of it. The intellect is stunned by the shock, and but gropingly gathers the meaning of the words. The power to realize their full import is mercifully wanting. The mind has a dumb sense of vast loss—that is all. It will take mind and memory months, and possibly years, to gather together the details, and thus learn and know the whole extent of the loss.

(NAR, October 5, 1906; Autob/NAR, p. 26)

clergymen

1880 The average clergyman, in all countries and of all denominations, is a very bad reader. One would think he would at least learn how to read the Lord's Prayer, by and by, but it is not so. He races through it as if he thought the quicker he got it in, the sooner it would be answered.

(Tramp Abroad, ch. 36, pp. 402-403)

Cleveland, Grover
(president of the United States, 1885–89, 1893–97)

1908 Of all our public men of today he stands first in my reverence & admiration, & the next one stands two-hundred-&-twenty-fifth. He is the only statesman we have now. . . . Cleveland *drunk* is a more valuable asset to this country than the whole batch of the rest of our public men *sober*. He is high-minded; all his impulses are great & pure & fine. I wish we had another of this sort.

(Letter to Jean Clemens, June 19, 1908, Ltrs-Love, p. 218)

climate

1897 It is your human environment that makes climate.

—Pudd'nhead Wilson's New Calendar

(Foll. Equat., ch. 9, p. 109)

clothes

1894 Clothes is well enough in school, and in towns, and at balls, too, but there ain't no sense in them when there ain't no civilization nor other kinds of bothers and fussiness around.   —[Huck Finn]

(Tom Sawyer Abrd., ch. 8, p. 60)

1897 We must put up with our clothes as they are—they have their reason for existing. They are on us to expose us—to advertise what we wear them to conceal. They are a sign; a sign of insincerity; a sign of repressed vanity; a pretense that we despise gorgeous colors and the graces of harmony and form; and we put them on to propagate that lie and back it up.

(Foll. Equat., ch. 37, p. 343)

1906 All human beings would like to dress in loose and comfortable and highly colored and showy garments, and they had their desire until a century ago, when a king, or some other influential ass, introduced sombre hues and discomfort and ugly designs into masculine clothing. The meek public surrendered to the outrage, and by consequence we are in that odious captivity to-day, and are likely to remain in it for a long time to come.

(NAR, April 5, 1907; Autob/NAR, p. 136)

1909 As for black clothes, my aversion for them is incurable.

(Letter to Frances Nunnally, March 28, 1909, Ltrs-Angelfish, p. 256)

cobra

1897 A snake whose bite kills where the rattlesnake's bite merely entertains.

(Foll. Equat., ch. 57, p. 546)

coffee

1869 Of all the unchristian beverages that ever passed my lips, Turkish coffee is the worst. The cup is small, it is smeared with grounds; the coffee is black, thick, unsavory of smell, and execrable in taste.

(Inn. Abroad, ch. 34, p. 380)

1880 In Europe, coffee is an unknown beverage. You can get what the European hotel keeper thinks is coffee, but it resembles the real thing as hypocrisy resembles holiness. It is a feeble, characterless, uninspiring sort of stuff, and almost as undrinkable as if it had been made in an American hotel. The milk used for it is what the French call "Christian" milk—milk which has been baptized.

(Tramp Abroad, ch. 49, p. 571)

1898 Vienna coffee! It was the first thing I thought of—that unapproachable luxury—that sumptuous coffee-house coffee, compared with which all other European coffee and all American hotel coffee is mere fluid poverty.

("At the Appetite Cure," MTCH&c, p. 154)

coffin

1883 "There's one thing in this world which isn't ever cheap. That's a coffin."
    —New Orleans undertaker
(Life on Miss., ch. 43, p. 437)

comfort

1889 It is the little conveniences that make the real comfort of life.   —[Hank Morgan]
(Conn. Yankee, ch. 7, p. 52)

1899 Shut the door. Not that it lets in the cold, but that it lets out the cosiness.
(MTP, ts 42, p. 70; MTN, p. 346)

THE LITTLE CONVENIENCES

59

communism

1879 Communism is idiotcy. They want to divide up the property. Suppose they did it—it requires brains to keep money as well as make it. In a precious little while the money would be back in the former owner's hands & Communist would be poor again. The division would have to be re-made every three years or it would do the communist no good.

(N&J-2, p. 302)

comparisons

1880 Comparisons are odious, but they need not be malicious ... .

("German Journals," Tramp Abroad, p. 628)

complaints

1902 I think a compliment ought always to precede a complaint, where one is possible, because it softens resentment and insures for the complaint a courteous & gentle reception.

(Letter to president of Western Union, August 1902, Ltrs/Paine, 2:723)

compliments

1865 A sincere compliment is always grateful to a lady, so long as you don't try to knock her down with it.

("Answers to Correspondents," ET&S-2, p. 180)

1894 An occasional compliment is necessary, to keep up one's self-respect. . . . When you cannot get a compliment in any other way, pay yourself one.

(MTP, ts 33, p. 55; MTN, p. 237)

1897 A dozen direct censures are easier to bear than one morganatic compliment.   —Pudd'nhead Wilson's New Calendar

(Foll. Equat., ch. 4, p. 65)

1897 Arguments are unsafe with wives, because they examine them; but they do not examine compliments. One can pass upon a wife a compliment that is three-fourths base metal; she will not even bite it to see if it is good; all she notices is the size of it, not the quality.

("Hellfire Hotchkiss," ch. 1, S&B, p. 185)

1902 You must not pay a person a compliment & then straight way follow it with a criticism.

(MTP, ts 45, p. 43; MTN, p. 379)

1902 Do not offer a compliment & ask a favor at the same time. A comp[liment] that is charged for is not valuable.

(Ibid., p. 380)

1906 Compliments make me vain: & when I am vain, I am insolent & overbearing. It is a pity, too, because I love compliments. I love them even when they are not so. . . . I can live on a good compliment two weeks with nothing else to eat.

(Letter to Gertrude Natkin, March 2, 1906, Ltrs-Angelfish, p. 16)

1907 The happy phrasing of a compliment is one of the rarest of human gifts, and the happy delivery of it another.

(NAR, March 15, 1907; Autob/NAR, p. 130)

conformity

1897 A round man cannot be expected to fit a square hole right away. He must have time to modify his shape.

(Foll. Equat., ch. 68, p. 689)

1900 It is our nature to conform; it is a force which not many can successfully resist. What is its seat? The inborn requirement of Self-Approval. We all have to bow to that; there are no exceptions.

("Corn-pone Opinions," WIM&OPW, pp. 93–94)

1902 "In this world one must be like everybody else if he doesn't want to provoke scorn or envy or jealousy." —Mrs. Stillman

(DBDS, bk. 1, ch. 2, p. 15)

Congress

1869 Shall we ever have a Congress a *majority* of whose members are hopelessly insane? Probably not. But it is possible—unquestionably such a thing is possible.

(Letter to Pamela A. Moffett, August 20, 1869, Ltrs-3, p. 311)

1874 "Even in these days, when people growl so much and the newspapers are so out of patience, there is still a very respectable minority of honest men in Congress." —Colonel Sellers

(Gilded Age, ch. 51, p. 466)

1878 Congressman is the trivialest distinction for a full grown man.

(N&J-2, p. 62)

1880 Moral coward & Congressman seem to be synonymous terms when there's an Irishman in the fence.

(Letter to Mary Fairbanks, February 6, 1880, Ltrs-Fairbanks, p. 237)

c. 1881 Reader, suppose you were an idiot. And suppose you were a member of Congress. But I repeat myself.

(Draft manuscript, quoted in MT:Biog, ch. 138, p. 724)

1907 Our Congresses consist of Christians. In their private life they are true to every obligation of honor; yet in every session they violate them all, and do it without shame. Because honor to party is above honor to themselves.

("Christian Science," Conclusion, WIM&OPW, p. 396)

1907 All Congresses and Parliaments have a kindly feeling for idiots, and a compassion for them, on account of personal experience and heredity.

(Autob/MTIE, p. 375)

congressman, ex-

1902 The poor fellow whose life has been ruined by a two-year taste of glory and of fictitious consequence; who has been superseded, and ought to take his heart-break home and hide it, but cannot tear himself away from the scene of lost little grandeur; and so he lingers, and still lingers, year after year, unconsidered, sometimes snubbed, ashamed of his fallen estate, and valiantly trying to look otherwise; dreary and depressed, but counterfeiting breeziness and gaiety, hailing with chummy familiarity, which is not always welcomed . . . That is the saddest figure I know of.

("Does the Race of Man Love a Lord?," CT-2, p. 522)

Connecticut Yankee (novel published in 1889)

1886 The story isn't a satire peculiarly, it is more especially a *contrast*. It merely exhibits under high lights, the daily life of the [*imaginary Arthurian*] time & that of to-day; & necessarily the bringing them into this immediate juxtaposition emphasizes the salients of both.

(Letter to Mary Fairbanks, November 16, 1886, Ltrs-Fairbanks, pp. 257–258)

1889 The book was not written for America, it was written for England. So many Englishmen have done their sincerest best to teach us something for our betterment, that it seems to me high time that some of us should substantially recognize the good intent by trying to pry up the English nation to a little higher level of manhood in turn.

(Letter to Andrew Chatto, July 16, 1889, Ltrs/Paine, 2:524)

1889 I'm not writing for those parties who miscal themselves critics, & I don't care to have them paw the book at all. It's my swan-song, my retirement from literature permanently, I wish to pass to the cemetery unclodded.

(Letter to W. D. Howells, August 24, 1889, Ltrs-Howells, 2:610–611)

63

conscience

1876 All the consciences *I* have ever heard of were nagging, badgering, fault-finding, execrable savages! Yes; and always in a sweat about some poor little insignificant trifle or other—destruction catch the lot of them, *I* say! I would trade mine for the small-pox and seven kinds of consumption, and be glad of the chance.

("The Facts Concerning the Recent Carnival of Crime in Connecticut," SWE, p. 118)

1884 It don't make no difference whether you do right or wrong, a person's conscience ain't got no sense, and just goes for him *anyway*.

—[Huck]

(Huck Finn, ch. 33, p. 290)

JUST GOES FOR HIM

1884 A man's *first* duty is to his own conscience & honor—the party & the country come second to that, & never first.

(Letter to W. D. Howells, September 17, 1884, Ltrs-Howells, 2:508)

1904 An uneasy conscience is a hair in the mouth.

(MTP, ts 47, p. 18; MTN, p. 392)

1906 Conscience—that independent Sovereign, that insolent absolute Monarch inside of a man who is the man's Master.   —Old Man

("What Is Man?," ch. 2, WIM&OPW, pp. 140–141)

1906 Man's moral medicine chest.

(Autob/MTA, 2:8)

conspiracy

1897 "It means laying for somebody—private. . . .

"Right? Right hasn't got anything to do with it. The wronger a conspiracy is, the better it is."   —Tom Sawyer

("Tom Sawyer's Conspiracy," HF&TS, ch. 1, p. 141)

1901 Conspiracies for good, like conspiracies for evil, are best conducted privately until success is sure.

("Skeleton Plan of a Proposed Casting Vote Party," E&E, p. 235)

Constantinople (capital of Turkey and the Ottoman Empire)

1867 You cannot conceive of anything so beautiful as Constantinople, viewed from the Golden Horn or the Bosphorus. I think it must be the handsomest city in the world.

(Letter to mother and family, September 1, 1867, Ltrs-2, p. 89)

1869 A street in Constantinople is a picture which one ought to see once—not oftener.

(Inn. Abroad, ch. 33, p. 359)

1869 The only solitary thing one does not smell when he is in the Great Bazaar, is something which smells good.

(Ibid., ch. 33, p. 367)

constellations

1897 Constellations have always been troublesome things to name. If you give one of them a fanciful name, it will always refuse to live up to it; it will always persist in not resembling the thing it has been named for.

(Foll. Equat., ch. 5, p. 80)

consuls, foreign

1868 They want to send me abroad, as a Consul or a Minister. . . . God knows I am mean enough and lazy enough, now, without being a foreign consul.

(Letter to mother and sister, February 6, 1868, Ltrs-2, *p. 179)*

contracts

1875 A mere verbal contract . . . is the weakest of all weak weapons. If you had only come sooner I could have given you priceless advice, viz.,—Never make a verbal contract with any man.

(Letter to Charles H. Webb, April 8, 1875, Ltrs-Publs, *p. 86)*

1906 Complexities annoy me; they irritate me; then this progressive feeling presently warms into anger. I cannot get far in the reading of the commonest and simplest contract—with its "parties of the first part" and "parties of the second part" and "parties of the third part,"—before my temper is all gone.

(NAR, October 19, 1906; Autob/NAR, p. 40)

conversation

1872 A good memory, and a tongue hung in the middle. This is a combination which gives immortality to conversation.

(Rough. It, ch. 35, p. 228)

convicts

1905 The law dresses a convict in a garb which makes him easily distinguishable from any moving thing in the world at a hundred and twenty-five yards, except a zebra.

(Letter to Harper's Weekly, October 18, 1905, MTSFH, p. 192)

65

Cooper, James Fenimore (American novelist)

1895 *Deerslayer* is not a work of art in any sense; it does seem to me that it is destitute of every detail that goes to the making of a work of art; in truth, it seems to me that *Deerslayer* is just simply a literary *delirium tremens.*

("Fenimore Cooper's Literary Offenses," CT-2, p. 191)

1895 Cooper's art has some defects. In one place in *Deerslayer*, and in the restricted space of two-thirds of a page, Cooper has scored 114 offenses against literary art out of a possible 115. It breaks the record.

(Ibid., CT-2, p. 180)

1895 Cooper hadn't any more invention than a horse; and I don't mean a high-class horse, either; I mean a clothes-horse. . . . Cooper's eye was splendidly inaccurate. Cooper seldom saw anything correctly. He saw nearly all things as through a glass eye, darkly.

(Ibid., p. 184)

copyright

1887 U.S. copyright laws are far & away the most idiotic that exist anywhere on the face of the earth . . .

(Letter to H. C. Christiancy, September 18, 1887, Ltrs/Paine, 2:481)

1903 Only one thing is impossible with God: to find any sense in any copyright law on the planet.

(MTP, ts 46, p. 19; MTN, p. 381)

1906 Perhaps no important American or English statutes are uncompromisingly and hopelessly idiotic except the copyright statutes of these two countries.

(Autob/MTIE, p. 373)

corn bread

1897–98 Perhaps no bread in the world is quite as good as Southern corn bread, and perhaps no bread in the world is quite so bad as the Northern imitation of it.

(NAR, March 1, 1907; Autob/NAR, p. 113)

corruption

1874 "There is no country in the world, sir, that pursues corruption as inveterately as we do. There is no country in the world whose representatives try each other as much as ours do, or stick to it as long on a stretch. I think there is something great in being a model for the whole civilized world . . ."   —Colonel Sellers

(Gilded Age, ch. 51, p. 468)

country

1889 You see my kind of loyalty was loyalty to one's country, not to its institutions or its office-holders. The country is the real thing, the substantial thing, the eternal thing; it is the thing to watch over, and care for, and be loyal to; institutions are extraneous, they are its mere clothing, and clothing can wear out, become ragged, cease to be comfortable, cease to protect the body from winter, disease, and death. To be loyal to rags, to shout for rags, to worship rags, to die for rags—that is a loyalty of unreason, it is pure animal; it belongs to monarchy, was invented by monarchy; let monarchy keep it.   —[Hank Morgan]

(Conn. Yankee, ch. 13, p. 113)

c. 1900–06 In a monarchy, the king and his family are the country; in a republic it is the common voice of the people.

("Passage from 'Glances at History,'" Fab. of Man, p. 392)

courage

1885 So sure of victory at last is the courage that can wait.

("The Private History of a Campaign That Failed," Merry Tales, p. 13)

1892 Through manifold experiences I have learned that no courage is absolutely perfect; that there is always some one who is able to modify his pluck.

(Autob/MTA, 1:235)

1894 Courage is resistance to fear, mastery of fear—not absence of fear. Except a creature be part coward it is not a compliment to say it is brave; it is merely a loose misapplication of the word.

—Pudd'nhead Wilson's Calendar

(Pudd. Wilson, ch. 12, PW&TET, p. 155)

1907 It is curious—curious that physical courage should be so common in the world, and moral courage so rare.

(Autob/MTIE, *p. 69*)

courtesy

1897 We require courteous speech from the children at all times and in all circumstances; we owe them the same courtesy in return; and when we fail of it we deserve correction.

("Which Was the Dream?," WWD&OSW, *p. 44*)

courtship

1899 Courtship lifts a young fellow far and away above his common earthly self, and by an impulse natural to those lofty regions he puts on his halo and his heavenly war-paint and plays archangel as if he was born to it. He is working a deception, but is not aware of it. His girl marries the archangel. In the course of time he recognises that his wings and his halo have disappeared, and that he is now no longer in the business; but it is a hundred to one that the wife, be she wise or be she otherwise, will keep her beautiful delusion all her life and always believe that the radiant outfit is still there.

("Indiantown," WWD&OSW, *p. 170*)

cowards

1877 You are a coward when you even *seem* to have backed down from a thing you openly set out to do.

(N&J-2, *p. 27*)

1907 The human race is a race of cowards; and I am not only marching in that procession but carrying a banner.

(Autob/MTIE, *Preface, p. xxix*)

coyotes

1872 The cayote is a living, breathing allegory of Want. He is *always* hungry. He is always poor, out of luck and friendless. The meanest creatures despise

ALLEGORY OF WANT

68

him, and even the fleas would desert him for a velocipede. He is so spir-
itless and cowardly that even while his exposed teeth are pretending a
threat, the rest of his face is apologizing for it. And he is *so* homely!—
so scrawny, and ribby, and coarse-haired, and pitiful.

(Rough. It, ch. 5, p. 31)

cranks

1897 The man with a new idea is a Crank until the idea succeeds.
—Pudd'nhead Wilson's New Calendar
(Foll. Equat., ch. 32, p. 297)

creeds

1869 Creeds mathematically precise, and hair-splitting niceties of doctrine, are absolutely necessary for the salvation of some kinds of souls,
but surely the charity, the purity, the unselfishness that are in the hearts
of men like these would save their souls though they were bankrupt in
the true religion—which is ours.

(Inn. Abroad, ch. 25, p. 261)

69

cremation

1882 For the rich, cremation would answer as well as burial; for the ceremonies connected with it could be made as costly and ostentatious as
a Hindoo *suttee*; while for the poor, cremation would be better than burial, because so cheap—so cheap until the poor got to imitating the rich,
which they would do by and by.

(Life on Miss., ch. 42, p. 435)

crickets

1880 It was as unlocatable as a cricket's noise; and where one thinks
that that is, is always the very place where it isn't.

(Tramp Abroad, ch. 13, p. 116)

crime

n.d. Nothing incites to money-crimes like great poverty or great wealth.

(More Max., p. 11)

1897 It could probably be shown by facts and figures that there is no distinctly native American criminal class except Congress.

—Pudd'nhead Wilson's New Calendar

(Foll. Equat., ch. 8, p. 99)

1897 A crime persevered in a thousand centuries ceases to be a crime, and becomes a virtue. This is the law of custom, and custom supersedes all other forms of law.

(Ibid., ch. 63, p. 624)

criticism

1889 One mustn't criticise other people on grounds where he can't stand perpendicular himself.   —[Hank Morgan]

(Conn. Yankee, ch. 26, p. 260)

1906 I like criticism, but it must be my way.

(NAR, September 7, 1906; Autob/NAR, p. 4)

critics

c. 1890 If a critic should start a religion it would not have any object but to convert angels, & they wouldn't need it.

(Letter to Andrew Lang, c. 1890, Ltrs/Paine, 2:527)

1895 I don't value the commendations of critics at as high a rate as I value the commendations of personal friends—for these latter are naturally in a state of solicitude and anxiety, and this makes them ever so much harder to please or move than the indifferent and disinterested stranger.

(Letter to H. H. Rogers, April 29, 1895, Ltrs-Rogers, p. 143)

1904 The critic's symbol: s[houl]d be the tumble-bug: he deposits his egg in somebody else's dung, otherwise he could not hatch it.

(MTP, ts 47, p. 18; MTN, p. 392)

1906 I believe that the trade of critic, in literature, music, and the drama, is the most degraded of all trades, and that it has no real value . . .

It is the will of God that we must have critics, and missionaries, and Congressmen, and humorists, and we must bear the burden. Meantime, I seem to have been drifting into criticism myself. But that is nothing.

At the worst, criticism is nothing more than a crime, and I am not unused to that.

(NAR, October 19, 1906; Autob/NAR, p. 37)

crucifixion

1898 For a God to take 3 days on a cross out of a life of eternal happiness & mastership of the Universe is a service which the least among us would be glad to do upon the like terms.

(MTP, ts 40, p. 28; MTN, p. 364)

Crusades

1894 As near as I could make out, most of the folks that shook farming to go crusading had a mighty rocky time of it.   —[Huck Finn]

(Tom Sawyer Abrd., ch. 1, p. 9)

crying

1880 It is the only efficient sewerage we've ever had.

(Speech in Hartford, October 26, 1880,
MT Speaking, p. 140)

cuckoo clocks

1880 Some sounds are hatefuler than others, but no sound is quite so inane, and silly, and aggravating as the "*hoo'*hoo" of a cuckoo clock . . .

(Tramp Abroad, ch. 26, p. 263)

cursing

1872 When it comes down to pure ornamental cursing, the native American is gifted above the sons of men.

(Rough. It, ch. 60, p. 415)

LEAKING.

Efficient sewerage

custom

1864 Custom is more binding, more impregnable, and more exacting than any law that was ever framed.

(Article in Call, *August 21, 1864;* Cl. of Call, *p. 242)*

1876 Often, the less there is to justify a traditional custom, the harder it is to get rid of it.

*(*Tom Sawyer, *ch. 5, p. 39)*

1897 Custom makes incongruous things congruous.

(Foll. Equat., ch. 44, p. 400)

1898 We have some insane customs, of course. All countries have insane customs. The stranger notices that they are insane, the native doesn't; he is used to them, hardened to them, they are matters of course to him.

(MTP, ts 40, p. 20; MTN, p. 360)

1899 Custom is a petrification: nothing but dynamite can dislodge it for a century.

("Diplomatic Pay and Clothes," CT-2, p. 346)

czars

1897 The Autocrat of Russia possesses more power than any other man in the earth; but he cannot stop a sneeze.

—Pudd'nhead Wilson's New Calendar

(Foll. Equat., ch. 35, p. 318)

1905 Who is it, what is it, that they worship? Privately, none knows better than I: it is my clothes. Without my clothes I should be as destitute of authority as any other naked person. Nobody could tell me from a parson, a barber, a dude. Then who is the real Emperor of Russia? My clothes! There is no other. —[Czar Nicholas II]

("The Czar's Soliloquy," CT-2, p. 642)

Dan'l Webster (the jumping frog)

1865 "You never see a frog so modest and straightfor'ard as he was, for all he was so gifted. And when it come to fair-and-square jumping on a dead level, he could get over more ground at one straddle than any animal of his breed you ever see." —Simon Wheeler

("Jim Smiley and His Jumping Frog,"
ET&S-2, p. 286)

1865 "I don't see no points about that frog that's any better'n any other frog." —The Stranger

(Ibid.)

MODEST AND STRAIGHTFORWARD

Darwinian theory

1909 I have been studying the traits and dispositions of the "lower animals" (so-called) and contrasting them with the traits and dispositions of man. . . . it obliges me to renounce my allegiance to the Darwinian theory of the Ascent of Man from the Lower Animals; since it now seems plain to me that that theory ought to be vacated in favor of a new and truer one, this new and truer one to be named the *Desc*ent of Man from the Higher Animals.

("The Lowest Animal," Lets. Earth, p. 223)

Davis, Jefferson (former president of the Confederacy)

1867 I am glad I am not Jefferson Davis, and I could show him a hundred good reasons why he ought to be glad he ain't me.

(Letter to Alta, May 17, 1867; MTTB, p. 168)

COMFORTING DAY-DREAMS

daydreams

1883 I had comforting day-dreams of a future when I should be a great and honored pilot, with plenty of money, and could kill some of those mates and clerks and pay for them.

(Life on Miss., ch. 4, p. 69)

dead, the

n.d. *It is a solemn thought:* Dead, the noblest man's meat is inferior to pork.

(More Max., p. 9)

1896 It is human to exaggerate the merits of the dead, & I find myself wondering if the praises in this multitude of letters have that defect.

(MTP, ts 39, p. 56; MTN, p. 321)

1909 The spirits of the dead hallow a house, for me.

("The Death of Jean," Autob/NAR, p. 249)

death

1864 I have a human distaste for death, as applied to myself, but I see nothing very solemn about it as applied to anybody—it is more to be dreaded than a birth or a marriage, perhaps, but it is really not as solemn a matter as either of these, when you come to take a rational, practical view of the case.

(Letter to Territorial Enterprise, February 5, 1864, MTOE, p. 152)

1883 Death, the refuge, the solace, the best and kindliest and most prized friend and benefactor of the erring, the forsaken, the old, and weary, and broken of heart, whose burdens be heavy upon them, and who would lie down and be at rest.

(Speech in Ottawa, May 23, 1883, MT Speaking, p. 180)

1894 Whoever has lived long enough to find out what life is, knows how deep a debt of gratitude we owe to Adam, the first great benefactor of our race. He brought death into the world.

—Pudd'nhead Wilson's Calendar

(Pudd. Wilson, ch. 3, PW&TET, p. 41)

1894 All say, "How hard it is that we have to die"—a strange complaint to come from the mouths of people who have had to live.

—Pudd'nhead Wilson's Calendar

(Ibid., ch. 10, p. 121)

1896 How lovely is death; & how niggardly it is doled out.

(Letter to Olivia Clemens, August 19, 1896, Ltrs-Love, p. 322)

c. 1906 The only earthly dignity that is not artificial—the only safe one. The others are traps that can beguile to humiliation.

(MTN, p. 398)

death, reports of

1863 There was a report about town, last night, that Charles Strong, Esq., Superintendent of the Gould & Curry, had been shot and very effectually killed. I asked him about it at church this morning. He said there was no truth in the rumor.

(Letter to Territorial Enterprise, *July 5, 1863, ET&S-1, p. 258)*

1897 James Ross Clemens, a cousin of mine, was seriously ill two or three weeks ago in London, but is well now.

The report of my illness grew out of his illness; the report of my death was an exaggeration.

(Note to London reporter, May 31, 1897, in Frank Marshall White,
"Mark Twain as a Newspaper Reporter," Outlook *[December 14, 1910];*
quoted in Shelley Fisher Fishkin, Lighting Out for the Territory
[New York: Oxford University Press, 1997], p. 134. Many versions of this
famous quip have been attributed to Mark Twain; the version reprinted here
appears to be the most authoritative.)

1907 Palmists, clairvoyants, seers and other kinds of fortune tellers all tell me that I am going to die, and I have the utmost admiration for their prediction. Perhaps they would convince me a little more of its truth if they told me the date. But I don't care so much about that. It was enough to know, on their authority, I was going to die. I at once went and got insured.

(Interview in New York Times, *June 30, 1907, MTSFH, p. 223)*

1907 For two years past I have been planning my funeral, but I have changed my mind and have postponed it.

(Interview in New York Times, *July 13, 1907, MTSFH, p. 225)*

1909 I hear the newspapers say I am dying. The charge is not true. I would not do such a thing at my time of life. I am behaving as good as I can.

(Letter to Associated Press, December 24, 1909, MT:Biog, ch. 289, p. 1549)

decorum

c. 1907 The world loses a good deal by the laws of decorum; gains a good deal, of course, but certainly loses a good deal.

(Autob/MTIE, p. 366)

degree, university

1888 I am the only literary animal of my particular sub-species who has ever been given a degree by any College in any age of the world, as far as I know.

(Letter to Charles H. Clarke, July 2, 1888, Ltrs/Paine, 2:495)

1907 A university degree is . . . a prize which I would go far to get at any time. I take the same childlike delight in a new degree that an Indian takes in a fresh scalp and I take no more pains to conceal my joy than the Indian does. . . .

It pleased me beyond measure when Yale made me a Master of Arts, because I didn't know anything about art; I had another convulsion of pleasure when Yale made me a Doctor of Literature, because I was not competent to doctor anybody's literature but my own . . . I rejoiced again when Missouri University made me a Doctor of Laws, because it was all clear profit, I not knowing anything about laws except how to evade them and not get caught. And now at Oxford I am to be made a Doctor of Letters—all clear profit, because what I don't know about letters would make me a multi-millionaire if I could turn it into cash.

(Autob/AMT, ch. 73, pp. 348–349)

delicacy

1889 To the unconsciously indelicate all things are delicate. King Arthur's people were not aware that they were indecent and I had presence of mind enough not to mention it. —[Hank Morgan]

(Conn. Yankee, ch. 4, p. 34)

delight

1897 A mixed ecstasy of deadly fright and unimaginable joy. I believe that this combination makes the perfection of human delight.

(Foll. Equat., ch. 56, p. 536)

dentistry

1880 I believed the average man dreaded tooth-pulling more than amputation, and that he would yell quicker under the former operation than he would under the latter.

(Tramp Abroad, ch. 23, p. 222)

desert

1872 The poetry was all in the anticipation—there is none in the reality. Imagine a vast, waveless ocean stricken dead and turned to ashes . . . This is the reality of it.

(Rough. It, ch. 18, p. 123)

desperado

1872 The true desperado is gifted with splendid courage, and yet he will take the most infamous advantage of his enemy; armed and free, he will stand up before a host and fight until he is shot all to pieces, and yet when he is under the gallows and helpless he will cry and plead like a child.

(Rough. It, ch. 11, p. 74)

detective

1876 One of those omniscient and awe-inspiring marvels, a detective . . .

(Tom Sawyer, ch. 24, p. 174)

1878 "A detective don't like to be told things—he likes to find them out."
—Simon Wheeler

("Simon Wheeler, Detective," ch. 2, S&B, p. 330)

THE DETECTIVE.

1897 "What's common sense got to do with detecting, you leather-head? It ain't got *anything* to do with it. What is wanted is genius and penetration and marvelousness. A detective that had common sense couldn't ever make a ruputation—couldn't even make his living."

—Tom Sawyer

("Tom Sawyer's Conspiracy," ch. 5, HF&TS, *p. 177)*

detective stories

1896 What a curious thing a "detective" story is. And was there ever one that the author needn't be ashamed of, except the "Murders in the Rue Morgue"?

(MTP, ts 38, p. 47; MTN, *p. 296)*

diamonds

1897 Let us not be too particular. It is better to have old second-hand diamonds than none at all.   —Pudd'nhead Wilson's New Calendar

*(*Foll. Equat., *ch. 34, p. 312)*

dictionaries

1897 The dictionary says a carbuncle is a kind of jewel. Humor is out of place in a dictionary.

*(*Foll. Equat., *ch. 1, p. 25)*

1905 Oh, that worthless, worthless book, that timid book, that shifty book, that uncertain book, that time-serving book that exasperating book, that unspeakable book, the Unlimited Dictionary! that book with but one object in life: to get in more words and shadings of the words than its competitors. With the result that nearly every time it gets done shading a good old useful word it means everything in general and nothing in particular.

("Three Thousand Years among the Microbes," ch. 4,
WWD&OSW, *p. 439n.)*

1906 Building a dictionary is exceedingly interesting work, but tough . . .

("Extract from Eve's Autobiography," Lets. Earth, *p. 89)*

diligence

1901 Diligence is a good thing, but taking things easy is much more—restful. My idea is that the employer should be the busy man and the employee the idle one. The employer should be the worried man, and the employee the happy one.

(Speech in New York City, March 30, 1901, Speeches/Paine, p. 235)

dingo (Australian dog)

1897 He is the most precious dog in the world, for he does not bark.

(Foll. Equat., ch. 19, p. 186)

direction

1897 The compass in my head has been out of order from my birth . . .

(Foll. Equat., ch. 59, p. 567)

disappearance

1878 "There is nothing in literature more romantic than such a fate. None is so mourned as such a victim, if he be young and persecuted by those who should have befriended him."   —Hugh Burnside

("Simon Wheeler, Detective," ch. 7, S&B, p. 398)

disappointment

1878 In my experience, previously counted chickens never *do* hatch. How many of mine I have counted!—& never a one of them but failed! It is much better to hedge disappointment by not counting. Unexpected money is a delight. The same sum is a bitterness when you expected more.

(Letter to Orion Clemens, March 23, 1878, Ltrs/Paine, 1:324)

1907 The one sensible thing to do with a disappointment is to put it out of your mind and think of something cheerfuler.

("Christian Science," bk. 2, ch. 10, WIM&OPW, pp. 347-348)

discharging

1870 I had rather discharge a perilous & unsound cannon than the soundest servant girl that ever was.

(Letter to in-laws, April 16, 1870, Ltrs-4, p. 110)

discovery

1869 What is it that confers the noblest delight? What is that which swells a man's breast with pride above that which any other experience can bring to him? Discovery! To know that you are walking where none others have walked; that you are beholding what human eye has not seen before; that you are breathing a virgin atmosphere. . . . To be the *first*— that is the idea.

(Inn. Abroad, ch. 26, p. 266)

discretion

1896 "Discretion hasn't anything to do with brains; brains are an obstruction to it, for it does not reason, it feels. Perfect discretion means absence of brains. Discretion is a quality of the heart—solely a quality of the heart; it acts upon us through feeling."   —Noël Rainguesson

(Joan of Arc, bk. 2, ch. 5, p. 96)

distance

1869 All distances in the East are measured by hours, not miles. A good horse will walk three miles an hour over nearly any kind of a road; therefore, an hour here always stands for three miles. . . . I cannot be positive about it, but I think that there, when a man orders a pair of pantaloons, he says he wants them a quarter of a minute in the legs and nine seconds around the waist.

(Inn. Abroad, ch. 50, p. 525)

1869 Imagination labors best in distant fields.

(Ibid., p. 527)

dogs

1894 If you pick up a starving dog and make him prosperous, he will not bite you. This is the principal difference between a dog and a man.

—Pudd'nhead Wilson's Calendar

(Pudd. Wilson, ch. 16, PW&TET, p. 214)

1899 The dog is a gentleman; I hope to go to his heaven, not man's.

(Letter to W. D. Howells, April 2–13, 1899, Ltrs-Howells, 2:692)

1910 Leave your dog outside. Heaven goes by favor. If it went by merit you would stay out and the dog would go in.

(Notes for advice on entering heaven, quoted in MT:Biog, ch. 292, p. 1567)

dollar

1889 We Americans worship the Almighty Dollar? Well it is a worthier god than Hereditary Privilege. The Dollar has no contempt for you but the other has.

(N&J-3, p. 520)

1891 A dollar picked up in the road is more satisfaction to you than the ninety-and-nine which you had to work for, and money won at faro or in stocks snuggles into your heart in the same way.

("At the Shrine of St. Wagner," WIM&OE, p. 219)

1902 It isn't merely the American that adores the Almighty Dollar, it is the human race. The human race has always adored the hatful of shells, or the bale of calico, or the half-bushel of brass rings, or the handful of steel fish-hooks, or the houseful of black wives, or the zareba full of cattle, or the two score camels and asses, or the factory, or the farm, or the block of buildings, or the railroad bonds, or the bank stock, or the hoarded cash, or—anything that stands for wealth and consideration and independence, and can secure to the possessor that most precious of all things, another man's envy.

("Does the Race of Man Love a Lord?," CT-2, p. 512)

Don Quixote (novel by Cervantes)

1869 Don Quixote is one of the most exquisite books that was ever written, & to lose it from the world's literature would be as the wresting of a constellation from the symmetry & perfection of the firmament—but neither it nor Shakespeare are proper books for virgins to read until some hand has culled them of their grossness.

(Letter to Olivia Langdon, March 2 [1], 1869, Ltrs-3, p. 132)

Douglas, Widow (character in *Tom Sawyer* and *Huckleberry Finn*)

1884 It was rough living in the house all the time, considering how dismal regular and decent the widow was in all her ways . . .   —[Huck]

(Huck Finn, ch. 1, p. 1)

drama

1900 The greatest of all the arts is to write a drama. It is a most difficult thing. It requires the highest talent possible and the rarest gifts. No, there is another talent that ranks with it—for anybody can write a drama—I had 499 of them—but to get one accepted requires real ability. And I have never had that felicity yet.

(Speech in London, June 9, 1900, MT Speaking, p. 339)

dreams

1897 While you are *in* a dream it *isn't* a dream—it is reality, and the bear-bite hurts; hurts in a perfectly real way.

("Which Was the Dream?," WWD&OSW, p. 47)

1910 Everything in a dream is more deep and strong and sharp and real than is ever its pale imitation in the unreal life which is ours when we go about awake and clothed with our artificial selves in this vague and dull-tinted artificial world.

("My Platonic Sweetheart," Mys. Stranger, p. 304)

drinking

1866 Never refuse to do a kindness unless the act would work great injury to yourself, & never refuse to take a drink—under any circumstances.

(N&J-1, p. 184)

1867 Didnt drink much in that ship—was like Congress—prohibit it save in Committee Rooms—carry it in in demijohns & carry it out in demagogues.

(N&J-1, p. 491)

1870 When I was two years of age she [*my grandmother*] asked me not to drink, and then I made a resolution of total abstinence. That I have adhered to it and enjoyed the beneficent effects of it through all time, I owe to my grandmother. I have never drunk a drop from that day to this of any kind of water.

("History Repeats Itself," SN&O, p. 272)

NICE AND CLEAN

drowning

1906 Drowning is so nice and clean, and writes up so well in a newspaper. But things ne'er do go smoothly in weddings, suicides, or courtships.

(Speech in New York City, February 7, 1906,
MT Speaking, p. 483)

83

dueling

1880 Much as the modern French duel is ridiculed by certain smart people, it is in reality one of the most dangerous institutions of our day. Since it is always fought in the open air, the combatants are nearly sure to catch cold.

(Tramp Abroad, ch. 8, p. 69)

1898 The *real* principals in any duel are not the duellists themselves, but their *families*. They do the mourning, the suffering, theirs is the loss and theirs the misery. They stake all that, the duellist stakes nothing but his life, and that is a trivial thing compared with what his death must cost those whom he leaves behind him.

(NAR, September 8, 1907; Autob/NAR, p. 204)

1907 I thoroughly disapprove of duels. I consider them unwise, and I know they are dangerous. Also, sinful. If a man should challenge me now,

NOT THE *REAL* PRINCIPALS

I would go to that man and take him kindly and forgivingly by the hand and lead him to a quiet retired spot, and *kill* him.

(NAR, December 21, 1906; Autob/NAR, p. 77)

c. 1909 I think I could wipe out a dishonor by crippling the other man, but I don't see how I could do it by letting him cripple me.

(Memorandum, quoted in MT:Biog, ch. 267, p. 1514)

dumb beasts

1906 Let us drop that lying phrase, and call them the Unrevealed Creatures; so far as we can know, there is no such thing as a dumb beast.

—Old Man

("What Is Man?," ch. 6, WIM&OPW, p. 194)

duty

n.d. Do your duty today and repent tomorrow.

(More Max., p. 6)

1897 Make it a point to do something every day that you don't want to do. This is the golden rule for acquiring the habit of doing your duty without pain. —Pudd'nhead Wilson's New Calendar

(Foll. Equat., ch. 58, p. 549)

1902 The human being's first duty—which is to think about himself until he has exhausted the subject, then he is in a condition to take up minor interests and think of other people.

(Ibid., ch. 3, p. 534)

1908 We never do *any* duty for the duty's sake but only for the mere personal satisfaction we get out of doing that duty.

(Autob/MTIE, p. 318)

dynamite

1897 We are not afraid of dynamite till we get acquainted with it.

(Foll. Equat., ch. 60, p. 582)

Earth

1870 I do not see how astronomers can help feeling exquisitely insignificant, for every new page of the Book of the Heavens they open reveals
to them more & more that the world we are so proud of is to the universe of careening globes as is one mosquito to the winged & hoofed
flocks & herds that darken the air & populate the plains & forests of all
the earth.

(Letter to Olivia Langdon, January 8, 1870, Ltrs-4, p. 12)

1897 The globe is a living creature, and the little stinking human race
and the other animals are the vermin that infest it—the microbes.

(Notebook entry, c. August 22, 1897, WWD&OSW, p. 13)

1909 "It is on the map. It is called the Wart."

—under clerk at a gate to Heaven

(Stormfield, ch. 1, p. 24)

earthquake

1865 I will set it down here as a maxim that the operations of the
human intellect are much accelerated by an earthquake. . . . There is no
incentive to rapid reasoning like an earthquake. . . . There is nothing
like an earthquake to hurry a man up when he starts to go anywhere.

("The Great Earthquake in San Francisco," ET&S-2, p. 304)

ecstasy

1900 A thing that will not go into words; it feels like music, and one
cannot tell about music so that another person can get the feeling of it.

("The Chronicle of Young Satan," ch. 2, Mys. Stranger Mss., p. 54)

Eddy, Mary Baker (founder of Christian Science)

1907 In several ways she is the most interesting woman that ever lived, and the most extraordinary. The same may be said of her career, and the same may be said of its chief result.

("Christian Science," bk. 2, ch. 1, WIM&OPW, p. 265)

1907 She has a perfectly astonishing talent for putting words together in such a way as to make successful inquiry into their intention impossible.

(Ibid., ch. 2, p. 276)

1909 She has no more intellect than a tadpole—until it comes to *business*—then she is a marvel!

(Letter to J. Wylie Smith, August 7, 1909, Ltrs/Paine, 2:832)

editors

1870 "I have been in the editorial business going on fourteen years, and it is the first time I ever heard of a man's having to know anything into order to edit a newspaper."   —Editor

("How I Edited an Agricultural Paper Once," CT-1, p. 416)

1906 No magazine editor can ever remember any part of a business talk except the part that's got graft in it for him and the magazine.

(Speech in New York City, September 19, 1906, Speeches/Paine, p. 317)

1910 They all look alike . . . They are conceited and troublesome, and don't pay enough. . . . They are full of envy and malice . . .

("How to Make History Dates Stick," WIM&OE, pp. 157–158)

education

1881 "Learning softeneth the heart and breedeth gentleness and charity."   —Prince Edward

(Prince & Pauper, ch. 4, p. 24)

1884 The self-taught man seldom knows anything accurately, and he does not know a tenth as much as he could have known if he had worked under teachers; and, besides, he brags, and is the means of fooling other thoughtless people into going and doing as he himself as done.

("Taming the Bicycle," WIM&OE, p. 290)

1899 Education consists mainly in what we have unlearned.

(MTP, ts 42, p. 70; MTN, *p. 346)*

1908 All schools, all colleges, have 2 great functions: to confer, & to conceal, valuable knowledge.

(MTP, ts 48, p. 22; MTN, *p. 398)*

eggs

1894 Behold, the fool saith, "Put not all thine eggs in the one basket"—which is but a manner of saying, "Scatter your money and your attention"; but the wise man saith, "Put all your eggs in the one basket and—WATCH THAT BASKET."
　　　　　—Pudd'nhead Wilson's Calendar
(Pudd. Wilson, ch. 14, PW&TET, *p. 197)*

A FINE VIEW

elephant

1897 I could easily learn to prefer an elephant to any other vehicle, partly because of that immunity from collisions, and partly because of the fine view one has from up there, and partly because of the dignity one feels in that high place, and partly because one can look in at the windows and see what is going on privately among the family.

(Foll. Equat., ch. 60, p. 582)

elevator

1891 Its rightful place is among the great ideas of our great age. It is an epoch maker. It is a concentrator of population, and economizer of room. It is going to build our cities skyward instead of toward the horizons.

("Some National Stupidities," E&E, *p. 181)*

1897 In Paris . . . they were using there what they thought was a lift. It held two persons, and traveled at such a slow gait that a spectator could not tell which way it was going. If the passengers were going to the sixth floor, they took along something to eat; and at night, bedding. Old peo-

eloquence

ple did not use it; except such as were on their way to the good place, anyhow.

("Letters to Satan," E&E, p. 217)

eloquence

1869 *People can always talk well when they are talking what they* FEEL. This is the secret of *eloquence.*

(Letter to Olivia Langdon, January 16, 1869, Ltrs-3, p. 46)

Emancipation Proclamation, The

1907 Lincoln's proclamation . . . not only set the black slaves free, but set the white man free also.

(Speech in London, July 4, 1907, Speeches/Paine, pp. 349-350)

emotion

1883 Emotions are among the toughest things in the world to manufacture out of whole cloth; it is easier to manufacture seven facts than one emotion.

(Life on Miss., ch. 27, p. 293)

c. 1894 All emotion is involuntary when genuine . . .

("Cooper's Prose Style," Lets. Earth, p. 142)

enemies

1885 One of the surest ways of begetting an enemy was to do some stranger an act of kindness which should lay upon him the irritating sense of an obligation.

(Autob/MTA, 1:59)

England

1872 Rural England is too absolutely beautiful to be left out doors—ought to be under a glass case.

(Letter to Mary Fairbanks, November 2, 1872, Ltrs-5, p. 206)

1879 Too grave a country. And its gravity soaks into the stranger and makes him as serious as everybody else. When I was there I couldn't seem to think of anything but deep problems of government, taxes, free trade, finance . . . she is not a good text for hilarious literature.

(*Interview in* **New York World,** *c. May 1879,* MTSFH, *p. 111*)

1889 There never was such a country for wandering liars; and they were of both sexes. —[Hank Morgan]

(**Conn. Yankee,** *ch. 11, p. 88*)

1890 England's coat of arms should be a lion's head & shoulders welded onto a cur's hindquarters.

(N&J-3, *p. 539*)

English, the

1878 The best English characteristic is its plucky & persistent & individual standing-up for its rights. No other people approaches England in this . . . admirable, this manliest of all traits. It . . . makes every man in the whole nation a policeman—the administration of law can never grow lax where every individual sees to it that it grows not lax in his own case or in cases which fall under his eyes.

(N&J-2, *p. 100*)

1883 What is an Englishman?

A person who does things because they have been done before.

What is an American (or difference between 'em.) A person who does things because they *haven't* been done before.

(N&J-3, *p. 39*)

1893 The English never play any game for amusement. If they can't make something or lose something,—they don't care which,—they won't play.

(*"The £1,000,000 Bank Note,"* CT-2, *p. 73*)

1897 The English are mentioned in the Bible: Blessed are the meek, for they shall inherit the earth. —Pudd'nhead Wilson's New Calendar

(**Foll. Equat.,** *ch. 17, p. 170*)

English language

1879 I do not speak English but American.—The main difference is that the main body of the English talk through their noses . . .

(N&J-2, *p. 295*)

1897 There is no such thing as "the Queen's English." The property has gone into the hands of a joint stock company and we own the bulk of the shares! —Pudd'nhead Wilson's New Calendar

(Foll. Equat., ch. 24, p. 230)

1897 I have traveled more than anyone else, and I have noticed that even the angels speak English with an accent.

—Pudd'nhead Wilson's New Calendar

(Foll. Equat., Conclusion, p. 710)

1907 I have a great respect for the English language. I am one of its supporters, its promoters, its elevators. I don't degrade it. A slip of the tongue would be the most that you would get from me.

(Speech in London, July 6, 1907, Speeches/Paine, p. 353)

envy

1897 Man will do many things to get himself loved, he will do all things to get himself envied. —Pudd'nhead Wilson's New Calendar

(Foll. Equat., ch. 21, p. 206)

1898 To be envied is the secret longing of pretty much all human beings—let us say *all*; to be envied makes them happy.

—[August Feldner]

(No. 44, ch. 5, p. 28)

1898 "To be envied is the human being's chiefest joy." —44

(Ibid., ch. 20, p. 103)

epitaphs

1870 Epitaphs are cheap, and they do a poor chap a world of good after he is dead, especially if he had hard luck while he was alive.

("A Curious Dream," CT-1, p. 362)

etiquette

n.d. Etiquette requires us to admire the human race.

(More Max., p. 7)

A WORLD OF GOOD

"Eureka!"

1872 I never did know what Eureka meant, but it seems to be as proper a word to heave in as any when no other that sounds pretty offers.

(Rough. It, ch. 42, p. 273)

Europe

1897 On the Continent you can't get a rare beefsteak—everything is as overdone as a martyr.

(MTN, p. 330)

1900 Europe is so sunk in superstitions & prejudices that it is an almost impossible thing to get her to do anything but scoff at a new thing—*unless it come from abroad*; as witness the telegraph, dentistry, &c.

(Letter to J. H. Twichell, January 8, 1900, Ltrs/Paine, 2:690)

"evasion"

1884 "When a prisoner of style escapes, it's called an evasion. It's always called so when a king escapes, frinstance. And the same with a king's son; it don't make no difference whether he's a natural one or an unnatural one." —Tom Sawyer

(Huck Finn, ch. 39, p. 333)

Eve

1906 "Wheresoever she was, *there* was Eden." —Adam

(Eve's Diary, p. 109)

Everest, Mount

1897 I did not see it; but I did not care, because I think that mountains that are as high as that are disagreeable.

(Foll. Equat., ch. 55, p. 532)

evil

1902 "[There is] no such thing as an evil deed. There are good *impulses*, there are evil impulses, and that is all. Half of the results of a good intention are evil; half the results of an evil intention are good. No man can command the results, nor allot them." —The Stranger

("The Dervish and the Offensive Stranger,"
Pen Warmed Up, p. 197)

EVOLUTION

evolution

1890 A truth ever since the globed suns and Planets of the solar system were but wandering films of meteor dust . . .

("Bible Teaching and Religious Practice,"
WIM&OPW, p. 72)

1901–02 Evolution is a blind giant who rolls a snowball down a hill. The ball is made of flakes—*circumstances.* They contribute to the mass without knowing it. They adhere without intention, and without foreseeing what is to result. When they see the result they marvel at the monster ball and wonder how the contriving of it came to be originally thought out and planned. Whereas there was *no such planning*, there was only a law: the ball once started, all the circumstances that happened to lie in its path would help to build it, in spite of themselves.

("The Secret History of Eddypus," bk. 2, ch. 7, Fab. of Man, *p. 378)*

example

1894 Few things are harder to put up with than the annoyance of a good example. —Pudd'nhead Wilson's Calendar

(Pudd. Wilson, ch. 19, PW&TET, p. 246)

excise tax

1867 Excise is a rife subject all over the land, and it does so exercise the people that I think they ought to add that middle syllable to the word.

(Letter to Alta, May 28, 1867; MTTB, p. 248)

exercise

1905 I have never taken any exercise, except sleeping and resting, and I never intend to take any. Exercise is loathsome. And it cannot be any benefit when you are tired; and I was always tired.

(Speech in New York City, December 5, 1905, Speeches/Paine, pp. 259–260)

existence

1898 "*Nothing* exists; all is a dream. God—man—the world—the sun, the moon, the wilderness of stars: a dream, all a dream, they have no existence. *Nothing exists save empty space—and you!* . . .

"And you are not you—you have no body, no blood, no bones, you are but a *thought.* . . .

"And You are but a Thought—a vagrant Thought, a useless Thought, a homeless Thought, wandering forlorn among the empty eternities."

—44
(No. 44, ch. 34, pp. 186–187)

expectations

1894 A thing long expected takes the shape of the unexpected when at last it comes.

(MTP, ts 33, p. 52; MTN, p. 236)

experience

1880 The most permanent lessons in morals are those which come, not of booky teaching, but of experience.

(Tramp Abroad, ch. 47, p. 554)

1897 We should be careful to get out of an experience only the wisdom that is in it—and stop there; lest we be like the cat that sits down on a hot stove-lid. She will never sit down on a hot stove-lid again—and that is well; but also she will never sit down on a cold one any more.

—Pudd'nhead Wilson's New Calendar
(Foll. Equat., ch. 11, p. 124)

1909 Experience is an author's most valuable asset; experience is the thing that put the muscle and the breath and the warm blood into the book he writes.

(ISD, ch. 4, p. 39)

explanations

1889 I hate explanations; they fog a thing up so you can't tell anything about it.

—[Hank Morgan]
(Conn. Yankee, ch. 11, p. 93)

F

facts

1889 The mere knowledge of a fact is pale; but when you come *realize* your fact, it takes on color. It is all the difference between hearing of a man being stabbed to the heart, and seeing it done.

—[Hank Morgan]
(Conn. Yankee, ch. 6, p. 44)

1907 I am not one of those who in expressing opinions confine themselves to facts. I don't know anything that mars good literature so completely as too much truth. Facts contain a deal of poetry, but you can't use too many of them without damaging your literature.

(Speech in London, July 6, 1907, Speeches/Paine, p. 354)

faith

1879 Religion consists in a set of things which the average man thinks he believes, & wishes he was certain.

(N&J-2, p. 305)

1897 There are those who scoff at the schoolboy, calling him frivolous and shallow. Yet it was the schoolboy who said "Faith is believing what you know ain't so."

—Pudd'nhead Wilson's New Calendar
(Foll. Equat., ch. 12, p. 132)

BELIEVING WHAT AIN'T SO

fame

1867 Fame is a vapor—popularity an accident—the only earthly certainty oblivion.

(N&J-1, p. 489)

1868 What is fame! Fame is an accident. Sir Isaac Newton discovered an apple falling to the ground—a trivial discovery, truly, and one which a million men had made before him—but his parents were influential, and so they tortured that small circumstance into something wonderful, and, lo! the simple world took up the shout, and, in almost the twinkling of an eye, that man was famous.

("My Late Senatorial Secretaryship," CT-1, p. 259)

1878 What nonsense fame is! In New York or London I am courteously invited into the banker's private office when I have business. Here [*Switzerland*] I am utterly unknown & must stand around & wait with Tom Dick & Harry—& lucky if not received at last with rude impertinence. . . .

The fact is, I am spoiled by 10 years' petting.—I needed to come to a country where I was unknown to get the tuck taken out of my self-complacency.

(N&J-2, p. 163)

familiarity

1894 Familiarity breeds contempt & children.

(MTP, ts 33, p. 55; MTN, p. 237)

1899 "Familiarity breeds contempt." How accurate that is. The reason we hold Truth in such respect is because we have so little opportunity to get familiar with it.

(MTP, ts 42, p. 64; MTN, p. 345)

fart

1876 "Hath it come to pass yt [that] a fart shall fart *itself*?"
—Queen Elizabeth
(1601, p. 34)

fault

n.d. Always acknowledge a fault frankly. This will throw those in authority off their guard and give you an opportunity to commit more.

(More Max., p. 5)

1894 It is easy to find fault, if one has that disposition. There was once a man who, not being able to find any other fault with his coal, complained that there were too many prehistoric toads in it.

—Pudd'nhead Wilson's Calendar
(Pudd. Wilson, ch. 9, PW&TET, p. 111)

fear

1904 Fears are worse than pains,—oh, much worse.

—[Aileen Mavourneen]

(Dog's Tale, ch. 3, p. 22)

feud

1878 "The feud itself was the only thing of consequence; how it originated was a circumstance of no interest." —Judge Griswold

("Simon Wheeler, Detective," ch. 1, S&B, p. 318)

1878 "In these hateful feuds a man's heart is cloven, but his wife's or
mother's is broken—so the guilty is released with an instant's pang; and
the long misery, the real suffering, falls upon the innocent."

—Mrs. Burnside

("Simon Wheeler, Detective," ch. 4, S&B, p. 343)

1884 "A feud is this way. A man has a quarrel with another man, and
kills him; then that other man's brother kills *him*; then the other brothers, on both sides, goes for one another; then the *cousins* chip in—and
by and by everybody's killed off, and there ain't no more feud. But it's
kind of slow, and takes a long time." —Buck Grangerford

(Huck Finn, ch. 18, p. 146)

figures

1870 Figures confuse & craze me in a little while. I haven't Livy's tranquil nerve in the presence of a financial complexity . . .

(Letter to Jervis Langdon, March 2–3, 1870, Ltrs-4, p. 82)

1897 Truly, nothing is so astonishing as figures, if they once get started.

(Foll. Equat., ch. 17, p. 172)

Finn, Huckleberry (title character of *Huckleberry Finn*)

1876 Huckleberry came and went, at his own free will. He slept on
doorsteps in fine weather and in empty hogsheads in wet; he did not have
to go to school or to church, or call any being master or obey anybody;
he could go fishing or swimming when and where he chose, and stay as
long as it suited him; nobody forbade him to fight; he could sit up as
late as he pleased; he was always the first boy that went barefoot in the

spring and the last to resume leather in the fall; he never had to wash, nor put on clean clothes; he could swear wonderfully. In a word, everything that goes to make life precious, that boy had. So thought every harassed, hampered, respectable boy in St. Petersburg.

(Tom Sawyer, ch. 6, p. 48)

1876 All careers were one to him . . .

(Ibid., ch. 13, p. 99)

1876 Huck was always willing to take a hand in any enterprise that offered entertainment and required no capital, for he had a troublesome superabundance of that sort of time which is *not* money.

(Ibid., ch. 25, p. 175)

Huck

1884 You don't know about me, without you have read a book by the name of "The Adventures of Tom Sawyer," but that ain't no matter. That book was made by Mr. Mark Twain, and he told the truth, mainly.

—[Huck]

(Huck Finn, ch. 1, p. 1)

1884 I see it warn't no use for me to try to learn to do right; a body that don't get *started* right when he's little, ain't got no show—when the pinch comes there ain't nothing to back him up and keep him to his work, and so he gets beat.   —[Huck Finn]

(Ibid., ch. 16, p. 127)

1905 Most honestly do I wish I could say a softening word or two in defence of Huck's character, since you wish it but really in my opinion, it is no better than those of Solomon, David, Satan, and the rest of the sacred brotherhood.

(Letter to A. Don Dickinson, November 21, 1905, in Autob/MTA, 2:336)

Finn, Pap (father of Huckleberry Finn)

1884 He was most fifty, and he looked it. His hair was long and tangled and greasy, and hung down, and you could see his eyes shining through like he was behind vines. It was all black, no gray; so was his long, mixed-up whiskers. There warn't no color in his face, where his face showed; it was white; not like another man's white, but a white to make a body sick, a white to make a body's flesh crawl—a tree-toad white, a fish-belly white. As for his clothes—just rags, that was all.

—[Huck]

(Huck Finn, ch. 5, p. 23)

firearms

1872 I was armed to the teeth with a pitiful little Smith & Wesson's seven shooter, which carried a ball like a homeopathic pill, and it took the whole seven to make a dose for an adult.

(Rough. It, ch. 2, p. 5)

1882 *Any*body can hit a relative, but a Gatling gun won't get a burglar.

(N&J-2, p. 469)

1882 Old unloaded firearms . . . are the most deadly and unerring things that have ever been created by man. . . . A youth who can't hit a cathedral at thirty yards with a Gatling gun in three-quarters of an hour, can take up an old empty musket and bag his grandmother every time, at a hundred.

(Address to Saturday Morning Club, Boston, April 15, 1882,
Speeches/Paine, p. 107)

firefighters

1892 The [*Berlin*] fire brigade march in rank, curiously uniformed, and so grave is their demeanor that they look like a Salvation Army under conviction of sin.

("The German Chicago," £1m Bank-note, p. 216)

1894 A village fire-company does not often get a chance to show off, and so when it does get a chance it makes the most of it. Such citizens of that village as were of a thoughtful and judicious temperament did not insure against fire; they insured against the fire-company.

(Pudd. Wilson, ch. 11, PW&TET, p. 154)

CHANCE TO SHOW OFF

98

fish

n.d. Do not tell fish stories where the people know you; but particularly, don't tell them where they know the fish.

(More Max., p. 7)

1876 The quicker a freshwater fish is on the fire after he is caught the better he is . . .

(Tom Sawyer, ch. 14, p. 108)

flag

1869 How tame a sight his country's flag is at home compared to what it is in a foreign land.

(Inn. Abroad, ch. 7, p. 64)

fleas

n.d. Nelson would have been afraid of ten thousand fleas, but a flea wouldn't be afraid of ten thousand Nelsons.

(More Max., p. 11)

1894 "They've got ever so much more sense, and brains, and brightness, in proportion to their size, than any other cretur in the world. A person can learn them 'most anything; and they learn it quicker than any other cretur, too. . . . S'pose you could cultivate a flea up to the size of a man, and keep his natural smartness a-growing and a-growing right along up, bigger and bigger, and keener and keener in the same proportion—where'd the human race be, do you reckon? That flea would be President of the United States, and you couldn't any more prevent it than you can prevent lightning."   —Tom

(Tom Sawyer Abrd., ch. 7, pp. 46-47)

1894 Consider the flea!—Incomparably the bravest of all the creatures of God, if ignorance of fear were courage. Whether you are asleep or awake, he will attack you, caring nothing for the fact that in bulk and strength you are to him as the massed armies of the earth to a sucking child; he lives both day and night and all days and nights in the very lap of peril and the immediate presence of death, and yet is no more afraid than is the man who walks the streets of a city that was threatened by an earthquake ten centuries before. When we speak of Clive, Nelson, and Putnam as men who "didn't know what fear was," we ought always to add the flea—and put him at the head of the procession.

—Pudd'nhead Wilson's Calendar

(Pudd. Wilson, ch. 12, PW&TET, p. 155)

1906 Fleas can be taught nearly anything that a Congressman can.

—Old Man

("What Is Man?," ch. 6, WIM&OPW, p. 193)

flies

n.d. Nothing is made in vain, but the fly came near it.

(More Max., p. 10)

c. 1900 The planning of the fly was an application of pure intelligence, morals not being concerned. Not one of us could have planned the fly, not one of us could have constructed him; and no one would have considered it wise to try, except under an assumed name. It is believed by some that the fly was introduced to meet a long-felt want. In the course of ages, for some reason or other, there have been millions of these persons, but out of this vast multitude there has not been one who has been willing to explain what the want was.

("Thoughts of God," Fab. of Man, p. 112)

1902 One fly makes a summer.   —Pudd'nhead Wilson's Calendar

("The Belated Russian Passport," MTCH&c, p. 353)

1903 The morals of a God ought to be minutely perfect. I would not worship a God that made the fly.

If God invented the fly, that is enough. It gives us the measure of His character. If a man had invented the fly, we should curse his name forever. And he would deserve it.

(Notebook 36, quoted in Fab. of Man, p. 110)

Florence, Italy

1869 My experiences of Florence were chiefly unpleasant. I will change the subject.

(Inn. Abroad, ch. 24, p. 249)

1892 No view that I am acquainted with in the world is at all comparable to this for delicacy, charm, exquisiteness, dainty coloring, & bewildering rapidity of change. It keeps a person drunk with pleasure all the time. Sometimes Florence ceases to be substantial, & becomes just a faint soft dream, with domes & towers of air, & one is persuaded that he might blow it away with a puff of his breath.

(Letter to Susan L. Crane, October 22, 1892, Ltrs/Paine, 2:573)

Florida, Missouri

1897–98 Recently some one in Missouri has sent me a picture of the house I was born in. Heretofore I have always stated that it was a palace, but I shall be more guarded now.

(Autob/MTA, 1:95)

flowers

1869 In all my experience I never saw an American in the street with flowers in his button-hole but he happened to be a fellow who had a weak spot about his head somewhere.

(Letter to Olivia Langdon, September 3, 1869, Ltrs-3, pp. 331-332)

'Fnobjectionbilltakuzhlcourssoreferred

1874 Habitués of the House [of Representatives] comprehended that this long, lightning-heeled word signified that if there was no objection, the bill would take the customary course of a measure of its nature, and be referred to the Committee on Benevolent Appropriations, and that it was accordingly so referred. Strangers merely supposed that the Speaker was taking a gargle for some affection of the throat.

(Gilded Age, ch. 43, p. 394)

Following the Equator (1897 travel book)

1897 I like the book myself. All this shows—what? That the common notion that a book infallibly reveals the man and his condition, is a mistake. This book has not exposed me. It pretends to an interest in its subject—which was mostly not the case. It pretends that it was freely spouted out of a contented heart—not the forced work of a rebellious prisoner fretting in chains. Well, Gott sei Dank it is over and done with; I would rather be hanged, drawn and quartered than write it again. All the heart I had was in Susy's grave and the Webster debts. And so, behold a miracle!—a book which does not give its writer away.

(Letter to H. H. Rogers, December 21, 1897, Ltrs-Rogers, p. 309)

1899 I wrote my last travel-book in hell; but I let on, the best I could, that it was an excursion through heaven. Some day I will read it, & if its lying cheerfulness fools me, then I shall believe it fooled the reader. How I did loathe that journey around the world!—except the sea-part & India.

(Letter to W. D. Howells, April 2–13, 1899, Ltrs-Howells, 2:690)

fools

n.d. The trouble ain't that there is too many fools, but that the lightning ain't distributed right.

(More Max., p. 13)

1876 "Old fools is the biggest fools there is."　　—Aunt Polly

(Tom Sawyer, ch. 1, p. 2)

1884 "Hain't we got all the fools in town on our side? and ain't that a big enough majority in any town?"　　—The King

(Huck Finn, ch. 26, p. 228)

1885 If all the fools in this world should die, lordly God how lonely I should be.

(Letter to Olivia Clemens, January 23, 1885, Ltrs-Love, p. 233)

1897 Let us be thankful for the fools. But for them the rest of us could not succeed.　　—Pudd'nhead Wilson's New Calendar

(Foll. Equat., ch. 28, p. 268)

forbidden

c. 1895 The more things are forbidden, the more popular they become.

(MTN, p. 257)

1896 There is a charm about the forbidden that makes it unspeakably desirable. It was not that A[dam] ate the apple's for the apple's sake, but *because* it was forbidden. It would have been better for us—O. infinitely better for us if the *serpent* had been forbidden.

(MTP, ts 36, p. 35; MTN, p. 275)

foreign language

1878 The idiotic fashion in America of teaching pupils only to read & write a foreign language . . . There may be a justifiable reason for this—God knows what it is. Any fool can teach *himself* to read a language—the only valuable thing a school can do is teach how to *speak* it.

(N&J-2, p. 184)

foreigners

1869 They spell it Vinci and pronounce it Vinchy; foreigners always spell better than they pronounce.

(Inn. Abroad, ch. 19, p. 185)

1895 A foreigner can photograph the exteriors of a nation, but I think that that is as far as he can get. I think that no foreigner can report its interior—its soul, its life, its speech, its thought. . . . Observation? Of what real value is it? One learns peoples through the heart, not the eyes or the intellect.

("What Paul Bourget Thinks of Us," CT-2, pp. 166–167)

Fort Pillow Massacre (Confederate slaughter of hundreds of black Union soldiers in Tennessee in 1864)

1883 Massacres are sprinkled with some frequency through the histories of several Christian nations, but this is almost the only one that can be found in American history; perhaps it is the only one which rises to a size correspondent to that huge and sombre title.

(Life on Miss., ch. 29, p. 311)

fountain pen

1884 Beware of the fountain pen! The worst stylograph is worth a million of the best fountains.

(Letter to Orion Clemens, December 26, 1884, MT:Bus. Man, p. 287)

1897 None of us can have as many virtues as the fountain-pen, or half its cussedness; but we can try.   —Pudd'nhead Wilson's New Calendar

(Foll. Equat., ch. 68, p. 686)

France

1878 France seems to interest herself mainly in high art & seduction.

(N&J-2, p. 101)

1895 I can't describe to you how poor & empty & offensive France is, compared to America—in my eyes. The minute I strike America I seem to wake out of an odious dream.

(Letter to Olivia Clemens, March 20–21, 1895, Ltrs-Love, p. 313)

Franklin, Benjamin (American statesman, writer, and inventor)

1869 The immortal axiom-builder, who used to sit up nights reducing the rankest old threadbare platitudes to crisp and snappy maxims that had a nice, varnished, original look in their regimentals . . .

("The Last Words of Great Men," CT-1, p. 317)

1870 He invented a stove that would smoke your head off in four hours by the clock. One can see the almost devilish satisfaction he took in it, by his giving it his name.

("The Late Benjamin Franklin," CT-1, p. 426)

1887 Franklin was sober because he lived in Philadelphia. . . . Franklin was frugal, and as he says himself, with becoming modesty, he had no vices, because, although he little suspected it, he made a vice of frugality.

(Speech in New York City, February 10, 1887, MT Speaking, pp. 216–217)

free speech

1873 There are laws to protect the freedom of the press's speech, but none that are worth anything to protect the people from the press.

(Paper delivered in Hartford, February 1873, Speeches/Paine, pp. 46–47)

1884 The surest way for a man to make of himself a target for almost universal scorn, obloquy, slander, and insult is to stop twaddling about these priceless independencies, and attempt to *exercise* one of them.

(Paper delivered in Hartford, late 1884, Speeches/Paine, p. 125)

1897 It is by the goodness of God that in our country we have those three unspeakably precious things: freedom of speech, freedom of conscience, and the prudence never to practice either of them.

—Pudd'nhead Wilson's New Calendar

(Foll. Equat., ch. 20, p. 195)

1905 In America—as elsewhere—free speech is confined to the dead.

(MTP, ts 48, p. 4; MTN, p. 393)

free will

1906 Free Will has always existed in *words*, but it stops there . . .

—Old Man

("What Is Man?," ch. 6, WIM&OPW, p. 199)

1907 Where there are two desires in a man's heart he has no choice between the two but must obey the strongest, there being no such thing as free will in the composition of any human being that ever lived.

(Autob/MTIE, p. 239)

freedom

1883 Of course the highest pleasure to be got out of freedom, and the having nothing to do[,] is labor.

(Letter to W. D. Howells, March 1, 1883, Ltrs-Howells, 1:427)

French, the

1879 French are the connecting link between man & the monkey. . . .
  Whatever is trivial to another man is important to a Frenchman. It is this that makes the French the most (artificially) polite nation.

(N&J-2, p. 320)

1879 In one thing the French stand almost alone. The spirit of massacre seems to be theirs by divine right.

(Lets. Earth, p. 184)

French language

1879 The language is right for the people—it is a mess of trivial sounds—words which run into each other (by law) & words which never end, but fade away. If one tried to be in earnest in such a language he could only be sophomoric & theatrical—& that is what a F[renchman] is when earnest—or what *he* thinks is in earnest. . . .

It is the language for lying compliment, for illicit love & for the conveying of exquisitely nice shades of meaning in bright graceful & trivial conversations—the conveying, especially, of double-meanings, a decent & indecent one so blended as—nudity thinly veiled, but gauzily & lovelily.

(N&J-2, p. 320)

1881 I speak French with timidity, and not flowingly—except when excited. When using that language I have often noticed that I have hardly ever been mistaken for a Frenchman, except, perhaps, by horses; never, I believe, by people.

(Speech in Montreal, December 8, 1881, MT Speaking, p. 160)

1900 "It is the official language [of hell]."   —Philip Traum

("The Chronicle of Young Satan," ch. 3,
Mys. Stranger Mss., p. 69)

c. 1907 Plainly a language likely to fail a person at the crucial moment.

(Autob/AMT, ch. 68, p. 330)

French Revolution

1889 Next to the 4th of July & its results, it was the noblest & the holiest thing & the most precious that ever happened in this earth.

(Letter to W. D. Howells, September 22, 1889, Ltrs-Howells, 2:613)

friends

1894 An enemy can partly ruin a man, but it takes a good-natured injudicious friend to complete the thing and make it perfect.

(Pudd. Wilson, ch. 5, PW&TET, p. 71)

1894 The holy passion of Friendship is of so sweet and steady and loyal and enduring a nature that it will last through a whole lifetime, if not asked to lend money.

—Pudd'nhead Wilson's Calendar
(Ibid., ch. 8, p. 93)

FRIENDS

1898–99 The proper office of a friend is to side with you when you are in the wrong. Nearly anybody will side with you when you are in the right.

(MTP, ts 42, p. 61; MTN, p. 344)

"fructifying"

1867 I don't really know the meaning of that word, but I heard it used somewhere yesterday, and it struck me as being an unusually good word. Any time that I put in a word that doesn't balance the sentence good, I would be glad if you would take it out and put in that one.

(Letter to Alta, May 20, 1867; MTTB, p. 207)

funerals

1872 Somebody has said that in order to know a community, one must observe the style of its funerals and know what manner of men they bury with most ceremony.

(Rough. It, ch. 47, p. 308)

1894 Why is it that we rejoice at a birth and grieve at a funeral? It is because we are not the person involved.

—Pudd'nhead Wilson's Calendar
(Pudd. Wilson, ch. 9, PW&TET, p. 111)

Galilee, Sea of

1869 The celebrated Sea of Galilee is not so large a sea as Lake Tahoe by a good deal . . . And when we come to speak of beauty, this sea is no more to be compared to Tahoe than a meridian of longitude is to a rainbow.

(Inn. Abroad, ch. 48, p. 507)

games

1906 In my experience, games played with a fiendish outfit furnish ecstacies of delight which games played with the other kind cannot match.

(NAR, November 1907; Autob/NAR, p. 227)

generosity

1907 The man who is born stingy can be taught to give liberally—with his hands; but not with his heart.

("Christian Science," bk. 2, ch. 10, WIM&OPW, p. 346)

Geneva, Switzerland

1880 That delightful city where accurate time-pieces are made for all the rest of the world, but whose own clocks never give the correct time of day by any accident.

(Tramp Abroad, ch. 47, p. 541)

genius

1866 Genius elevates a man to ineffable sp[h]eres far above the vulgar world, & fills his soul with a regal contempt for the gross & sordid things of earth[.]

It is probably on account of this that people who have genius do not pay their board, as a general thing.

(N&J-1, p. 250)

1904 Dahomey could not find an Edison out; in Dahomey an Edison could not find himself out. Broadly speaking, genius is not born with sight, but blind; and it is not itself that opens its eyes, but the subtle influences of a myriad of stimulating exterior circumstances.

("Saint Joan of Arc," CT-2, p. 592)

1907 A genius is not very likely to ever discover himself; neither is he very likely to be discovered by his intimates.

(Autob/MTIE, p. 359)

1907 Thousands of geniuses live and die undiscovered—either by themselves or by others. But for the Civil War, Lincoln and Grant and Sherman and Sheridan would not have been discovered.

(Ibid., p. 360)

gentlemen

1901–02 "No real gentleman will tell the naked truth in the presence of ladies."

("The Secret History of Eddypus," bk. 2, ch. 1, Fab. of Man, p. 339)

1906 I had never in my life uttered in print a definition of that word—a word which once had a concrete meaning, but has no clear and definite meaning now, either in America or elsewhere.

(Speech, c. February–March 1906, Speeches/Paine, p. 297)

1906 I don't know what a gentleman is—a gentleman on the indefinite modern plan. It's the fourth dimension to me, with the unsquared circle and the nebular theory added.

(Ibid., p. 299)

1906 I don't remember that I ever defined a gentleman, but it seems to me that if any man has just merciful and kindly instincts he would be a gentleman, for he would need nothing else in the world.

(Speech in New York City, March 4, 1906, Speeches/Paine, p. 283)

gentleness

1879 It is hard to *seem* gentle when you are not, but only *ought* to be.

(Letter to Mary Fairbanks, September 23, 1879, Ltrs-Fairbanks, p. 233)

Genuine Mexican Plug
(horse purchased by *Roughing It*'s narrator)

1872 Everybody I loaned him to always walked back; they never could get enough exercise any other way. Still, I continued to loan him to anybody who was willing to borrow him, my idea being to get him crippled, and throw him on the borrower's hands, or killed, and make the borrower pay for him. But somehow nothing ever happened to him. . . . Of course I had tried to sell him; but that was a stretch of simplicity which met with little sympathy. . . . Finally I tried to *give* him away. But it was a failure. Parties said earthquakes were handy enough on the Pacific coast—they did not wish to own one.

(Rough. It, ch. 24, pp. 163–164)

German language

1878 Some of the words are so long that they have a perspective. When one casts his glance along down one of these, it gradually tapers to a point like the receding lines of a railway track.

(N&J-2, p. 81)

1878 With prayer & a dictionary one may wade through most any sentence[.]

(Ibid., p. 254)

1880 Surely there is not another language that is so slip-shod and systemless, and so slippery and elusive to the grasp.

("The Awful German Language," Tramp Abroad, p. 601)

1880 I heard a Californian student in Heidelberg say, in one of his calmest moods, that he would rather decline two drinks than one German adjective.

(Ibid., p. 606)

1880 In German, all the Nouns begin with a capital letter. Now that is a good idea; and a good idea in this language is necessarily conspicuous from its lonesomeness.

(Ibid.)

1880 Every noun has a gender, and there is no sense or system in the distribution . . . In German, a young lady has no sex, while a turnip has. Think what overwrought reverence that shows for the turnip, and what callous disrespect for the girl.

(Ibid., p. 607)

1899 It is easier for a cannibal to enter the Kingdom of heaven through the eye of a rich man's needle than it is for any other foreigner to read the terrible German script.

(MTP, ts 42, p. 70; MTN, p. 346)

1907 The language which enables a man to travel all day in one sentence without changing cars.

("Christian Science," bk. 1, ch. 1, WIM&OPW, p. 216)

Germans

1878 The chief German characteristic seems to be kindness, good will to men.

(N&J-2, p. 100)

1880 Where and how did we get the idea that the Germans are a stolid, phlegmatic race? In truth they are widely removed from that. They are warm-hearted, emotional, impulsive, enthusiastic, their tears come at the mildest touch, and it is not hard to move them to laughter. They are the very children of impulse. We are cold and self-contained, compared to the Germans.

(Tramp Abroad, ch. 10, pp. 92–93)

Germany

1878 It is pleasant to be in a country where you can break the Sabbath without sin.

(N&J-2, p. 120)

1891 I don't believe there is anything in the whole earth that you can't learn in Berlin except the German language. It is a desperate language.

(MTP, ts 31, p. 11; MTN, p. 219)

germs

1905 Men and germs are not widely different from each other. Of germs there are many nationalities, and there are many languages, just as it is with mankind.

("Three Thousand Years among the Microbes," ch. 3, WWD&OSW, p. 437)

Gilded Age, The
(novel by Mark Twain and Charles Dudley Warner published in 1874)

1873 Chas. Dudley Warner . . . & I have written a bulky novel in partnership. He has worked up the fiction & I have hurled in the facts. I consider it one of the most astonishing novels that ever was written. Night after night I sit up reading it over & over again & crying.

(Letter to Daily Graphic, *April 17, 1873, Ltrs-5, pp. 342–343)*

1873 We both think this is going to be no slouch of a novel, as Solomon said to the Hebrew Children.

(Letter to Olivia Clemens, April 26, 1873, Ltrs-5, p. 357)

Gillis, Steve (prospector friend of Mark Twain)

1906 Steve was a Gillis, and when a Gillis confronted a man and had a proposition to make, the proposition always contained business.

(NAR, December 21, 1906; Autob/NAR, p. 77)

A CURIOUS KIND OF A FOOL

girls

1876 "What a curious kind of a fool a girl is. . . . Girls' faces always tell on them. They ain't got any backbone." —Tom

(Tom Sawyer, ch. 20, p. 149)

1906 Girls are charming creatures. I shall have to be twice seventy years old before I change my mind as to that.

(NAR, November 16, 1906; Autob/NAR, p. 62)

1909 I wish I *was* a pretty girl. However, it is no use to try; we all have our limitations.

(Letter to Frances Nunnally, August 27, 1909,
Ltrs-Angelfish, p. 263)

glacier

1880 I have traveled by canal-boat, ox-waggon, raft, and by the Ephesus and Smyrna railway; but when it comes down to good solid honest slow motion, I bet my money on the glacier. As a means of passenger transportation, I consider the glacier a failure; but as a vehicle for slow freight, I think she fills the bill.

(Tramp Abroad, ch. 39, p. 457)

glass

1889 It is a little thing—glass is—until it is absent, then it becomes a big thing. —[Hank Morgan]

(Conn. Yankee, ch. 7, p. 54)

glory

1906 The glory which is built upon a lie soon becomes a most unpleasant incumbrance.

(NAR, January 4, 1907; Autob/NAR, p. 87)

goat

c. 1907 We do not say to the ram and the goat, "Thou shalt not commit adultery," for we know that ineradicably embedded in their temperament—that is to say in their born nature—God has said to them, "Thou *shalt* commit it." . . .

When we think of the goat, unchastity occurs to us and no other trait. . . .

(Autob/AMT, ch. 63, p. 307)

God

1880 Men are more compassionate/(nobler)/magnanimous/generous than God; for men forgive the dead, but God does not.

(N&J-2, p. 416)

1888 God himself exhibits no originality. Look at people; all alike, & he keeps repeating them.

(N&J-3, p. 305)

1896 It is said that the ways of God are not like ours. Let us not contest this point.

(MTP, ts 37, p. 49; MTN, p. 290)

1898–99 What God lacks is convictions—stability of character. He ought to be a Presbyterian or a Catholic or *something*,—not try to be everything.

(MTP, ts 42, p. 63; MTN, p. 344)

1902 None of us can be as great as God, but any of us can be as good.

(MTP, ts 45, p. 40; MTN, p. 379)

1904 God, so atrocious in the Old Testament, so attractive in the New—the Jekyll & Hyde of sacred romance.

(MTP, ts 47, p. 18; MTN, p. 392)

1908 God made man, without man's consent, and made his nature, too; made it vicious instead of angelic, and then said, Be angelic, or I will punish you and destroy you. But no matter, God is responsible for everything man does, all the same; He can't get around that fact. There is only one Criminal, and it is not man. —Mr. Hollister

("Little Bessie," ch. 2, Fab. of Man, p. 38)

1908 It is most difficult to understand the disposition of the Bible God, it is such a confusion of contradictions; of watery instabilities and iron firmnesses; of goody-goody abstract morals made out of words, and concerted hell-born ones made out of *acts*; of fleeting kindnesses repented of in permanent malignities.

(Ibid., p. 425)

gondolas and gondoliers

1869 This the famed gondola and this the gorgeous gondolier!—the one an inky, rusty old canoe with a sable hearse-body clapped on to the middle of it, and the other a mangy, barefooted guttersnipe with a portion of his raiment on exhibition which should have been sacred from public scrutiny.

(Inn. Abroad, ch. 22, p. 218)

AVOIDING LONESOMENESS

goodness

n.d. All the talk used to be about doing people good, now it is about doing people.

(More Max., p. 5)

n.d. Do good when you can, and charge when you think they will stand it.

(Ibid., p. 6)

1883 It is very wearing to be good.

(Life on Miss., ch. 55, p. 540)

1889 I am privileged to infer that there is *far* more goodness than ungoodness in man, for if it were not so man would have exterminated himself before this.

(Letter to Olivia Clemens, July 17, 1889, Ltrs-Love, p. 253)

1897 Be good & you will be lonesome.

(Foll. Equat., flyleaf)

Gould, Jay (corrupt American financier)

1905 If Jay Gould had been Adam he would have owned the planet. He would have got the apple, too, & no punishment, because he would have worked out a way to beat the judgment.

(Working notes to "Refuge of the Derelicts," Fab. of Man, p. 461)

1906 The mightiest disaster which has ever befallen this country.

(Autob/MTIE, p. 77)

government

1890 That gov[ernmen]t is not best which best secures mere life & property—there is a more valuable thing—Manhood.

(N&J-3, p. 541)

1900 "All forms of government—including republican and democratic— are rich in funny shams and absurdities, but their supporters do not see it."   —Philip Traum

("The Chronicle of Young Satan," ch. 10,
Mys. Stranger Mss., p. 165)

c. 1900–06 The Government is merely a *servant*—merely a temporary servant; it cannot be its prerogative to determine what is right and what is wrong, and decide who is a patriot and who isn't. Its function is to obey orders, not originate them. . . .

Only when a republic's *life* is in danger should a man uphold his government when it is in the wrong. There is no other time.

("Passage from 'Glances at History,'" Fab. of Man, p. 392)

graft

n.d. Wherefore being all of one mind, we do highly resolve that government of the grafted by the grafter for the grafter shall not perish from the earth.

(More Max., p. 14)

grammar

1881 To save a single moment's time, & a single word, I will gladly break any rule of grammar, when the matter is not for print.

(Letter to Orion Clemens, November 21, 1881, MT:Bus. Man, p. 177)

1898 Perfect grammar—persistent, continuous, sustained—is the fourth dimension, so to speak; many have sought it, but none has found it.

(Autob/MTA, 1:173)

Grant, Ulysses S.

1907 No one can write perfect English and keep it up through a stretch of ten chapters. It has never been done.

("Christian Science," bk. 2, ch. 2, WIM&OPW, p. 273)

Grant, Ulysses S.
(Civil War commander and president of the United States, 1869–77)

1904 I can't rise to General Grant's lofty place in the estimation of this nation, but it is a deep happiness to me to know that when it comes to epistolary literature he can't sit in the front seat along with me.

(NAR, September 21, 1906; Autob/NAR, p. 21)

Grant, Memoirs of
(book published by Mark Twain's own company in 1886)

1887 General Grant's book is a great, and in its peculiar department unique and unapproachable literary masterpiece.

(Speech at Army & Navy Club, April 27, 1887, MT Speaking, p. 226)

1894 That terrible book! which made money for everybody concerned but me.

(Letter to Pamela A. Moffett, February 25, 1894, Ltrs-Publs, p. 364)

c. 1907 I had been comparing the memoirs with Caesar's "Commentaries" and was . . . able to say in all sincerity that the same high merits distinguished both books—clarity of statement, directness, simplicity, unpretentiousness, manifest truthfulness, fairness and justice toward friend and foe alike, soldierly candor and frankness and soldierly avoidance of flowery speech.

(Autob/AMT, ch. 50, p. 252)

gratitude

1894 Gratitude and treachery are merely the two extremities of the same procession. You have seen all of it that is worth staying for when the band and the gaudy officials have gone by.

—Pudd'nhead Wilson's Calendar

(Pudd. Wilson, ch. 18, PW&TET, p. 225)

INGRATITUDE

Gridley, David

(fictional character whom Mark Twain modeled on himself)

1899 It is not easy to describe David Gridley, there being two of him—the one that God made, and another one. The one that God made was a sufficiently indifferent piece of work, but it was at least not a sham—all its parts were genuine; but the other one was all sham; there was not a genuine fibre in it. It was the work of Mrs. Gridley. . . . he was just a piece of honest kitchen furniture transferred to the drawing-room and glorified and masked from view in gorgeous cloth of gold.

("Indiantown," WWD&OSW, pp. 166–167)

grief

1873 I'm an old hand at grief. Grief makes me hump myself when I'm *alone*, but that is taking advantages. When my family is around I am superior to it.

(Letter to Olivia Clemens, April 26, 1873, Ltrs-5, p. 358)

1897 Nothing that grieves us can be called little: by the eternal laws of proportion a child's loss of a doll and a king's loss of a crown are events of the same size.

("Which Was the Dream?," WWD&OSW, p. 46)

1905–06 Grief is repetitious; and this kind of wear eventually blunts a listener's interest and discourages the teller, then both parties retire within their shells and feed upon that slow-starving diet, Introspection.

("The Refuge of the Derelicts," ch. 9, Fab. of Man, p. 222)

grottoes

1869 It seems curious that personages intimately connected with the Holy Family always lived in grottoes—in Nazareth, in Bethlehem, in imperial Ephesus—and yet nobody else in their day and generation thought of doing any thing of the kind. . . . It is exceedingly strange that these tremendous events all happened in grottoes—and exceedingly fortunate, likewise, because the strongest houses must crumble to ruin in time, but a grotto in the living rock will last forever.

(Inn. Abroad, ch. 50, p. 528)

growth

1884 What is the most rigorous law of our being? *Growth.* No small-est atom of our moral, mental or physical structure can stand still a *year.* . . . In other words, we *change*—and *must* change, constantly, and keep on changing as long as we live.

(Paper delivered in Hartford, late 1884, Speeches/Paine, p. 121)

guides, tour

1869 These are the people that make life a burthen to the tourist. Their tongues are never still. They talk forever and forever, and that is the kind of billingsgate they use. . . . they interrupt every dream, every pleasant train of thought, with their tiresome cackling.

**(Inn. Abroad, *ch. 19, p. 183)*

118

habits

1877 The habits of all peoples are determined by their circumstances. The Bermudians lean upon barrels because of the scarcity of lamp-posts.

("Some Rambling Notes of an Idle Excursion," part 3, SWE, p. 66)

NOTHING SO NEEDS REFORMING

1894 Habit is habit, and not to be flung out of the win-dow by any man, but coaxed downstairs a step at a time.
—Pudd'nhead Wilson's Calendar
(Pudd. Wilson, ch. 6, PW&TET, p. 77)

1894 Nothing so needs reforming as other people's habits.

—Pudd'nhead Wilson's Calendar
(Ibid., ch. 15, p. 197)

1897 A man may have no bad habits and have worse.
—Pudd'nhead Wilson's New Calendar
(Foll. Equat., ch. 1, p. 25)

1905 We have no permanent habits until we are forty. Then they begin to harden, presently they petrify, then business begins.
(Speech in New York City, December 5, 1905, Speeches/Paine, p. 257)

Hadleyburg (fictitious town)

1899 A new word to the dictionary—*Hadleyburg*, synonym for *incorruptible*—destined to live in dictionaries forever!
("The Man That Corrupted Hadleyburg," CT-2, p. 402; also in MTCH&c)

happiness

1897 There are people who can do all fine and heroic things but one! keep from telling their happiness to the unhappy.
—Pudd'nhead Wilson's New Calendar
(Foll. Equat., ch. 26, p. 251)

c. 1899 Happiness is a Swedish sunset—it is there for all, but most of us look the other way and lose it.
(MTN, p. 371)

1900 "Every man is a suffering-machine and a happiness-machine combined. The two functions work together harmoniously, with a fine and delicate precision, on the give-and-take principle. For every happiness turned out in the one department the other stands ready to modify it with a sorrow or a pain—maybe a dozen. In most cases the man's life is about equally divided between happiness and unhappiness. When this is not the case the unhappiness predominates—always; never the other."
—Philip Traum
("The Chronicle of Young Satan," ch. 6, Mys. Stranger Mss., p. 112)

1900 "Sanity and happiness are an impossible combination[.] No sane man can be happy, for to him life is real, and he sees what a fearful thing it is. Only the mad can be happy, and not many of those."
—Philip Traum
("The Chronicle of Young Satan," ch. 10,
Mys. Stranger Mss., pp. 163–164)

1900 When you climb the hill of happiness, may you never meet a friend.

(MTP, ts 43, p. 16; MTN, *p. 373)*

1907 The one sole condition that makes spiritual happiness and preserves it is the absence of doubt.

(Autob/MTIE, p. 339)

1909 "Happiness ain't a *thing in itself*—it's only a *contrast* with something that ain't pleasant. That's all it is. There ain't a thing you can mention that is happiness in its own self—it's only so by contrast with the other thing." —Sam Bartlett

(Stormfield, ch. 1, pp. 43–44)

1910 Up to 18 we don't know. Happiness consists in not knowing.

(Notebook 39, quoted in Ltrs-Angelfish, *p. 278)*

Harris, Joel Chandler

(author of Uncle Remus stories)

1906 He was the bashfulest grown person I have ever met. When there were people about he stayed silent, and seemed to suffer until they were gone. But he was lovely, nevertheless; for the sweetness and benignity of the immortal Remus looked out from his eyes, and the graves and sincerities of his character shone in his face.

*(*NAR, *November 1907;* Autob/NAR, *p. 222)*

Harte, Bret

(western writer and one-time friend of Mark Twain)

1866 Though I am generally placed at the head of my breed of scribblers in this part of the country, the place belongs properly to Bret Harte . . .

(Letter to mother and sister, January 20, 1866, Ltrs-1, *p. 328)*

1877 I don't believe Hart ever had an idea that he came by honestly. He is the most abandoned thief that defiles the earth.

(Letter to W. D. Howells, August 3, 1877, Ltrs-Howells, *1:192)*

UNCLE REMUS

1906 One of the pleasantest men I have ever known. He was also one of the unpleasantest men I have ever known. He was showy, meretricious, insincere; and he constantly advertised these qualities in his dress. . . . He hadn't a sincere fibre in him. I think he was incapable of emotion, for I think he had nothing to feel with. I think his heart was merely a pump and had no other function.

(Autob/MTIE, pp. 264–265)

1907 An invertebrate without a country. He hadn't any more passion for his country than an oyster has for its bed; in fact not so much and I apologize to the oyster. The higher passions were left out of Harte; what he knew about them he got from books.

(Ibid., p. 286)

Hartford, Connecticut

1897 To us, our [*Hartford*] house was not unsentient matter—it had a heart, & a soul, & eyes to see us with; & approvals, & solicitudes, & deep sympathies, it was of us, & we were in its confidence, & lived in its grace & in the peace of its benediction.

(Letter to J. H. Twichell, January 19, 1897, Ltrs/Paine, 2:641)

Hawaii

1881 It is the only supremely delightful place on earth.

(Letter to W. D. Howells, October 26, 1881, Ltrs-Howells, 1:378)

1889 That peaceful land, that beautiful land, that far-off home of profound repose, and soft indolence, and dreamy solitude, where life is one long slumberous Sabbath, the climate one long delicious summer day, and the good that die experience no change, for they but fall asleep in one heaven and wake up in another.

(Speech in New York City, April 5, 1889, MT Speaking, p. 244)

1908 The loveliest fleet of islands that lies anchored in any ocean.

(Letter to H. P. Wood, November 30, 1908, Ltrs/Paine, 2:824)

Hawaiian language

1889 The native language is soft, and liquid and flexible, and in every way efficient and satisfactory—till you get mad; then there you are; there isn't anything in it to swear with.

(Speech in New York City, April 5, 1889, MT Speaking, p. 245)

Hawaiians

1866 Down there in the islands they have exploded one of our most ancient and trusted maxims. . . . *Be virtuous and you will be happy.* The Kanakas are not virtuous . . . and yet they are the happiest creatures the sun shines on. They are as happy as the day is long.

(Sandwich Islands lecture, MT Speaking, pp. 14–15)

1866 They will lie for a dollar when they could get a dollar and a half for telling the truth.

(Sandwich Islands lecture, Speeches/Paine, pp. 7–8)

Hay, John (American statesman)

1879 The presence of such a man in politics is like a vase of attar of roses in a glue-factory—it can't extinguish the stink, but it modifies it.

(Letter to W. D. Howells, October 27, 1879, Ltrs-Howells, 1:277)

headaches

1897 Do not undervalue the headache. While it is at its sharpest it seems a bad investment; but when relief begins, the unexpired remainder is worth $4 a minute.   —Pudd'nhead Wilson's New Calendar

(Foll. Equat., ch. 54, p. 517)

healing

1889 Any mummery will cure, if the patient's faith is strong in it.

—[Hank Morgan]

(Conn. Yankee, ch. 26, p. 256)

health

1872 Me sick? The idea! I would as soon expect a wooden image to get sick. I don't know what sickness is.

(Letter to Olivia Clemens, January 4, 1872, Ltrs-5, p. 6)

1897 He had had much experience of physicians, and said "the only way to keep your health is to eat what you don't want, drink what you don't like, and do what you'd druther not."

—Pudd'nhead Wilson's New Calendar

(Foll. Equat., ch. 49, p. 459)

1909 I have what is technically termed a "tobacco" heart. This will move even the wise to laugh at me, for in my vanity I have often bragged that tobacco couldn't hurt me. Privately & between you & me, I am well aware that I ought to laugh at *myself*—& would if I were a really honest person.

However the victory over me is not much of a victory after all, for it has taken 63 years to build this disease. I was immune *that* long, anyway.

(Letter to Frances Nunnally, July 15, 1909,
Ltrs-Angelfish, p. 262)

ME SICK?

heart

1889 You can't reason with your heart; it has its own laws, and thumps about things which the intellect scorns.

—[Hank Morgan]

(Conn. Yankee, ch. 20, p. 183)

123

1899 The heart is the real Fountain of Youth. While that remains young the Waterbury of Time must stand still.

(MTP, ts 42, p. 69; MTN, p. 346)

Heaven

1870 We have reason to believe that there will be laboring men in heaven; and also a number of negroes, and Esquimaux, and Tierra del Fuegans, and Arabs, and a few Indians, and possibly even some Spaniards and Portuguese. All things are possible with God.

("About Smells," WIM&OPW, p. 48)

1893 This serene and noiseless life out here [*Florence, Italy*], with the unimaginable beauty of the view . . . is heaven, & I want to stay in this one when I die, on account of doubts about being a pet in the other one, there's so many people gone there who know about me & will talk . . .

(Letter to Mary Fairbanks, January 18, 1893, Ltrs-Fairbanks, p. 269)

1894 When I reflect upon the number of disagreeable people who I know have gone to a better world, I am moved to lead a different life.

—Pudd'nhead Wilson's Calendar

(Pudd. Wilson, ch. 13, PW&TET, p. 166)

1903 We may not doubt that society in heaven consists mainly of undesirable persons.

(MTP, ts 46, p. 11; MTN, p. 381)

1908 When you consider that heaven, and how crushingly charged it is with everything that is repulsive to a human being, how *can* we believe a human being invented it?

("Letters from the Earth," WIM&OPW, p. 413)

1909 "This is Russia—only more so. There's not the shadow of a republic about it anywhere. There are ranks, here. There are viceroys, princes, governors, sub-governors, sub-sub-governors, and a hundred orders of nobility, grading along down from grand-ducal archangels, stage by stage, till the general level is struck, where there ain't any titles."
—Sandy McWilliams
(Stormfield, ch. 2, pp. 81–82)

heedlessness

1906 I was always heedless. I was born heedless; and therefore I was constantly, and quite unconsciously, committing breaches of the minor proprieties, which brought upon me humiliations which ought to have humiliated me, but didn't, because I didn't know anything had happened. But Livy knew . . . She was very sensitive about me. It distressed her to see me do heedless things which could bring me under criticism, and so she was always watchful and alert to protect me from the kind of transgressions which I have been speaking of.

(NAR, December 7, 1906; Autob/NAR, p. 65)

Heidelberg, Germany

1880 One thinks Heidelberg by day—with its surroundings—is the last possibility of the beautiful; but when he sees Heidelberg by night, a fallen Milky Way, with that glittering railway constellation pinned to the border, he requires time to consider upon the verdict.

(Tramp Abroad, ch. 2, p. 31)

Hell

1866 The heaven and hell of the wildcat religions are vague and ill defined but there is nothing mixed about the Presbyterian heaven and hell. The Presbyterian hell is all misery; the heaven all happiness—nothing to do. But when a man dies on a wildcat basis, it will never rightly know hereafter which department he is in—but he will think he is in hell anyhow, no matter which place he goes to; because in the good place they pro-gress, pro-gress, pro-gress—study, study, study, all the time—and if this isn't hell I don't know what is; and in the bad place he will be worried by remorse of conscience.

("Reflections on the Sabbath," Sketch in Golden Era,
March 18, 1866, WIM&OPW, p. 40)

1890 Dying man couldn't make up his mind which place to go to—both have their advantages, "heaven for climate, hell for company!"

(N&J-3, p. 538)

1908 The first time the Deity came down to earth he brought life and death; when he came the second time, he brought hell.

("Letters from the Earth," WIM&OPW, p. 442)

Henry VIII (16th-century king of England)

1884 "My, you ought to seen old Henry the Eight when he was in bloom. He *was* a blossom. He used to marry a new wife every day, and chop off her head next morning. And he would do it just as indifferent as if he was ordering up eggs. . . . And he made every one of them tell him a tale every night; and he kept that up till he had hogged a thousand and one tales that way, and then he put them all in a book, and called it Domesday Book—which was a good name, and stated the case."   —Huck

(Huck Finn, ch. 23, p. 199)

hereafter

1889 I don't *know* anything about the hereafter, but I am not afraid of it. The further I get away from the superstitions in which I was born & mis-trained, the more the idea of a hereafter commends itself to me & the more I am persuaded I shall find things comfortable when I get there.

HENRY VIII IN BOSTON

(Letter to Olivia Clemens, July 17, 1889, Ltrs-Love, p. 254)

heroes

n.d. Person in a book who does things which he can't and girl marries him for it.

(More Max., p. 8)

1866 Unpoetical history says he [*Lono*] was a favorite god on the island of Hawaii—a great king who had been deified for meritorious services—just our own fashion of rewarding heroes, with the difference that we would have made him a postmaster instead of a god, no doubt.

(Ltrs-Hawaii, Letter 22, p. 243)

1909 Unconsciously we all have a standard by which we measure other men, and if we examine closely we find that this standard is a very simple one, and is this: we admire them, we envy them, for great qualities which we ourselves lack. Hero worship consists in just that. Our heroes are the men who do things which we recognize, with regret, and sometimes with a secret shame, that we cannot do. We find not much in ourselves to admire, we are always privately wanting to be like somebody else. If everybody was satisfied with himself, there would be no heroes.

(Autob/MTA, 1:263–264)

A SHINING HERO

heroine

n.d. Girl who is perfectly charming to live with, in a book.

(More Max., p. 8)

n.d. Girl in a book who is saved from drowning by a hero and marries him next week, but if it was to be over again ten years later it is likely she would rather have a life-belt and he would rather have her have it.

(Ibid., p. 8)

Hinduism

1897 It is a good and gentle religion, but inconvenient.

(Foll. Equat., ch. 49, p. 464)

Hindus

1897 The Hindoo has a childish and unreasoning aversion to being turned into an ass. It is hard to tell why. One could properly expect an ass to have an aversion to being turned into a Hindoo. One could understand that he could lose dignity by it; also self-respect, and nine-tenths of his intelligence. But the Hindoo changed into an ass wouldn't lose anything, unless you count his religion.

(Foll. Equat., ch. 51, pp. 493–494)

1897 It is a curious people. With them, all life seems to be sacred except human life.

(Ibid., ch. 52, p. 503)

history

1897 The very ink with which all history is written is merely fluid prejudice. —Pudd'nhead Wilson's New Calendar

(Foll. Equat., ch. 69, p. 699)

1897 History is better than prophecy. In fact history *is* prophecy. And history says that wherever a weak and ignorant people possess a thing which a strong and enlightened people want, it must be yielded up peaceably. —Pudd'nhead Wilson's New Calendar

(More Tramps, ch. 6, p. 45)

1901–02 One of the most admirable things about history is, that almost as a rule we get as much information out of what it does not say as we get out of what it does say.

("The Secret History of Eddypus," bk. 2, ch. 1, Fab. of Man, p. 338)

1907 It is not worth while to try to keep history from repeating itself, for man's character will always make the preventing of the repetitions impossible.

(Autob/MTIE, p. 66)

c. 1909 A historian who would convey the truth has got to lie. Often he must enlarge the truth by diameters, otherwise his reader would not be able to see it.

(Memorandum, quoted in MT:Biog, ch. 267, p. 1514)

hogs

1884 Hogs likes a puncheon floor in summer-time because it's cool. If you notice, most folks don't go to church only when they've got to; but a hog is different. —[Huck]

(Huck Finn, ch. 18, p. 148)

Holmes, Sherlock
(fictional detective created by Arthur Conan Doyle)

1902 "He can't detect a crime except when he plans it all out beforehand and arranges the clews and hires some fellow to commit it according to instructions." —Fetlock Jones

(DBDS, bk. 1, ch. 1, p. 96)

Holy Grail, the

1889 It was just the Northwest Passage of that day, as you may say; that was all. Every year expeditions went out holy grailing, and next year relief expeditions went out to hunt for *them*. There was worlds of reputation in it, but no money. —[Hank Morgan]

(Conn. Yankee, ch. 9, p. 78)

Holy Land, the

1867 This is a country of disappointments. Nothing in it is as extraordinary as one expects it to be.

(Letter to Alta, September 1867; TWIA, p. 306)

1869 If all the poetry and nonsense that have been discharged upon the fountains and the bland scenery of this region were collected in a book, it would make a most valuable volume to burn.

(Inn. Abroad, ch. 47, p. 495)

homage

1891 By common consent of all the nations and all the ages the most valuable thing in this world is the homage of men, whether deserved or undeserved.

("At the Shrine of St. Wagner," WIM&OE, p. 220)

home

1892 There is a trick about an American house that is like the deep-lying untranslatable idioms of a foreign language—a trick uncatchable by the stranger, a trick incommunicable and indescribable; and that elusive trick, that intangible something, whatever it is, is just the something that gives the home look and the home feeling to an American house and makes it the most satisfying refuge yet invented by men—and women, mainly women.

(Autob/MTA, 1:226)

1894 A home without a cat—and a well-fed, well-petted and properly revered cat—may be a perfect home, perhaps, but how can it prove title?

(Pudd. Wilson, ch. 1, PW&TET, p. 18)

1906 What is a home without a child?

(Letter to Dorothy Quick, August 9, 1907, Ltrs-Angelfish, p. 49)

honesty

n.d. Every man is wholly honest to himself and to God, but not to anyone else.

(More Max., p. 7)

n.d. Honesty *was* the best policy.

(Ibid., p. 8)

1885 All men are liars, partial hiders of facts, half tellers of truths, shirks, moral sneaks.—When a merely *honest* man appears, he is a comet—his fame is eternal—needs no genius, no talent—mere honesty—Luther, Christ, & maybe God has made 2 others—or one—besides me.

(N&J-3, p. 144)

1897 There are people who think that honesty is always the best policy. This is a superstition; there are times when the appearance of it is worth six of it.

(Foll. Equat., ch. 5, p. 78)

honor

1906 We never become really and genuinely our entire and honest selves until we are dead—and not then until we have been dead years and years. People ought to start dead, and then they would be honest so much earlier.

(Autob/MTIE, p. 203)

honor

1895 Honor is a harder master than the law. It cannot compromise for less than one hundred cents on a dollar, and its debts are never outlawed.

(Statement released in August 1895, Speeches/Paine, p. 197)

honors

1902 On the whole it is better to deserve honors & not have them than have them & not deserve them.

(MTP, ts 45, p. 43; MTN, p. 380)

1903 I am a Missourian, & so I shrink from distinctions which have to be arranged beforehand & with my privity; for I then become a party to my own exalting.

(Letter to T. F. Gatts, June 8, 1903, Ltrs/Paine, 2:740)

"hoopilimeaai" (ho'o pili mea'ai; Hawaiian term for fawning over a superior for self-gain)

1866 That long native word means—well, it means Uriah Heep boiled down—it means the soul and spirit of obsequiousness.

(Ltrs-Hawaii, Letter 16, p. 164)

horses

1866 I never mount a horse without experiencing a sort of dread that I may be setting out on that last mysterious journey which all of us must take sooner or later, and I never come back in safety from a horseback trip without thinking of my latter end for two or three days afterward.

(Ltrs-Hawaii, Letter 6, p. 44)

1869 The new horse is not much to boast of, I think. One of his hind legs bends the wrong way, and the other one is as straight and stiff as a tent-pole. Most of his teeth are gone, and he is as blind as a bat. His nose has been broken at some time or other, and is arched like a culvert now. His under lip hangs down like a camel's, and his ears are chopped off close to his head. I had some trouble at first to find a name for him, but I finally concluded to call him Baalbec, because he is such a magnificent ruin.

(Inn. Abroad, ch. 45, p. 476)

1870 My custom heretofore, when I wanted to break a horse, was to do it with a rail. You cannot get hurt then—unless of course the horse bites you.

*(Letter to Theodore W. Crane,
April 22, 1870, Ltrs-4, p. 116)*

THAT LAST MYSTERIOUS JOURNEY

1900 I would have been a Rough Rider if I could have gone to war on an automobile—but not on a horse! No, I know the horse too well; I have known the horse in war and in peace, and there is no place where a horse is comfortable. . . . The horse has too many caprices, and he is too much given to initiative. He invents too many new ideas. No, I don't want anything to do with a horse.

(Speech in New York City, November 10, 1900, MT Speaking, p. 351)

Hotchkiss, Mr. (character based on Orion Clemens)

1898 He was a broad man in many ways; hospitable to new facts and always seeking them; to new ideas, and always examining them; to new opinions and always adopting them; a man ready to meet any novelty half way and give it a friendly trial. He changed his principles with the moon, his politics with the weather, and his religion with his shirt.

("Schoolhouse Hill," ch. 3, Mys. Stranger Mss., p. 190)

Howells, William Dean
(writer, editor, and close friend of Mark Twain)

1879 Possibly you will not be a fully accepted classic until you have been dead a hundred years,—it is the fate of the Shakspeares & of all genuine prophets,—but *then* your books will be as common as Bibles, I

131

believe. You ain't a weed, but an oak; you ain't a summer-house, but a cathedral.

(Letter to W. D. Howells, January 21, 1879, Ltrs-Howells, 1:245–246)

1885 You are really my only author; I am restricted to you; I wouldn't give a damn for the rest.

(Letter to W. D. Howells, July 21, 1885, Ltrs-Howells, 2:533)

1902 Howells has a peculiar gift for seeing the merits of people, and he has always exhibited them in my favor. Howells has never written anything about me that I couldn't read six or seven times a day; he is always just and always fair; he has written more appreciatively of me than anyone in this world.

(Speech in New York City, November 28, 1902, Speeches/Paine, p. 248)

1906 In the sustained exhibition of certain great qualities—clearness, compression, verbal exactness, and unforced and seemingly unconscious felicity of phrasing—he is, in my belief, without his peer in the English-writing world.

("William Dean Howells," WIM&OE, p. 228)

Huckleberry Finn, Adventures of (1884 novel)

1884 Persons attempting to find a motive in this narrative will be prosecuted; persons attempting to find a moral in it will be banished; persons attempting to find a plot in it will be shot.

(Huck Finn, "Notice," p. xxv)

human beings

1897 "There are three kinds of people—Commonplace Men, Remarkable Men, and Lunatics." —Sydney wool-broker

(Foll. Equat., ch. 13, p. 150)

1898 The human being is a stupidly-constructed machine. He may have been a sufficiently creditable invention in the early and ignorant times, but to-day there is not a country in Christendom that would grant a patent on him.

(Letter to H. H. Rogers, May 31, 1898, Ltrs-Rogers, p. 348)

1899 Damn these human beings; if I had invented them I would go hide my head in a bag.

(Letter to W. D. Howells, May 12–13, 1899, Ltrs-Howells, 2:695)

1905–06 "Every human being has a weak place in him, a soft spot. In one it is avarice—you buy him with money; in another it is vanity—you beguile him through that; in another it is a compassionate heart—you work him to your will through that . . ."   —David

("The Refuge of the Derelicts," ch. 1, Fab. of Man, p. 165)

1906 The human being always looks down when he is examining another person's standard, he never finds one that he has to examine by looking up.

("What Is Man?," ch. 5, WIM&OPW, p. 176)

1907 I am only human, although I regret it.

(NAR, March 15, 1907; Autob/NAR, pp. 129–130)

human nature

1865 It is **human nature** to yearn to be what we were never intended for. It is singular, but it is so. I wanted to be a pilot or preacher, & I was about as well calculated for either as is poor Emperor Norton for Chief Justice of the United States.

(Letter to Orion and Mollie Clemens, October 19–20, 1865, Ltrs-1, p. 323)

1884 Isn't human nature the most consummate sham & lie that was ever invented? Isn't man a creature to be ashamed of in pretty much all his aspects? Is he really fit for anything but to be stood up on the street corner as a convenience for dogs? Man, "Know thyself"—& then thou wilt despise thyself, to a dead moral certainty.

(Letter to W. D. Howells, August 31, 1884, Ltrs-Howells, 2:501)

1889 We speak of nature; it is folly; there is no such thing as nature; what we call by that misleading name is merely heredity and training. We have no thoughts of our own, no opinions of our own: they are transmitted to us, trained into us.   —[Hank Morgan]

(Conn. Yankee, ch. 18, p. 162)

1907 A person's nature never changes. What it is in childhood, it remains. Under pressure, or a change of interest, it can partially or wholly disappear from sight, and for considerable stretches of time, but nothing can ever permanently modify it, nothing can ever remove it.

("Christian Science," bk. 2, ch. 7, WIM&OPW, *p. 297)*

1908 It seems to be a law of the human constitution that those that deserve shall not have and those that do not deserve shall get everything that is worth having. It is a sufficiently crazy arrangement, it seems to me.

(Autob/MTIE, p. 305)

human race

1899 The human race consists of the damned & the ought-to-be damned.

(MTP, ts 42, p. 67; MTN, *p. 346)*

1899 I have been reading the morning paper. I do it every morning—well knowing that I shall find in it the usual depravities & basenesses & hypocrisies & cruelties that make up Civilization, & cause me to put in the rest of the day pleading for the damnation of the human race. I cannot seem to get my prayers answered, yet I do not despair.

(Letter to W. D. Howells, April 2–13, 1899, Ltrs-Howells, *2:691)*

1902 The human race consists of the dangerously insane & such as are not.

(MTP, ts 45, p. 43; MTN, *p. 380)*

1906 If we would learn what the human race really *is* at bottom, we need only observe it in election times.

(Autob/MTA, 2:11)

1906 The last quarter of a century of my life has been pretty constantly and faithfully devoted to the study of the human race—that is to say, the study of myself, for, in my individual person, I am the entire human race compacted together. I have found that there is no ingredient of the race which I do not possess in either a small way or a large way. . . . my private and concealed opinion of myself is not of a complimentary sort. It follows that my estimate of the human race is the duplicate of my estimate of myself.

(NAR, November 1907; Autob/NAR, *p. 225)*

1907 There isn't any way to libel the intelligence of the human race.

(Autob/MTIE, p. 18)

1907 The human race was always interesting, and we know by its past that it will always continue so. Monotonously. It is always the same; it never changes. Its circumstances change from time to time, for better or worse, but the race's *character* is permanent, and never changes.

(Autob/MTIE, p. 66)

humility

1893 "There's a breed of humility which is *itself* a species of showing-off . . ."

—*Lasca ("The Esquimau Maiden's Romance," CT-2, p. 121)*

1899 The humble-minded are vain of their humility without suspecting it—the vainest of the vain.

("Indiantown," WWD&OSW, pp. 160–161)

humor

1878 By far The *very* funniest things that ever happened or were ever said, are unprintable (in our day). A great pity. It was no[t] so in the freer age of Boccaccio & Rabelais.

(N&J-2, p. 87)

1879 The funniest things are the forbidden.

(Ibid., p. 304)

1897 Everything human is pathetic. The secret source of Humor itself is not joy but sorrow. There is no humor in heaven.

—Pudd'nhead Wilson's New Calendar
(Foll. Equat., ch. 10, p. 119)

1901 I have never examined the subject of humor until now. I am surprised to find how much ground it covers. I have got its divisions and frontiers down on a piece of paper. I find it defined as a production of the brain, as the power of the brain to produce something humorous, and the capacity of perceiving humor.

(Speech in New York City, November 30, 1901, MT Speaking, p. 423)

1905 People forget that no man is all humor, just as they fail to remember that every man is a humorist.

(Interview in New York Times, *November 26, 1905,* MTSFH, *p. 196)*

humorists

1876 When a humorist ventures upon the grave concerns of life he must do his job better than another man or he works harm to his cause.

(Letter to W. D. Howells, August 23, 1876, Ltrs-Howells, *1:146)*

1905 A humorous *subject* illustrated *seriously* is all right, but a *humorous artist* is no fit person for such work. You see, the humorous writer pretends to absolute seriousness (when he knows his trade) then for an artist to step in & give his calculated gravity all away with a funny picture—oh, my land! It gives me the dry gripes just to think of it.

(Letter to F. A. Duneka, October 7, 1905, Ltrs/Paine, *2:779)*

1906 Humorists of the "mere" sort cannot survive. Humor is only a fragrance, a decoration. Often it is merely an odd trick of speech and of spelling. . . . Humor must not professedly teach, and it must not professedly preach, but it must do both if it would live forever. By forever, I mean thirty years. . . . I have always preached. That is the reason that I have lasted thirty years.

(Autob/MTIE, p. 202)

HUNGER IS ALWAYS RESPECTABLE

hunger

1881 "A full belly is little worth where the mind is starved, and the heart."
—Prince Edward
(Prince & Pauper, ch. 4, p. 24)

1897 Hunger is the handmaid of genius.
—Pudd'nhead Wilson's New Calendar
(Foll. Equat., ch. 43, p. 392)

1898 "A bad person can be as hungry as a good one, and hunger is always respectable." —Heinrich Stein
(No. 44, ch. 3, p. 18)

hymn books

1876 When a Sunday-school superintendent makes his customary little speech, a hymn-book in the hand is as necessary as is the inevitable sheet of music in the hand of a singer who stands forward on the platform and sings a solo at a concert—though why is a mystery: for neither the hymn-book nor the sheet of music is ever referred to by the sufferer.

(Tom Sawyer, ch. 4, p. 31)

hypocrisy

1900 "The first man was a hypocrite and a coward, qualities which have not yet failed in his line; it is the foundation upon which all civilizations have been built." —Philip Traum

("The Chronicle of Young Satan," ch. 8, Mys. Stranger Mss., p. 138)

1905 If any teacher tries to persuade you that hypocrisy is not a part of your blood and bone and flesh, and can therefore be trained out of you by determined and watchful and ceaseless and diligent application to the job, do not you heed him; ask him to cure himself first, then call again.

("Three Thousand Years among the Microbes," ch. 7, WWD&OSW, p. 460)

ideals

c. 1909 It is at our mother's knee that we acquire our noblest & truest & highest ideals, but there is seldom any money in them.

(Memorandum, quoted in MT:Biog, ch. 267, p. 1513)

ideas

1889 Inherited ideas are a curious thing, and interesting to observe and examine. —[Hank Morgan]

(Conn. Yankee, ch. 8, p. 65)

idols

1890 If I were required to guess off-hand, and without collusion with higher minds, what is the bottom cause of the amazing material and intellectual advancement of the last fifty years, I should guess that it was the modern-born and previously non-existent disposition on the part of men to believe that a new idea can have value.

("A Majestic Literary Fossil," £1m Bank-note, p. 241)

1891 The slowness of one section of the world about adopting the valuable ideas of another section of it is a curious thing and unaccountable. This form of stupidity is confined to no community, to no nation; it is universal.

("Some National Stupidities," E&E, p. 175)

1908 It is an astonishing thing that after all these ages the world goes on thinking the human brain-machinery can *originate* a thought.

It can't. It has never done it. In *all* cases, little & big, the thought is born of a suggestion; & in *all* cases the suggestion comes to the brain *from the outside*. . . . In all my life I have never originated an idea, & neither has . . . anybody else.

(Letter to F. V. Christ, August 1908, Ltrs/Paine, 2:813–814)

138

idols

1872 It [is] a glorious thing to be a boy's idol, for it is the only worship one can *swear* to, as genuine . . .

(Letter to Thomas Nast, December 10, 1872, Ltrs-5, p. 249)

ignorance

1864 We do object to a man's parading his ignorance with an air of overbearing egotism which shows you that he is proud of it. True merit is modest, and why should not ignorance be?

(Article in Call, June 28, 1864; ET&S-2, p. 429)

1875 I would rather have my ignorance than another man's knowledge, because I have got so much more *of* it.

(Letter to W. D. Howells, February 10, 1875, Ltrs-Howells, 1:65)

1897 Nothing is so ignorant as a man's left hand, except a lady's watch.
—Pudd'nhead Wilson's New Calendar
(Foll. Equat., ch. 22, p. 214)

1899 One should be gentle with the ignorant, for they are the chosen of God.
(Letter to W. D. Howells, May 12–13, 1899, Ltrs-Howells, 2:697)

illusions

1897 Don't part with your illusions. When they are gone you may still exist, but you have ceased to live.
—Pudd'nhead Wilson's New Calendar
(Foll. Equat., ch. 59, p. 567)

1899 There is no accounting for a woman's illusions. Every woman has one or more that flatly contradict her whole character, her whole mental and moral make-up.
("Indiantown," WWD&OSW, p. 169)

imagination

1892 "Well, no doubt it's a blessed thing to have an imagination that can always make you satisfied, no matter how you are fixed."
—Polly Sellers
(Amer. Claim., ch. 4, p. 56)

1898–99 You can't depend on your judgment when your imagination is out of focus.
(MTP, ts 42, p. 61; MTN, p. 344)

imitation

1894 "Imitation is the bane of courts—I thank God that this one is free from the contamination of that vice . . . "   —Judge Sim Robinson
("Those Extraordinary Twins," ch. 5, PW&TET, p. 393)

1906 In the matter of slavish imitation, man is the monkey's superior all the time. The average man is destitute of independence of opinion.

immortality

He is not interested in contriving an opinion of his own, by study and reflection, but is only anxious to find out what his neighbor's opinion is and slavishly adopt it.

(NAR, October 19, 1906; Autob/NAR, p. 36)

immortality

1902 One of the "proofs" of the immortality of the soul is that myriads have believed it. They have also believed the world was flat.

(MTP, ts 45, p. 38; MTN, p. 379)

c. 1907 I have long ago lost my belief in immortality—also my interest in it. . . . I have sampled this life and it is sufficient. . . . Annihilation has no terrors for me, because I have already tried it before I was born— a hundred million years—and I have suffered more in an hour, in this life, than I remember to have suffered in the whole hundred million years put together.

(Autob/AMT, ch. 49, p. 249)

impossibility

1878 To man all things are possible but one—he cannot have a hole in the seat of his breeches & keep his fingers out of it.

(Letter to W. D. Howells, June 27, 1878, Ltrs-Howells, 1:237)

"In God We Trust"

1907 The motto stated a lie. If this nation has ever trusted in God, that time has gone by; for nearly a half century almost its entire trust has been in the Republican party and the dollar—mainly the dollar.

(Autob/MTIE, p. 50)

1908 That motto on the coin is an overstatement. . . .

There was never a nation in the world that put its whole trust in God. It is a statement made on insufferable evidence.

(Speech in New York City, May 14, 1908, Speeches/Paine, p. 379)

inanimate objects

1869 We bestow thoughtful care upon inanimate objects, but none upon ourselves.

(Inn. Abroad, ch. 19, p. 187)

indecency

1896 Each race determines for itself what indecencies are. Nature knows no indecencies; man invents them.

(MTP, ts 37, p. 27; MTN, p. 288)

independence

1888 Independence—which is loyalty to one's best self & principles, & this is often disloyalty to the general idols & fetishes.

(N&J-3, p. 415)

India

1897 There is only one India! It is the only country that has a monopoly of grand and imposing specialties. When another country has a remarkable thing, it cannot have it all to itself—some other country has a duplicate. But India—that is different. Its marvels are its own; the patents cannot be infringed; imitations are not possible. And think of the size of them, the majesty of them, the weird and outlandish character of the most of them!

(Foll. Equat., ch. 43, p. 397)

1897 So far as I am able to judge, nothing has been left undone, either by man or Nature, to make India the most extraordinary country that the sun visits on his round. Nothing seems to have been forgotten, nothing overlooked. Always, when you think you have come to the end of her tremendous specialties and have finished hanging tags upon her as the Land of the Thug, the Land of the Plague, the Land of Famine, the Land of Giant Illusions, the Land of Stupendous Mountains, and so forth, another specialty crops up and another tag is required. . . . Perhaps it will be simplest to throw away the tags and generalize her with one all-comprehensive name, as the Land of Wonders.

(Foll. Equat., ch. 57, p. 544)

1906 The only foreign land I ever daydream about or deeply long to see again.

(Autob/MTIE, p. 312)

Indians, American

1869 It isn't worth while, in these practical times, for people to talk about Indian poetry—there never was any in them—except in the Fenimore Cooper Indians. But *they* are an extinct tribe that never existed.

(Inn. Abroad, ch. 20, p. 205)

1877 Knowledge of Indians, & humanity, are seldom found in the same individual . . .

(Letter to W. D. Howells, February 22, 1877, Ltrs-Howells, 1:172)

inhumanity

1898–99 God's inhumanity to man makes countless thousands mourn.

(MTP, ts 42, p. 61; MTN, p. 344)

THE INNOCENT TRAVELER

Innocents Abroad, The (1869 travel book)

1869 The irreverence of the volume appears to be a tip-top good feature of it, diplomatically speaking, though I wish with all my heart there wasn't an irreverent passage in it.

(Letter to Elisha Bliss, September 3, 1869, Ltrs-3, p. 329)

1870 To say that the *Innocents Abroad* is a curious book, would be to use the faintest language—would be to speak of the Matterhorn as a neat elevation or of Niagara as being "nice" or "pretty." "Curious" is too tame a word wherewith to describe the imposing insanity of this work.

("An Entertaining Article," $30k Bequest, p. 218)

1886 When the Lord finished the world, he pronounced it good. That is what I said about my first work, too. But Time, I tell you, Time takes the confidence out of these incautious early opinions. It is more than likely that He thinks about the world now pretty much as I think about the *Innocents Abroad.* The fact is, there is a trifle too much water in both.

(Letter to unidentified person, November 6, 1886, PortMT, *p. 763)*

insane asylums

1897 All human rules are more or less idiotic, I suppose. It is best so, no doubt. The way it is now, the asylums can hold the sane people, but if we tried to shut up the insane we should run out of building materials.

(Foll. Equat., ch. 50, p. 477)

insanity

1870 Insanity certainly is on the increase in the world, and crime is dying out. There are no longer any murders—none worth mentioning, at any rate. Formerly, if you killed a man, it was possible that you were insane—but now, if you, having friends and money, kill a man it is *evidence* that you are a lunatic. . . .

Really, what we want now, is not laws against crime, but a law against *insanity.* That is where the true evil lies.

("A New Crime," SN&O, *pp. 190–191)*

1907 Let us consider that we are all partially insane. It will explain us to each other; it will unriddle many riddles; it will make clear and simple many things which are involved in haunting and harassing difficulties and obscurities now.

("Christian Science," bk. 1, ch. 5, WIM&OPW, *p. 234)*

1907 All democrats are insane, but not one of them knows it; none but the republicans and mugwumps know it. All the republicans are insane, but only the democrats and mugwumps can perceive it. The rule is perfect: *in all matters of opinion our adversaries are insane.*

(Ibid., p. 235)

instinct

1894 For all the brag you hear about knowledge being such a wonderful thing, instink is worth forty of it for real unerringness.

—[Huck Finn]

(Tom Sawyer Abrd., ch. 13, p. 99)

1897–98 Whenever we have a strong and persistent and ineradicable instinct, we may be sure that it is not original with us, but inherited—inherited from away back, and hardened and perfected by the petrifying influence of time.

(NAR, September 7, 1906; Autob/NAR, p. 5)

1906 It is merely *petrified thought*; thought solidified and made inanimate by habit; thought which was once alive and awake, but is become unconscious—walks in its sleep, so to speak.   —Old Man

("What Is Man?," ch. 6, WIM&OPW, p. 190)

instruction

1863 It is a good thing, perhaps, to write for the amusement of the public, but it is a far higher and nobler thing to write for their instruction—their profit—their actual and tangible benefit.

("How to Cure a Cold," ET&S-1, p. 298)

insurance

1874 Certainly there is no nobler field for human effort than the insurance line of business—especially accident insurance. . . .

There is nothing more beneficent than accident insurance. I have seen an entire family lifted out of poverty and into affluence by the simple boon of a broken leg. . . . I have seen nothing so seraphic as the look that comes into a freshly mutilated man's face when he feels in his vest pocket with his remaining hand and finds his accident ticket all right.

(Speech in Hartford, October 12, 1874, SN&O, pp. 229-230)

insurrection

1897 Tom explained what it was, but there didn't seem to be any way to work it. He had to give in, himself, that there wasn't anything definite about an insurrection. It wasn't either one thing nor t'other, but only just the middle stage of a tadpole. With its tail on, it was only just a riot; tail gone, it was an insurrection; tail gone and legs out, it was a revolution.   —[Huck Finn]

("Tom Sawyer's Conspiracy," HF&TS, ch. 1, p. 140)

interest, new

1880 A great and priceless thing is a new interest! How it takes possession of a man! how it clings to him! how it rides him!

(Tramp Abroad, ch. 35, p. 381)

interview

1888 For several quite plain and simple reasons, an "interview" must, as a rule, be an absurdity, and chiefly for this reason—It is an attempt to use a boat on land or a wagon on water, to speak figuratively. Spoken speech is one thing, written speech is quite another. Print is the proper vehicle for the latter, but it isn't for the former. The moment "talk" is put into print you recognize that it is not what it was when you heard it; you perceive that an immense something has disappeared from it. This is its soul. You have nothing but a dead carcass left on your hands. Color, play of feature, the varying modulations of the voice, the laugh, the smile, the informing inflections, everything that gave that body warmth, grace, friendliness and charm and commended it to your affections—or, at least, to your tolerance—is gone and nothing is left but a pallid, stiff and repulsive cadaver.

(Letter to Edward W. Bok, July 25, 1888,
Ltrs/Paine, 2:504; date corrected in UCCL)

invention

1870 An inventor is a poet—a true poet—and nothing in any degree less than a high order of poet—wherefore his noblest pleasure dies with the stroke that completes the creature of his genius, just as the painter's & the sculptor's & other poets' highest pleasure ceases with the touch that finishes their work—& so only he can understand or appreciate the *legitimate* "success" of his achievement, littler minds being able to get no higher than a comprehension of a vulgar moneyed success.

(Letter to Pamela A. Moffett, June 12, 1870,
Ltrs-4, p. 151)

145

POETIC INVENTOR

Irish, the

1880 There is a difference between invention & application.—The ancients invented; the modern spirit invents <u>&</u> applies.

(N&J-2, p. 417)

1888 The thing which has made Labor great & powerful is labor-saving machinery—& nothing else in the world could have done it. It has been Labor's savior, benefactor; but Labor doesn't know it, & would ignorantly crucify it. But that is human, & natural. Every great invention takes a livelihood away from 50,000 men—& within ten years *creates* a livelihood for *half a million*. But you can't make Labor appreciate that . . .

(Letter to W. D. Howells, March 31, 1888, Ltrs-Howells, 2:597)

1906 I have invented a good many useful things in my time, but never anything better than that of getting money out of people who don't want to part with it.

(Speech in New York City, March 29, 1906, MT Speaking, p. 507)

LINED WITH COPPER

Irish, the

1883 "Give an Irishman lager for a month, and he's a dead man. An Irishman is lined with copper, and the beer corrodes it. But whisky polishes the copper and is the saving of him, sir." —Irish vendor on steamboat

(Life on Miss., ch. 23, p. 260)

irreverence

1888 Irreverence is the champion of liberty, & its only sure defence.

(N&J-3, p. 392)

1897 True irreverence is disrespect for another man's god.

—Pudd'nhead Wilson's New Calendar

(Foll. Equat., ch. 53, p. 507)

1898 "Irreverence is *another person's* disrespect to *your* god; there isn't any word that tells what your disrespect to *his* god is."   —44

(No. 44, ch. 30, p. 168)

1909 When a thing is sacred to me it is impossible for me to be irreverent toward it. I cannot call to mind a single instance where I have ever been irreverent, except toward the things which were sacred to other people.

(ISD, ch. 12, p. 134)

Italians

1880 It seems that the heavy work in the quarries and the new railway gradings [*in Germany*] is done mainly by Italians. That was a revelation. We have the notion in our country that Italians never do heavy work at all, but confine themselves to the lighter arts, like organ-grinding, operatic singing, and assassination.

(Tramp Abroad, ch. 17, p. 155)

italics

1863 I never knew a girl in my life who could write consecutive sentences without italicising a word. They can't do it . . .

("Mark Twain—More of Him," ET&S-1, p. 309)

Italy

1869 She is to-day one vast museum of magnificence and misery. . . . It is the wretchedest, princeliest land on earth.

(Inn. Abroad, ch. 25, p. 258)

1878 Italy the home of art & swindling; home of religion & moral rottenness . . .

(N&J-2, p. 182)

1904 The best country in the world to live in.

(Interview in New York Times, April 10, 1904, MTSFH, p. 189)

147

jackass

1899 Concerning the difference between man & the jackass. Some observers hold that there isn't any. But this wrongs the jackass.

(MTP, ts 42, p. 72; MTN, p. 347)

Jackson, Andrew

(president of the United States when Mark Twain was born)

1883 The war had ended, the two nations were at peace, but the news had not yet reached New Orleans. If we had had the cable telegraph in those days, this blood would not have been spilt, those lives would not have been wasted; and better still, Jackson would probably never have been president. We have gotten over the harms done us by the War of 1812, but not over some of those done us by Jackson's presidency.

(Life on Miss., ch. 48, p. 476)

James, Jesse (western outlaw killed in 1882)

1883 According to [*cheap histories*], he was the most marvellous creature of his kind that had ever existed. It was a mistake. Murel was his equal in boldness; in pluck; in rapacity; in cruelty, brutality, heartlessness, treachery, and in general and comprehensive vileness and shamelessness; and very much his superior in some larger aspects. James was a retail rascal; Murel wholesale.

(Life on Miss., ch. 29, p. 312)

Jerusalem

1869 No landscape exists that is more tiresome to the eye than that which bounds the approaches to Jerusalem. The only difference between the roads and the surrounding country, perhaps, is that there are rather more rocks in the roads than in the surrounding country.

(Inn. Abroad, ch. 52, p. 555)

1869 Jerusalem is mournful, and dreary, and lifeless. I would not desire to live here.

(Ibid., ch. 53, p. 560)

Jesuits

1867 The true Jesuit wisdom . . . says that ignorance is bliss and progress is sedition.

(Letter to Alta, June 19, 1867; TWIA, p. 5)

Jews

1879 The Jews have the best average brain of any people in the world. The Jews are the only race in the world who work wholly with their brains & never with their hands. There are no Jew beggars, no Jew tramps, no Jew ditchers, hod-carriers day laborers or followers of toil-some mechanical traders. They are peculiarly & conspicuously the world's intellectual aristocracy.

(N&J-2, p. 302)

Jim (character in *Huckleberry Finn* and other stories)

1884 He was right; he was most always right; he had an uncommon level head, for a nigger. —[Huck]

(Huck Finn, ch. 14, p. 93)

1884 I . . . got to thinking over our trip down the river; and I see Jim before me, all the time . . . But somehow I couldn't seem to strike no places to harden me against him, but only the other kind. I'd see him standing my watch on top of his'n, stead of calling me—so I could go on sleeping; and see him how glad he was when I come back out of the fog; and when I come to him agin in the swamp, up there where the feud was; and such-like times; and would always call me honey, and pet me, and do everything he could think of for me, and how good he always was . . . —[Huck]

(Ibid., pp. 269–270)

Joan of Arc (15th-century French national heroine)

1896 Whatever thing men call great, look for it in Joan of Arc, and there you will find it.

(Joan of Arc, bk. 2, ch. 29, p. 245)

1896 It took six thousand years to produce her; her like will not be seen in the earth again in fifty thousand.

(Ibid., bk. 3, ch. 6, p. 349)

1904 The Wonder of the Ages. . . . Taking into account . . . all the circumstances—her origin, youth, sex, illiteracy, early environment, and the obstructing conditions under which she exploited her high gifts and made her conquests in the field and before the courts that tried her for her life—she is easily and by far the most extraordinary person the human race has ever produced.

("Saint Joan of Arc," CT-2, p. 591)

Joan of Arc, Personal Recollections of (1896 novel)

1895 I judged that this end of the book would be hard work, and it turned out so. I have never done any work before that cost so much thinking and weighing and measuring and planning and cramming, or so much cautious and painstaking execution. . . .

Possibly the book may not sell, but that is nothing—it was written for love.

(Letter to H. H. Rogers, January 29, 1895, Ltrs-Rogers, pp. 124–125)

c. 1908 I liked *Joan of Arc* best of all my books; and it is the best; I know it perfectly well.

(Autobiographical dictation, quoted in Ltrs-Angelfish, p. xxiv)

journals

1869 At certain periods it becomes the dearest ambition of a man to keep a faithful record of his performances in a book; and he dashes at this work with an enthusiasm that imposes on him the notion that keeping a journal is the veriest pastime in the world, and the pleasantest. But if he only lives twenty-one days, he will find out that only those rare natures that are made up of pluck, endurance, devotion to duty for duty's sake, and invincible determination, may hope to venture upon so tremendous an enterprise as the keeping of a journal and not sustain a shameful defeat.

(Inn. Abroad, ch. 4, p. 40)

1869 If you wish to inflict a heartless and malignant punishment upon a young person, pledge him to keep a journal a year.

(Ibid., p. 42)

joy

1869 And what is *any* joy (except the miser's,) without companionship?

(Letter to Olivia Langdon, May 17, 1869, Ltrs-3, *p. 240)*

1897 Grief can take care of itself; but to get the full value of a joy you must have somebody to divide it with.

—Pudd'nhead Wilson's New Calendar

(Foll. Equat., ch. 48, p. 447)

Jubilee Singers (African American choir)

1897 In the Jubilees and their songs America has produced the perfectest flower of the ages; and I wish it were a foreign product, so that she would worship it and lavish money on it and go properly crazy over it.

(Letter to J. H. Twichell, August 22, 1897, Letters/Paine, *2:646)*

Judas (apostle who betrayed Christ)

1873 To my mind Judas Iscariot was nothing but a low, mean, premature Congressman.

(Letter to New York Tribune, *March 10, 1873,* MTSFH, *p. 76)*

July Fourth

1894 Statistics show that we lose more fools on this day than in all the other days of the year put together. This proves, by the number left in stock, that one Fourth of July per year is now inadequate, the country has grown so. —Pudd'nhead Wilson's Calendar

(Pudd. Wilson, ch. 17, PW&TET, *p. 221)*

1897 Eight grown Americans out of ten dread the coming of the Fourth, with its pandemonium and its perils, and they rejoice when it is gone—if still alive.

(Foll. Equat., ch. 16, p. 163)

Jumping frog story (1865 sketch published under several titles)

1866 I never tried to tell it myself, without making a botch of it.

(Letter to mother and sister, June 21, 1866, Ltrs-1, *p. 344)*

1906 It certainly had a wide celebrity . . . but I was aware that it was only the frog that was celebrated. It wasn't I.

(NAR, September 21, 1906; Autob/NAR, *p. 13)*

151

jury system

1872 The jury system puts a ban upon intelligence and honesty, and a premium upon ignorance, stupidity and perjury.

(Rough. It, ch. 48, p. 321)

1873 The humorist who invented trial by jury played a colossal practical joke upon the world, but since we have the system we ought to try to respect it.

(Letter to New York Tribune, March 10, 1873, MTSFH, p. 76)

1873 We have a criminal jury system which is superior to any in the world; and its efficiency is only marred by the difficulty of finding twelve men every day who don't know anything and can't read. And I may observe that we have an insanity plea that would have saved Cain.

(Speech in London, July 4, 1873, SN&O, pp. 180–181)

justice

1864 It is better to save than to destroy, and that justice is most righteous which is tempered by mercy.

(Article in Call, July 17, 1864; Cl. of Call, p. 220)

Keller, Helen (blind and deaf author and friend of Mark Twain)

1896 It won't *do* for America to allow this marvelous child to retire from her studies because of poverty. If she can go on with them she will make a fame that will endure in history for centuries. Along her special lines she is the most extraordinary product of all the ages.

(Letter to Emilie Rogers, November 26, 1896, Ltrs-Rogers, p. 253)

1909 She is the most marvelous person of her sex that has existed on this earth since Joan of Arc.

(Speech in Norfolk, Virginia, April 3, 1909, Speeches/Paine, *p. 393)*

Kilauea (volcano on the island of Hawaii)

1872 I have seen Vesuvius since, but it was a mere toy, a child's volcano, a soup-kettle, compared to this.

*(*Rough. It, *ch. 74, p. 507)*

killing

1900 "Two centuries from now it will be recognised that all the competent killers are Christians; then the pagan world will go to school to the Christian: not to acquire his religion, but his guns."

—Philip Traum

("The Chronicle of Young Satan," ch. 8, Mys. Stranger Mss., *p. 137)*

153

kings

1884 "All kings is mostly rapscallions, as fur as I can make out." —Huck

*(*Huck Finn, *ch. 23, p. 199)*

1884 "Kings is kings, and you got to make allowances. Take them all around, they're a mighty ornery lot. It's the way they're raised." —Huck

(Ibid., p. 200)

1889 A king is a mere artificiality, and so a king's feelings, like the impulses of an automatic doll, are mere artificialities; but as a man, he is a reality, and his feelings, as a man, are real, not phantasms.

—[Hank Morgan]

*(*Conn. Yankee, *ch. 35, pp. 350–351)*

1897 "Kings ain't in our line; we ain't used to them, and wouldn't know how to keep them satisfied and

A RAPSCALLION

quiet; and they don't seem to do anything much for the wages, anyway, and don't pay no rent."

—Tom Sawyer

("Tom Sawyer's Conspiracy," HF&TS, ch. 1, p. 140)

1898 A king is a king by accident; the reason the rest of us are not kings is merely due to another accident; we are all made out of the same clay, and it is a sufficiently poor quality.

("The Memorable Assassination," WIM&OE, p. 174)

Kipling, Rudyard (English writer and friend of Mark Twain)

c. 1906 Kipling's name and Kipling's words always stir me now, stir me more than do any other living man's. . . .

I know Kipling's . . . better than I know anybody else's books. They never grow pale to me; they keep their color; they are always fresh.

(Autob/AMT, ch. 59, pp. 286, 288)

1906 Between us, we cover all knowledge; he knows all that can be known, and I know the rest.

(Autob/MTIE, p. 311)

kleptomania

Kleptomania.

1870 In these days, too, if a person of good family and high social standing steals anything, they call it *kleptomania*, and send him to the lunatic asylum.

("A New Crime," SN&O, p. 190)

knights

1889 If knights errant were to be believed, not all castles were desirable places to seek hospitality in. As a matter of fact, knights errant were *not* persons to be believed—that is, measured by modern standards of veracity; yet measured by the standards of their own time, and scaled accordingly, you got the truth.

—[Hank Morgan]

(Conn. Yankee, ch. 16, p. 138)

1889 Knight-errantry is a most chuckle-headed trade, and it is tedious hard work, too, but I begin to see that there *is* money in it, after all, if you have luck.

(Ibid., ch. 19, p. 177)

1889 As a rule, a knight is a lummox, and sometimes even a labrick, and hence open to pretty poor arguments when they come glibly from a superstition-monger.

(Ibid., ch. 30, p. 292)

knowledge

1870 "The less a man knows the bigger the noise he makes and the higher the salary he commands." —Editor

("How I Edited an Agricultural Paper Once," CT-1, p. 416)

Ladies Home Journal (American magazine)

1898 It is a mere literary night-cart. I would rather steal nickels for a living than earn it writing for such a rag as that. It is full of Wanamaker and his Sunday schools and other hypocricies. It ought to be medicated, and restricted [to] the Bleeding Piles Hospital.

(Letter to H. H. Rogers, October 18, 1898, Ltrs-Rogers, p. 370)

"lagniappe"

1883 We picked up one excellent word—a word worth travelling to New Orleans to get; a nice limber, expressive handy word—"Lagniappe." They pronounce it lanny-*yap*. . . . It is the equivalent of the thirteenth roll in a "baker's dozen." It is something thrown in, gratis, for good measure.

(Life on Miss., ch. 44, p. 450)

language

1897 Language is a treacherous thing, a most unsure vehicle, and it can seldom arrange descriptive words in such a way that they will not inflate the facts—by help of the reader's imagination, which is always ready to take a hand, and work for nothing, and do the bulk of it at that.

(Foll. Equat., ch. 59, p. 571)

1906 What is the real function, the essential function, the supreme function, of language? Isn't it merely to convey ideas and emotions?

(Speech in New York City, September 19, 1906, Speeches/Paine, p. 319)

last words

1869 A distinguished man should be as particular about his last words as he is about his last breath. He should write them out on a slip of paper and take the judgment of his friends on them. He should never leave such a thing to the last hour of his life, and trust to an intellectual spurt at the last moment to enable him to say something smart with his latest gasp and launch into eternity with grandeur. . . . There is hardly a case on record where a man came to his last moment unprepared and said a good thing—hardly a case where a man trusted to that last moment and did not make a solemn botch of it and go out of the world feeling absurd.

("The Last Words of Great Men," CT-1, p. 315)

1880 Relevancy was a matter of no consequence in last words, what you wanted was thrill.

(Tramp Abroad, ch. 8, p. 71)

latitude, lines of

1897 There isn't a Parallel of Latitude but thinks it would have been the Equator if it had had its rights.

—Pudd'nhead Wilson's New Calendar
(Foll. Equat., ch. 69, p. 699)

laughter

1899 Laughter which cannot be suppressed is catching. Sooner or later it washes away our defences, and undermines our dignity, and we join in it—ashamed of our weakness, and embittered against the cause of its exposure, but no matter, we have to join in, there is no help for it.

("Indiantown," WWD&OSW, *p. 172)*

1900 "Your race, in its poverty, has unquestionably one really effective weapon—laughter. Power, Money, Persuasion, Supplication, Persecution—these can lift at a colossal humbug—push it a little—crowd it a little—weaken it a little, century by century: but only Laughter can blow it to rags and atoms at a blast. Against the assault of Laughter nothing can stand." —Philip Traum

("The Chronicle of Young Satan," ch. 10, Mys. Stranger Mss., *pp. 165–166)*

law

1889 There are written laws—they perish; but there are also unwritten laws—*they* are eternal. —[Hank Morgan]

(Conn. Yankee, ch. 33, p. 328)

1897 To succeed in the other trades, capacity must be shown; in the law, concealment of it will do. —Pudd'nhead Wilson's New Calendar

(Foll. Equat., ch. 37, p. 331)

lawyers

1876 The more I see of lawyers, the more I despise them. They seem to be natural, born *cowards*, and on top of that they are God damned idiots. I suppose *our* law firm are above average; and yet it would be base flattery to say that *their* heads contain anything more valuable than can be found in a new tripe.

(Letter to James R. Osgood, January 25, 1876,
Ltrs-Publs, *p. 95)*

laziness

1867 I am not as lazy as I was—but I am lazy enough yet, for two people.

(Letter to Mary Fairbanks, December 12, 1867,
Ltrs-2, *p. 134)*

1869 I thought I was lazy, but I am a steam-engine compared to a Constantinople dog.

(Inn. Abroad, ch. 34, p. 372)

BORN LAZY

1906 I was born lazy. I am no lazier now than I was forty years ago, but that is because I reached the limit forty years ago. You can't go beyond possibility.

(Autob/MTIE, p. 256)

A DISMAL SORT OF BUSINESS

lecturing

1869 I most cordially hate the lecture field. And, after all, I shudder to think that I may never get out of it.

(Letter to family, June 4, 1869, Ltrs-3, p. 259)

1870 I'm out of the lecture field permanently, I hope. It is a dismal sort of business, even to a lazy man like me—it would kill a nervous thunderbolt like you.

(Letter to Frank Fuller, April 26, 1870, Ltrs-4, p. 120)

1880 There's a great moral difference between a lecture and a speech . . . for when you deliver a lecture you get good pay, but when you make a speech you don't get a cent.

(Speech in Hartford, October 26, 1880, MT Speaking, p. 139)

1896 Why, there *isn't* any slavery that is so exacting and so infernal.

(Letter to H. H. Rogers, July 22, 1896, Ltrs-Rogers, p. 227)

left-handedness

1878 "Pretty much all the murders are done by left-handed people."
—Simon Wheeler

("Simon Wheeler, Detective," ch. 7, S&B, p. 411)

1902 "A fact which you must have often noticed in the great detective narratives—that *all* assassins are left-handed."   —Sherlock Holmes

(DBDS, bk. 2, ch. 3, pp. 131–132)

legislatures

1866 I have seen a number of legislatures, and there was a comfortable majority in each of them that knew just about enough to come in when it rained, and that was all. Few men of first-class ability can afford to let their affairs go to ruin while they fool away their time in legislatures for months on a stretch. Few men care for the small-beer distinctions one is able to achieve in such a place.

(Ltrs-Hawaii, *Letter 12, p. 109*)

1866 This [*Hawaiian*] Legislature is like all other legislatures. A woodenhead gets up and proposes an utterly absurd something or other, and he and half a dozen other woodenheads discuss it with windy vehemence for an hour, the remainder of the house sitting in silent patience the while, and then a sensible man—a man of weight—a big gun—gets up and shows the foolishness of the matter in five sentences; a vote is taken and the thing is tabled.

(Ibid., *pp. 111–112*)

1873 I think I can say, and say with pride, that we have some legislatures that bring higher prices than any in the world.

(Speech in London, *July 4, 1873*, SN&O, *p. 181*)

1875 I think that when a man has unsuccessfully aspired to be a legislator, and is capable of mentioning it where people could not otherwise find it out, he is manifestly telling the petrified truth.

(Letter to Hartford Courant, *c. October 1, 1875*, MTSFH, *p. 100*)

Leopold II (king of Belgium and owner of the Congo Free State)

1906 A wild beast . . . who for money's sake mutilates, murders and starves half a million of friendless and helpless poor natives in the Congo State every year, and does it by the silent consent of all the Christian powers except England . . . [A] moldy and piety-mouthing hypocrite, this bloody monster whose mate is not findable in human history anywhere, and whose personality will surely shame hell itself when he arrives there—which will be soon, let us hope and trust.

(Autob/MTIE, *pp. 211–212*)

letter writing

1863 Nothing but that deep & abiding sense of duty which is a second nature with me, prompts me to write even to my gay & sprightly mother. It is misery to me to write letters.

(Letter to mother, *April 16, 1863*, Ltrs-1, *p. 251*)

1869 The most useful and interesting letters we get here from home are from children seven or eight years old. . . . They write simply and naturally and without strain for effect. They tell all they know, and stop.

(Article in Grass Valley, California, Daily National,
December 6, 1869; MTSFH, p. 58)

1871 The reason I dread writing letters is because I am so apt to get to slinging wisdom & forget to let up. Thus much precious time is lost.

(Letter to James Redpath, June 15, 1871, Ltrs-4, p. 409)

1879 I mightily like to get letters from you, & I mightily like to answer them, too, after I get started, but I do so hate to start! Why ain't people constructed so that they will *like* to write letters? I don't mind taking a bath, after I am once *in*, but I do hate to get in.

(Letter to Mary Fairbanks, March 6, 1879, Ltrs-Fairbanks, pp. 223, 225)

1885 My correspondence is the despair of my life. Suppose *you* had to have 15 teeth pulled every day; & every time you lost 3 days—a thing that happens once a fortnight on an average—must have 45 pulled at one sitting?

(Letter to Pamela A. Moffett, June 12, 1885, MT:Bus. Man, p. 325)

c. 1907 The frankest and freest and privatest product of the human mind and heart is a love letter; the writer gets his limitless freedom of statement and expression from his sense that no stranger is going to see what he is writing.

(Autob/MTA, Preface, 1:xv)

Letters from the Earth, The
(unfinished book by Mark Twain first published in 1962)

1909 This book will never be published—in fact it couldn't be, because it would be felony to soil the mails with it, for it has much Holy Scripture in it of the kind that prostitutes & Christians like, but which can't properly be read aloud, except from the pulpit and in family worship. Paine enjoys it, but Paine is going to be damned one of these days, I suppose.

(Letter to Elizabeth Wallace, November 13, 1909, Ltrs/Paine, 2:834)

letters, publication of

1865 You had better shove this [*letter*] in the stove—for if we strike a bargain I don't want any absurd "literary remains" & "unpublished letters of Mark Twain" published after I am planted.

(Letter to Orion and Mollie Clemens, October 19–20, 1865, Ltrs-1, *p. 322)*

libraries

1894 Books are the liberated spirits of men, and should be bestowed in a heaven of light and grace and harmonious color and sumptuous comfort . . . instead of in the customary kind of public library, with its depressing austerities and severities of form and furniture and decoration. A public library is the most enduring of memorials, the trustiest monument for the preservation of an event or a name or an affection; for it, and it only, is respected by wars and revolutions, and survives them.

(Letter to the Millicent Library, February 22, 1894, MTSFH, *p. 146)*

lies

1865 Good little boys must never tell lies when the truth will answer just as well. In fact, real good little boys will never tell lies at all—not at all—except in case of the most urgent necessity.

("Advice for Good Little Boys," ET&S-2, *p. 242)*

1867 Nobody can have confidence in cold, monotonous, inanimate utterances, though they were teeming with truth and wisdom. Manner is everything in these cases—matter is nothing. The most outrageous lies that can be invented will find believers if a man only tells them with all his might.

(Letter to Alta, *May 17, 1867,* MTTB, *p. 175)*

1881 "A wise man does not waste so good a commodity as lying for naught."   —Hugo

(Prince & Pauper, ch. 18, p. 160)

1882 No fact is more firmly established than that lying is a necessity of our circumstances,—the deduction that it is then a Virtue goes without saying. No virtue can reach its highest usefulness

without careful and diligent cultivation,—therefore, it goes without saying, that this one ought to be taught in the public schools—at the fireside—even in the newspapers. What chance has the ignorant, uncultivated liar against the educated expert? . . . *Judicious* lying is what the world needs. I sometimes think it were even better and safer not to lie at all than to lie injudiciously. An awkward, unscientific lie is often as ineffectual as the truth.

("On the Decay of the Art of Lying," SWE, *p. 218)*

1882 The young ought to be temperate in the use of this great art until practice and experience shall give them that confidence, elegance, and precision which alone can make the accomplishment graceful and profitable.

(Address to Saturday Morning Club, Boston,
April 15, 1882, Speeches/Paine, *p. 105)*

1882 An awkward, feeble, leaky lie is a thing which you ought to make it your unceasing study to avoid; such a lie as that has no more real permanence than an average truth. Why, you might as well tell the truth at once and be done with it. A feeble, stupid, preposterous lie will not live two years—except it be a slander upon somebody.

(Ibid., p. 106)

1889 In all lies there is wheat among the chaff . . . —[Hank Morgan]

(Conn. Yankee, ch. 11, p. 90)

1894 It is often the case that the man who can't tell a lie thinks he is the best judge of one. —Pudd'nhead Wilson's Calendar

(Pudd. Wilson, ch. 13, PW&TET, p. 166)

1897 The only difference that I know of between a silent lie and a spoken one is, that the silent lie is a less respectable one than the other. And it can deceive, whereas the other can't—as a rule.

(Foll. Equat., ch. 39, pp. 360–361)

1897 There are 869 different forms of lying, but only one of them has been squarely forbidden. Thou shalt not bear false witness against thy neighbor. —Pudd'nhead Wilson's New Calendar

(Ibid., ch. 55, p. 524)

1899 Almost all lies are acts, and speech has no part in them. . . . all people are liars from the cradle onward, without exception, and . . . they begin to lie as soon as they wake in the morning, and keep it up, without rest or refreshment, until they go to sleep at night.

("My First Lie, and How I Got Out of It," CT-2, pp. 439–440)

1899 The universal conspiracy of the silent-assertion lie is hard at work always and everywhere, and always in the interest of a stupidity or a sham, never in the interest of a thing fine or respectable.

(Ibid., p. 441)

1901 Another instance of unconscious humor was of the Sunday school boy who defined a lie as "An abomination before the Lord and an ever present help in time of trouble." That may have been unconscious humor, but it looked more like hard, cold experience and knowledge of facts.

(Speech in New York City, November 30, 1901, MT Speaking, p. 424)

1902 What is the difference between lying with your eyes and lying with your mouth? There is none; and if you would reflect a moment you would see that it is so. There isn't a human being that doesn't tell a gross of lies every day of his life . . .

("Was It Heaven? or Hell?," CT-2, ch. 3, p. 536)

life

n.d. What is human life? The first third a good time; the rest remembering about it.

(More Max., p. 14)

1876 What a curious thing life is. We delve away, through years of hardship, wasting toil, despondency; then comes a little butterfly season of wealth, ease, & clustering honors.—Presto! the wife dies, a daughter marries a spendthrift villain, the heir & hope of the house commits suicide, the laurels fade & fall away. Grand result of a hard-fought, successful career & a blameless life. Piles of money, tottering age, & a broken heart.

(Letter to Mary Fairbanks, June 3, 1876, Ltrs-Fairbanks, pp. 199–200)

1894 Let us endeavor so to live that when we come to die even the undertaker will be sorry.   —Pudd'nhead Wilson's Calendar

(Pudd. Wilson, ch. 6, PW&TET, p. 77)

1898 "Oh, this human life, this earthy life, this weary life! It is so groveling, and so mean; its ambitions are so paltry, its prides so trivial, its vanities so childish; and the glories that it values and applauds—lord, how empty!"   —Emil Schwarz

(No. 44, ch. 27, p. 151)

1903 It is not in the least likely that any life has ever been lived which was not a failure, in the secret judgment of the person who lived it.

It is not likely that there has ever been a civilized person 65 years old who would consent to live his life over again.

(MTP, ts 46, p. 35; MTN, p. 385)

1905 A man's experiences of life are a book, and there was never yet an uninteresting life. Such a thing is an impossibility. Inside of the dullest exterior there is a drama, a comedy, and a tragedy.

("The Refuge of the Derelicts," ch. 4, Fab. of Man, p. 197)

lightning

1880 The fear of lightning is one of the most distressing infirmities a human being can be afflicted with. It is mostly confined to women; but now and then you find it in a little dog, and sometimes in a man. It is a particularly distressing infirmity, for the reason that it takes the sand out of a person to an extent which no other fear can, and it can't be *reasoned* with, neither can it be shamed out of a person.

("Mrs. McWilliams and the Lightning," Merry Tales, p. 144)

1908 Thunder is good, thunder is impressive; but it is lightning that does the work.

(Letter to Henry W. Ruoff, August 28, 1908, Ltrs/Paine, 2:818)

light-year

c. 1907 This is without doubt the most stupendous and impressive phrase that exists in any language.

(Autob/AMT, ch. 56, p. 277n.)

Lincoln, Abraham (president of the United States, 1861–1865)

1901 The greatest citizen, and the noblest and the best, after Washington, that this land or any other has yet produced.

(Speech in New York City, February 11, 1901, Speeches/Paine, p. 231)

literature

1877 Delicacy—a sad, sad false delicacy—robs literature of the two best things among its belongings: Family-circle narratives & obscene stories. But no matter; in that better world which I trust we are all going to I have the hope & belief that they will not be denied us.

(Letter to W. D. Howells, September 19, 1877, Ltrs-Howells, *1:203)*

1881 To my mind, that literature is best and most enduring which is characterized by a noble simplicity . . .

(Speech in Montreal, December 8, 1881, MT Speaking, *p. 160)*

1885 An *art*, not an inspiration. It is a *trade*, so to speak, & must be *learned*—one cannot "pick it up." Neither can one learn it in a year, nor in five years. And its capital is *experience.* . . . Whatever you have *lived*, you can write—& by hard work & a genuine apprenticeship, you can learn to write well; but what you have not lived you cannot write, you can only pretend to write it . . .

(Letter to Mrs. Whiteside, quoted in letter to Olivia Clemens, c. January 10, 1885, Ltrs-Love, *p. 228)*

1899 Literature is well enough, as a time-passer, and for the improvement and general elevation and purification of mankind, but it has no practical value.

(Letter to H. H. Rogers, January 24, 1899, Ltrs-Rogers, *p. 386)*

MALE LOBBYIST $3,000.

1903 I have never been able to get up high enough to be at home with high literature.

(Letter to W. D. Howells, April 29, 1903, Ltrs-Howells, *2:769)*

1906 Read it aloud. I may be wrong, still it is my conviction that one cannot get out of finely wrought literature all that is in it by reading it mutely[.]

("William Dean Howells," WIM&OE, *p. 230)*

FEMALE LOBBYIST $3,000.

lobbyists

1874 Laura was on excellent terms with a great many members of Congress, and there was an undercurrent of suspicion in some quarters that she was one of that detested class known as "lobbyists"; but what belle could escape slander in such a city?

(Gilded Age, ch. 34, p. 315)

HIGH MORAL SENATOR $3,000.

locusts

1897 Nature makes the locust with an appetite for crops; man would have made him with an appetite for sand.

—Pudd'nhead Wilson's New Calendar

(Foll. Equat., ch. 30, p. 285)

London, England

1872 You can walk, but it is best to go in a cab, for there is no place in London which is less than two miles and a half from any other place.

("From an English Notebook," Lets. Earth, *p. 176)*

lotteries

1882 A State that permits a lottery is pretty far behind the age. (La.).

(N&J-2, p. 483)

Louis XIV (17th-century French king)

n.d. We have to grant that God made this royal hog; we may also be permitted to believe that it was a crime to do so.

(Marginal note in book, quoted in MT:Biog, *ch. 287, p. 1537)*

BAIT WITH THE HEART

love

1894 Love seems the swiftest but is the slowest of all growths. No man and woman really know what perfect love is until they have been married a quarter of a century.

(MTP, ts 33, p. 48; MTN, *p. 235)*

1898 Love is a madness; if thwarted it develops fast . . .

("The Memorable Assassination," WIM&OE, *p. 171)*

1899 When you fish for love, bait with your heart, not your brain.

(MTP, ts 42, p. 68; MTN, *p. 346)*

1906 This kind of love is not a product of reasonings and statistics. It just *comes*—none knows whence—and cannot explain itself. And doesn't need to. —[Eve]

(Eve's Diary, p. 103)

loyalty

1888 Loyalty is a word which has worked vast harm; for it has been made to trick men into being "loyal" to a thousand iniquities whereas the true loyalty should have been to themselves—in which case there would have ensued a rebellion & the throwing off of that deceptive yoke.

(N&J-3, p. 414)

luck

1892 The very best thing in all this world that can befall a man is to be born lucky.

("Luck," Merry Tales, p. 75)

1894 When ill luck begins, it does not come in sprinkles, but in showers.

(Pudd. Wilson, ch. 14, PW&TET, p. 181)

1897 My own luck has been curious all my literary life; I never could tell a lie that anybody would doubt, nor a truth that anybody would believe.

(Foll. Equat., ch. 62, p. 610)

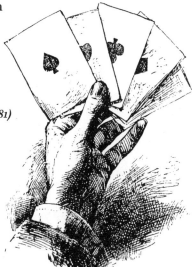

THE BEST THING IN THIS WORLD

lynchings

1902 It is always the way with lynchings; when they find out it is a mistake they are sorry, but it is too late . . .

(DBDS, bk. 2, ch. 4, p. 163)

madness

1864 Unconscious madness must be better than conscious mental distress . . .

(Article in Call, *July 8, 1864; Cl. of Call, p. 140)*

c. 1898 When we remember that we are all mad, the mysteries disappear & life stands explained.

(MTP, ts 42, p. 66; MTN, p. 345)

1898 One of the commonest forms of madness is the desire to be noticed, the pleasure derived from being noticed. Perhaps it is not merely common, but universal.

("The Memorable Assassination," WIM&OE, p. 171)

magazines

1870 Do you know, Madam, that I would rather write for a Magazine for $2 a page than for a newspaper at $10? I *would*. One takes more pains, the "truck" looks nicer in print, & one has a pleasanter audience. It is the difference between lecturing in "the States" & doing the same thing in delectable Nevada.

(Letter to Mary Fairbanks, May 29, 1870, Ltrs-4, p. 145)

1899 In my view, a person who published things in a mere newspaper could not properly claim recognition as a Literary Person: he must rise away above that; he must appear in a magazine. He would then be a Literary Person; also, he would be famous—right away.

("My Début As a Literary Person," MTCH&c, p. 84)

magnolias

1883 The scent of the flower is very sweet, but you want distance on it, because it is so powerful. They are not good bedroom blossoms—they might suffocate one in his sleep.

(Life on Miss., ch. 40, p. 416)

mail train

1874 [*The New York to Washington*] mail train . . . has never run over a cow since the road was built, for the reason that it has never been able to overtake one.

(*Gilded Age, ch. 43, p. 391*)

majority

1905 Whenever you find that you are on the side of the majority, it is time to reform. or (pause & reflect.)

(*MTP, ts 48, p. 4; MTN, p. 393*)

UNABLE TO OVERTAKE THE COW

maliciousness

1882 A malignant book would hurt nobody but the fool who wrote it.

(*Letter to W. D. Howells, January 28, 1882, Ltrs-Howells, 1:387*)

1908 There is more real pleasure to be gotten out of a malicious act, where your heart is in it, than out of thirty acts of a nobler sort.

(*Autob/MTIE, p. 297*)

man

1895 Man is merely & exclusively the Immodest Animal, for he is the only one that covers his nakedness, the only one with a soiled mind, the only one under the dominion of a false shame.

(*MTP, ts 34, p. 9; MTN, p. 242*)

1899 I suspect that to you there is still dignity in human life, & that Man is not a joke—a poor joke—the poorest that was ever contrived—an April-fool joke, played by a malicious Creator with nothing better to waste his time upon.

(*Letter to W. D. Howells, April 2-13, 1899, Ltrs-Howells, 2:689*)

1900 "A museum of disgusting diseases, a home of impurities; he comes to-day and is gone to-morrow;, he begins as dirt and departs as a stench . . . And man has the *Moral Sense*."   —Philip Traum

(*"The Chronicle of Young Satan," ch. 2, Mys. Stranger Mss., p. 55*)

169

1900 "I know your race. It is made up of sheep. It is governed by minorities, seldom or never by majorities. It suppresses its feelings and its beliefs and follows the handful that makes the most noise."

—Philip Traum

(Ibid., ch. 9, p. 154)

1900 Really, when a man can prove that he is not a jackass, I think he is in the way to prove that he is no legitimate member of the race.

(Letter to J. H. Twichell, January 8, 1900, Ltrs/Paine, 2:691)

1903 Man was made at the end of the week's work when God was tired.

(MTP, ts 46, p. 16; MTN, p. 381)

1903 If man had created man, he would be ashamed of his performance.

(MTP, ts 46, p. 35; MTN, p. 385)

1906 He was not made for any useful purpose . . . he hasn't served any . . . For his history, in all climes, all ages and all circumstances, furnishes oceans and continents of proof that of all the creatures that were made he is the most detestable. Of the entire brood he is the only one— the solitary one—that possesses malice.

That is the basest of all instincts, passions, vices—the most hateful. That one thing puts him below the rats, the grubs, the trichinae. He is the only creature that inflicts pain for sport, knowing it to *be* pain. . . . Also—in all the list he is the only creature that has a nasty mind.

(Autob/MTA, 2:7)

1906 "The noblest work of God?" Man.
"Who found it out?" Man.

(More Max., p. 7)

1907 Every man is a master and also a servant, a vassal. There is always someone who looks up to him and admires and envies him; there is always someone to whom he looks up and whom he admires and envies.

(Autob/MTIE, p. 67)

c. 1907 In matters concerning religion and politics a man's reasoning powers are not above the monkey's.

(Ibid., p. 345)

1909 There is this difference between man and the higher animals: he is avaricious and miserly, they are not.

("The Lowest Animal," Lets. Earth, *p. 224)*

manure

1880 Manure is evidently the Black Forester's main treasure—his coin, his jewel, his pride, his Old Master, his keramics, his bric-a-brac, his darling, his title to public consideration, envy, veneration, and his first solicitude when he gets ready to make his will.

(Tramp Abroad, ch. 22, p. 210)

Mardi Gras

1883 It is a thing which could hardly exist in the practical North . . . For the soul of it is the romantic, not the funny and the grotesque. Take away the romantic mysteries, the kings and knights and big-sounding titles, and Mardi-Gras would die, down there in the South. The very feature that keeps it alive in the South—girly-girly romance—would kill it in the North or in London.

(Life on Miss., ch. 46, pp. 466-467)

Marie Antoinette (French queen executed in 1793)

1880 Martyrdom made a saint of the trivial and foolish Marie Antoinette, and her biographers still keep her fragrant with the odor of sanctity to this day, while unconsciously proving upon almost every page they write that the only calamitous instinct which her husband lacked, she supplied—the instinct to root out and get rid of an honest, able, and loyal official, wherever she found him.

(Tramp Abroad, ch. 26, p. 261)

"Mark Twain" (pen name of Samuel L. Clemens)

1871 I lay awake all last night aggravating myself with this prospect of seeing my hated nom de plume (for I do loathe the very sight of it,) in print *again* every month.

(Letter to Orion Clemens, March 11, 1871, Ltrs-4, p. 350)

"BY THE MARK TWAIN!"

171

1881 Capt. Sellers used the signature, "Mark Twain," himself when he used to write up the antiquities in the way of river reminiscences for the New Orleans Picayune. He hated me for burlesquing them in an article in the True Delta; so four years later, when he died, I robbed the corpse—that is, I confiscated the nom de plume. I have published this vital fact 3,600 times now. But no matter, it is good practice; it is about the only fact that I can tell the same way every time.

(Letter to John B. ["Major Jack"] Downing, August 28? 1881,
Ltrs/Paine, 2:496; date corrected in UCCL*)*

1883 I was a fresh new journalist, and needed a *nom de guerre*; so I confiscated the ancient mariner's discarded one, and have done my best to make it remain what it was in his hands—a sign and symbol and warrant that whatever is found in its company may be gambled on as being the petrified truth; how I have succeeded, it would be not be modest in me to say.

(Life on Miss., ch. 50, p. 498)

marriage

1852 What a world of trouble those who never marry escape!

("Connubial Bliss," ET&S-1, p. 86)

1866 Marry be d----d. I am too old to marry. I am nearly 31. I have got gray hairs in my head. Women appear to like me, but d--n them, they don't *love* me.

(Letter to Will Bowen, August 25, 1866, Ltrs-1, p. 359)

1867 I want a good wife—I want a couple of them if they are particularly good—but where is the wherewithal? . . .

   If I were settled I would quit all nonsense & swindle some girl into marrying me. But I wouldn't expect to be "*worthy*" of her. I wouldn't *have* a girl that *I* was worthy of. *She* wouldn't do. She wouldn't be respectable enough.

(Letter to Mary Fairbanks, December 12, 1867, Ltrs-2, pp. 133-134)

1870 If all of one's married days are as happy as these new ones have been to me, I have deliberately fooled away 30 years of my life. If it were to do over again I would marry in early infancy instead of wasting time cutting teeth & breaking crockery.

(Letter to Robert M. and Louise M. Howland, March 6, 1870, Ltrs-4, p. 87;
written after Mark Twain had been married for a month)

1888 Both marriage & death ought to be welcome; the one promises happiness, doubtless the other assures it.

(Letter to Will Bowen, November 4, 1888, Ltrs/Paine, *2:501)*

1889 People talk about beautiful friendships between two persons of the same sex. What is the best of that sort, as compared with the friendship of man and wife, where the best impulses and highest ideals of both are the same? There is no place for comparison between the two friendships; the one is earthly, the other divine.   —[Hank Morgan]

(Conn. Yankee, ch. 41, p. 435)

1894 The first year of marriage—the most trying year for any young couple, for then the mutual failings are coming one by one to light, and the necessary adjustments are being made in pain and tribulation . . .

("In Defense of Harriet Shelley," How to Tell a Story, *p. 26)*

1908 Marriage—yes, it *is* the supreme felicity of life, I concede it. And it is also the supreme tragedy of life. The deeper the love the surer the tragedy.

(Letter to Father Fitz-Simon, June 5, 1908, Ltrs/Paine, *2:811;*
written on the fourth anniversary of his wife's death)

Marseilles, France

1869 In Marseilles they make half the fancy toilet soap we consume in America, but the Marseillaise only have a vague theoretical idea of its use, which they have obtained from books of travel, just as they have acquired an uncertain notion of clean shirts, and the peculiarities of the gorilla, and other curious matters.

(Inn. Abroad, ch. 19, p. 189)

marsupials

1897 A marsupial is a plantigrade vertebrate whose specialty is its pocket. In some countries it is extinct, in others it is rare. The first American marsupials were Stephen Girard, Mr. Astor, and the opossum; the principal marsupials of the Southern Hemisphere are Mr. Rhodes, and the kangaroo. I, myself, am the latest marsupial. Also, I might boast that I have the largest pocket of them all. But there is nothing in that.

(Foll. Equat., ch. 29, p. 283)

martyr paintings

1869 It seemed that when I had seen one of these martyrs I had seen them all. They all have a marked family resemblance to each other, they dress alike, in coarse monkish robes and sandals, they are all bald headed, they all stand in about the same attitude, and without exception they are gazing heavenward . . .

(Inn. Abroad, ch. 23, p. 237)

martyrdom

1880 Martyrdom is the luckiest fate that can befall some people. Louis XVI did not die in his bed, consequently history is very gentle with him; she is charitable toward his failings, and she finds in him high virtues which are not usually considered to be virtues when they are lodged in kings. She makes him out to be a person with a meek and modest spirit the heart of a female saint, and a wrong head. None of these qualities are kingly but the last. Taken together they make a character which would have fared harshly at the hands of history if its owner had had the ill luck to miss martyrdom.

(Tramp Abroad, ch. 26, p. 265)

1903 Martyrdom covers a multitude of sins.

(MTP, ts 46, p. 16; MTN, p. 381)

masturbation

1879 Of all the various kinds of sexual intercourse, this has the least to recommend it. As an amusement it is too fleeting. As an occupation it is too wearing. As a public exhibition, there is no money in it.

("Some Thoughts on the Science of Onanism," speech in Paris, spring 1879,
MT Speaking, p. 126)

1879 "It is the bulwark of virginity." —Elizabeth I

(Ibid., p. 125)

matches

1884 They were the convenientest things in the world . . . —[Huck]

("Huck Finn and Tom Sawyer Among the Indians,"
HF&TS, ch. 2, p. 39)

174

mathematics

1906 There are too many statistics and figure[s] for me. I never could do anything with figures, never had any talent for mathematics, never accomplished anything in my efforts at that rugged study, and to-day, the only mathematics I know is multiplication, and the minute I get away up in that, as soon as I reach nine times seven—

(Speech in New York City, March 29, 1906, Speeches/Paine, p. 307)

Mauritius (Indian Ocean island)

1897 Apparently, there has been only one prominent event in the history of Mauritius, and that one didn't happen.

(Foll. Equat., ch. 62, p. 618)

maxims

1897 It is more trouble to make a maxim than it is to do right.
—Pudd'nhead Wilson's New Calendar

(Foll. Equat., ch. 3, p. 48)

1897 What are the proper proportions of a maxim? A minimum of sound to a maximum of sense. —Pudd'nhead Wilson's New Calendar

(More Tramps, ch. 23, p. 132)

Maxims, Pudd'nhead Wilson

1897 These wisdoms are for the luring of youth toward high moral altitudes. The author did not gather them from practice, but from observation. To be good is noble; but to show others how to be good is nobler and no trouble.

(Foll. Equat., Preface, p. 5)

memory

1881 "Remember all thou canst—*seem* to remember all else."
—Lord Saint John

(Prince & Pauper, ch. 6, p. 42)

1882 I never remember anything whatever except humiliation.

(Letter to G. W. Cable, October 12, 1882, Ltrs-Cable, p. 85)

175

1883 My memory was never loaded with anything but blank cartridges.

(*Life on Miss., ch. 6, p. 88*)

1883 Astonishing things can be done with the human memory if you will devote it faithfully to one particular line of business.

(*Ibid., ch. 13, p. 155*)

1887 *Nothing* remains the same: when the man goes back to look at the house of his childhood, it has always *shrunk*: there is no instance of such house being as big as the picture in memory & imagination call for. Shrunk how? Why, to its correct dimensions: the *house* hasn't altered; this is the first time it has been in focus.

(*Letter to W. D. Howells, August 22, 1887, Ltrs-Howells, 2:595-596*)

1896 We are so strangely made; the memories that could make us happy pass away; it is the memories that break our hearts that abide.

(*Joan of Arc, bk. 3, ch. 22, p. 439*)

1897–98 For many years I believed that I remembered helping my grandfather drink his whisky toddy when I was six weeks old but I do not tell about that any more, now; I am grown old and my memory is not as active as it used to be. When I was younger I could remember anything, whether it happened or not; but my faculties are decaying, now, & soon I shall be so I cannot remember any but the latter. It is sad to go to pieces like this, but we all have to do it.

(*NAR, March 1, 1907; Autob/NAR, pp. 112–113.*
Corrected against original manuscript in the MTP.)

1903 A grown person's memory-tablet is a palimpsest, with hardly a bare space upon which to engrave a phrase.

(*Letter to Helen Keller, March 17, 1903, Ltrs/Paine, 2:732*)

1905 Certainly memory is a curious machine and strangely capricious. It has no order, it has no system, it has no notion of values, it is always throwing away gold and hoarding rubbish.

(*"Three Thousand Years among the Microbes," ch. 6, WWD&OSW, p. 456*)

1906 The truth is, a person's memory has no more sense than his conscience, and no appreciation whatever of values and proportions.

(*NAR, January 4, 1907; Autob/NAR, p. 81*)

Menken, Ada Isaacs (popular actress and notorious libertine whom Mark Twain met in the west)

1867 The poor woman who has got so much money, but not any clothes. . . .

Menken is a good-hearted, free-handed, charitable soul—a woman who does white deeds enough, kindly Christian deeds enough, every day of her life to blot out a swarming multitude of sins; but, Heaven help us, what desperate chances she takes on her reputation!

(Letter to Alta, *May 17, 1867;* MTTB, *pp. 169, 170)*

mental telegraphy

1891 I have never seen any mesmeric or clairvoyant performances or spiritual manifestations which were in the least degree convincing—a fact which is not of consequence, since my opportunities have been meagre; but I am forced to believe that one human mind (still inhabiting the flesh) can communicate with another, over any sort of a distance, and without any *artificial* preparation of "sympathetic conditions" to act as a transmitting agent.

("Mental Telegraphy," CT-2, p. 38)

1900 Mental Telegraphy will be greatly respected a century hence.

(Letter to J. H. Twichell, January 8, 1900, Ltrs/Paine, 2:689)

Merlin (figure of Arthurian legends)

1889 He was an old numskull; a magician who believed in his own magic; and no magician can thrive who is handicapped with a superstition like that.   —[Hank Morgan]

(Conn. Yankee, ch. 22, p. 209)

1889 He was the worst weather-failure in the kingdom. Whenever he ordered up the danger-signals along the coast there was a week's dead calm, sure, and every time he prophesied fair weather it rained brickbats.

(Ibid., ch. 23, p. 218)

metropolis

1906 I never write "metropolis" for seven cents, because I can get the same money for "city."

(Speech in New York City, September 19, 1906, Speeches/Paine, p. 318)

177

Michael, Grand Duke of Russia
(brother of Czar Alexander II)

1869 The princeliest figure in Russia. . . . He looks like a great-hearted fellow who would pitch an enemy into the river in a moment, and then jump in and risk his life fishing him out again.

(Inn. Abroad, ch. 37, pp. 396-397)

Michelangelo

1894 Even popularity can be overdone. In Rome, along at first, you are full of regrets that Michelangelo died; but by and by, you only regret that you didn't see him do it. —Pudd'nhead Wilson's Calendar

(Pudd. Wilson, ch. 17, PW&TET, p. 221)

microbes

1897–98 I doubt if God has given us any refreshment which, taken in moderation, is unwholesome, except microbes.

(NAR, March 1, 1907; Autob/NAR, p. 114)

mind

1869 I must have a prodigious quantity of mind; it takes me as much as a week sometimes to make it up.

(Inn. Abroad, ch. 7, p. 65)

1871 I am different from other women. They have their monthly period once a month, but I have mine once a week, & sometimes oftener. That is to say, my mind changes that often. People who *have* no mind, can easily be steadfast & firm; but when a man is loaded down to the guards with it, as I am, every heavy sea of foreboding, or inclination, or mayhap indolence, shifts his cargo.

(Letter to James Redpath, August 8, 1871, Ltrs-4, pp. 440-441)

1906 Your mind is merely a machine, nothing more. You have no command over it, it has no command over itself—it is worked *solely from the outside*. That is the law of its make; it is the law of all machines. —Old Man

("What Is Man?," ch. 1, WIM&OPW, p. 129)

1906 It is merely a thermometer: it registers the heat and the cold, and cares not a farthing about either. —Old Man

(Ibid., ch. 6, p. 200)

mining

1897 I had been a gold miner myself, in my day, and knew substantially everything that those people [*South Africans*] knew about it, except how to make money at it.

(Foll. Equat., ch. 68, p. 687)

miracles

1905 There is nothing more awe-inspiring than a miracle, except the credulity that can take it at par.

(MTP, ts 48, p. 4; MTN, p. 393)

1909 "If it is a Miracle, any sort of evidence will answer, but if it is a Fact, proof is necessary." . . .

"There has never been a Miracle that noticeably resembled a Fact." . . .

"The difference between a Miracle and a Fact is exactly the difference between a mermaid and a seal." —Hiram Bledso

("Official Report to the I.I.A.S.," Lets. Earth, pp. 149–150)

mirrors

1863 I have a great regard for a good house, and a girlish passion for mirrors.

(Letter to Territorial Enterprise, January 31, 1863, MTOE, p. 50)

1906 Ugly! I was never ugly in my life! Forty years ago I was not so good-looking. A looking glass then lasted me three months. Now I can wear it out in two days.

(Unidentified newspaper interview, February 1906; quoted in Autob/MTA, 2:202)

misfortune

1906 The size of a misfortune is not determinable by an outsider's measurement of it, but only by the measure-

GIRLISH PASSION FOR MIRRORS

ments applied to it by the person specially affected by it. The king's lost crown is a vast matter to the king, but of no consequence to the child. The lost toy is a great matter to the child, but in the king's eyes it is not a thing to break the heart about.

(NAR, October 5, 1906; Autob/NAR, p. 30)

missionaries

1881 Infatuation for a filthy prostitute can make a man rival the Jesuit missionaries at their grandest & finest.

(Letter to Olivia Clemens, November 29, 1881, Ltrs-Love, p. 206)

c. 1897 The first thing a missionary teaches a savage is indecency.

(MTN, p. 325)

1901 A man who is pretty nearly all heart, else he would not be in a calling which requires of him such large sacrifices of one kind and another. He is made up of faith, zeal, courage, sentiment, emotion, enthusiasm; and so he is a mixture of poet, devotee, and knight errant.

("To My Missionary Critics," E&E, p. 295)

c. 1905 We are all missionaries (propagandists of *our* views). Each of us disapproves of the other missionaries; in fact detests them, as a rule. I am one of the herd myself.

(MTN, pp. 393-394)

"Mississippi"

1874 . . . the Mississiipi (dang that word, it is worse than type or Egypt) . . .

(Letter to W. D. Howells, December 3, 1874, Ltrs-Howells, 1:47)

Mississippi River

1883 The Mississippi is well worth reading about. It is not a commonplace river, but on the contrary is in all ways remarkable.

(Life on Miss., ch. 1, p. 21)

1883 The Mississippi is a just and equitable river; it never tumbles one man's farm overboard without building a new farm just like it for that man's neighbor. This keeps down hard feelings.

(Ibid., ch. 25, p. 280)

1907 The Mississippi will always have its own way; no engineering skill can persuade it to do otherwise . . .

(Autob/MTIE, *p. 18*)

mistakes

1908 One is not blameable for mistakes, we all make them. A mistake is not a crime, it is only a miscarriage of judgment.

(Letter to Louise Paine, September 30, 1908, Ltrs-Angelfish, p. 210)

mobs

1884 "The pitifulest thing out is a mob; that's what an army is—a mob; they don't fight with courage that's born in them, but with courage that's borrowed from their mass, and from their officers. But a mob without any *man* at the head of it is *beneath* pitifulness." —Colonel Sherburn

(Huck Finn, *ch. 22, pp. 190–191*)

Model Boys

1883 The Model Boy of my time—we never had but the one—was perfect: perfect in manners, perfect in dress, perfect in conduct, perfect in filial piety, perfect in exterior godliness; but at bottom he was a prig; and as for the contents of his skull, they could have changed place with the contents of a pie, and nobody would have been the worse off for it but the pie. This fellow's reproachlessness was a standing reproach to every lad in the village. He was the admiration of all the mothers, and the detestation of all their sons.

(Life on Miss., *ch. 54, pp. 538–539*)

1906 I remember his [*schoolmaster John Dawson's*] boy, Theodore who was as good as he could be. In fact he was inordinately good, extravagantly good, offensively good, detestably good—and he had pop-eyes—and I would have drowned him if I had had a chance.

THE MODEL BOY

(NAR, *August 2, 1907*; Autob/NAR, *p. 194*)

181

modesty

1889 I was born modest; not all over, but in spots; and this was one of the spots. —[Hank Morgan]

(Conn. Yankee, ch. 16, p. 145)

1897 The man who is ostentatious of his modesty is twin to the statue that wears a fig-leaf. —Pudd'nhead Wilson's New Calendar

(Foll. Equat., ch. 50, p. 475)

1897 Without doubt modesty is nothing less than a holy feeling; and without doubt the person whose rule of modesty has been transgressed feels the same sort of wound that he would feel if something made holy to him by his religion had suffered a desecration.

(Ibid., p. 476)

1899 The statue that advertises its modesty with a fig-leaf really brings its modesty under suspicion.

("Diplomatic Pay and Clothes," CT-2, p. 345)

1906 I was born modest, but it didn't last.

(Speech in New York City, March 4, 1906, Speeches/Paine, p. 282)

1908 The convention miscalled Modesty has no standard, and cannot have one, because it is opposed to nature and reason, and is therefore an artificiality and subject to anybody's whim, anybody's diseased caprice.

("Letters from the Earth," WIM&OPW, p. 417)

c. 1909 Modesty died when clothes were born.

(Memorandum, quoted in MT:Biog, ch. 267, p. 1513)

Moffett, Pamela A. (Mark Twain's sister)

1869 My sister is a good woman, familiar with grief, though bearing it bravely & giving no sign upon the surface; & she is kind-hearted, void of folly or vanity, perfectly unacquainted with deceit or dissimulation, diffident about her own faults, & slow to discover those of others.

(Letter to Olivia Langdon, March 6, 1869, Ltrs-3, p. 145)

Mona Lisa (painting by Leonardo da Vinci)

1891 To me it was merely a serene and subdued face, and there an end. There might be more in it, but I could not find it. The complexion was bad; in fact, it was not even human; there are no people of that color. I finally concluded that maybe others still saw in the picture faded and vanished marvels which *had* been there once and were now forever vanished.

("Down the Rhône," E&E, p. 143)

monarchy

1888 There are shams & shams, there are frauds & frauds, but the transparentest of all is the sceptred one. We see monarchs meet & go through solemn ceremonies [(]farces[)] with straight countenances; but it is not possible to imagine them meeting in private & not laughing in each other's faces.

(N&J-3, p. 401)

1888 Monarchy & nobility (hereditary) is a laughable departure from the law of survival of the fittest—a law obeyed in all other cases.

(Ibid., p. 410)

1889 Surely the grotesquest of all the swindles ever invented by man—monarchy. It is enough to make a graven image laugh . . . When our great brethren the disenslaved Brazilians frame their Declaration of Independence, I hope they will insert this missing link: "We hold these truths to be self-evident: that all monarchs are usurpers, & descendants of usurpers."

(Letter to Sylvester Baxter, November 20, 1889, Ltrs/Paine, 2:519-520)

1890 It is out of date. It belongs to the stage of culture that admires a ring in your nose, a head full of feathers, & your belly painted blue.

(N&J-3, p. 540)

1891 The first gospel of all monarchies should be Rebellion; the second s[houl]d be Rebellion; & the third & all gospels & the only gospel in any monarchy s[houl]d be Rebellion against Church & State.

(MTP, ts 31, pp. 2-3; MTN, p. 217)

1907 Republics have lived long but monarchy lives forever.

(Autob/MTIE, p. 68)

THE ROOT OF ALL EVIL

money

n.d. The lack of money is the root of all evil.

(More Max., p. 10)

1898–99 Some men worship rank, some worship heroes, some worship power, some worship God, & over these ideals they dispute & cannot unite—but they all worship money.

(MTP, ts 42, p. 58; MTN, p. 343)

1906 It is merely a symbol, it has no *material* value; you think you desire it for its own sake, but it is not so. You desire it for the spiritual content it will bring . . .   —Old Man

("What Is Man?," ch. 6, WIM&OPW, p. 203)

1906 Like all the other nations, we worship money and the possessors of it—they being our aristocracy, and we have to have one.

(NAR, January 4, 1907; Autob/NAR, p. 80)

monkeys

1906 I believe that our Heavenly Father invented man because he was disappointed in the monkey.

(Autob/MTIE, p. 372)

1906 In discarding the monkey and substituting man, our Father in Heaven did the monkey an undeserved injustice.

(Ibid., p. 375)

Mono Lake (alkaline lake in California)

1872 A white man cannot drink the water of Mono Lake, for it is nearly pure lye. It is said that the Indians in the vicinity drink it sometimes, though. It is not improbable, for they are among the purest liars I ever saw.

(Rough. It, ch. 38, p. 247)

monuments

1897 It's just the way, in this world. One person *does* the thing, and the other one gets the monument. —[Huck Finn]

("Tom Sawyer's Conspiracy," HF&TS, ch. 1, p. 138)

moons

1897 Every one is a moon, and has a dark side which he never shows to anybody. —Pudd'nhead Wilson's New Calendar

(Foll. Equat., ch. 66, p. 654; see also
"The Refuge of the Derelicts," ch. 6, Fab. of Man, p. 206)

moral sense, the

1897 There is a Moral Sense, and there is an Immoral Sense. History shows us that the Moral Sense enables us to perceive morality and how to avoid it, and that the Immoral Sense enables us to perceive immorality and how to enjoy it. —Pudd'nhead Wilson's New Calendar

(Foll. Equat., ch. 16, p. 161)

c. 1900 It is a degradation, a disaster. Without it one cannot do wrong; with it, one can. Therefore it has but one office, only one—to teach how to do wrong. It can teach no other thing—no other thing whatever. It is the *creator* of wrong; wrong cannot exist until the Moral Sense brings it into being.

("That Day in Eden," E&E, p. 344)

1901 The Moral Sense teaches us what is right, and how to avoid it—when unpopular.

("The United States of Lyncherdom," E&E, p. 244)

1909 Since the Moral Sense has but the one office, the one capacity—to enable man to do wrong.—it is plainly without value to him.

("The Lowest Animal," Lets. Earth, p. 181)

morality

n.d. The low level which commercial morality has reached in America is deplorable. We have humble God fearing Christian men among us who will stoop to do things for a million dollars that they ought not to be willing to do for less than 2 millions.

(More Max., p. 10)

185

morals

n.d. Morals consist of political morals, commercial morals, ecclesiastical morals, and morals.

(More Max., p. 10)

1894 A man should not be without morals . . . it is better to have bad morals than none at all.

(MTP, ts 33, p. 56; MTN, p. 237)

1899 It is not best that we use our morals weekdays, it gets them out of repair for Sundays.

(MTP, ts 42, p. 67; MTN, p. 345)

1899 Theoretical morals are the sort you get on your mother's knee, in good books, and from the pulpit. You gather them in your head, and not in your heart; they are theory without practice.

(Speech in London, June 29, 1899, MT Speaking, p. 331)

1905 Morals are an acquirement—like music, like a foreign language, like piety, poker, paralysis—no man is born with them. I wasn't myself, I started poor. I hadn't a single moral.

(Speech in New York City, December 5, 1905, Speeches/Paine, p. 260)

1906 There are two kinds of Christian morals, one private and the other public. These two are so distinct, so unrelated, that they are no more kin to each other than are archangels and politicians.

(Speech in New York City, January 22, 1906, Speeches/Paine, pp. 276–277)

1906 It's my opinion that every one I know has morals, though I wouldn't like to ask. I know I have. But I'd rather teach them than practice them any day.

(Speech in New York City, March 7, 1906, Speeches/Paine, p. 284)

1907 The political and commercial morals of the United States are not merely food for laughter, they are an entire banquet.

(Autob/MTIE, p. 81)

1907 It has always been a peculiarity of the human race that it keeps two sets of morals in stock—the private and real, and the public and artificial.

(Ibid., p. 382)

Morgan, Hank

(title character of *Connecticut Yankee*)

1889 "I am a Yankee of the Yankees—and practical; yes, and nearly barren of sentiment, I suppose—or poetry, in other words. My father was a blacksmith, my uncle was a horse-doctor, and I was both, along at first. Then I went over to the Colt great arms-factory and learned my real trade; learned all there was to it; learned to make everything: guns, revolvers, cannon, boilers, engines, all sorts of labor-saving machinery. Why, I could make anything a body wanted—anything in the world, it didn't make any difference what; and if there wasn't any quick new-fangled way to make a thing, I could invent one—and do it as easy as rolling off a log."   —Hank Morgan

(Conn. Yankee, Preface, p. 4)

morgues

1869 The Morgue, that horrible receptacle for the dead who die mysteriously and leave the manner of their taking off a dismal secret.

(Inn. Abroad, ch. 14, p. 132)

multiplication table, the

1909 That odious and confusing and unvanquishable and unlearnable and shameless invention, the multiplication table[.]

("Marjorie Fleming, the Wonder Child," E&E, p. 369)

murder

1897 If the desire to kill and the opportunity to kill came always together, who would escape hanging.

—Pudd'nhead Wilson's New Calendar

(Foll. Equat., ch. 46, p. 426)

MUSIC WITHOUT MUSIC

188

music

n.d. We often feel sad in the presence of music without words; and often more than that in the presence of music without music.

(More Max., p. 14)

1877 Age enlarges and enriches the powers of some musical instruments,—notably those of the violin,—but it seems to set a piano's teeth on edge.

("Some Rambling Notes of an Idle Excursion,"
part 4, SWE, p. 79)

1880 I suppose there are two kinds of music,—one kind which one feels, just as an oyster might, and another sort which requires a higher faculty, a faculty which must be assisted and developed by teaching. Yet if base music gives certain of us wings, why should we want any other?

(Tramp Abroad, ch. 24, p. 237)

1896 The power of music, that magician of magicians; who lifts his wand and says his mysterious word and all things real pass away and the phantoms of your mind walk before you clothed in flesh.

(Joan of Arc, bk. 2, ch. 36, pp. 282-283)

Muslims

1869 Mosques are plenty, churches are plenty, graveyards are plenty, but morals and whisky are scarce. The Koran does not permit Mohammedans to drink. Their natural instincts do not permit them to be moral.

(Inn. Abroad, ch. 34, p. 368)

1894 When I asked him [*Tom Sawyer*] what a Moslem was, he said it was a person that wasn't a Presbyterian. So there is plenty of them in Missouri, though I didn't know it before.   —[Huck Finn]

(Tom Sawyer Abrd., ch. 13, p. 98)

mystery

1897 Tom said . . . glory was grand and valuable; but for solid satisfaction, mystery laid over it. —[Huck Finn]

("Tom Sawyer's Conspiracy," HF&TS, ch. 1, pp. 140–141)

nakedness

n.d. Clothes make the man. Naked people have little or no influence in society.

(More Max., p. 6)

1905 There is no power without clothes. It is the power that governs the human race. Strip its chiefs to the skin, and no State could be governed; naked officials could exercise no authority; they would look (and be) like everybody else—commonplace, inconsequential.

—[Czar Nicholas II]

("The Czar's Soliloquy," CT-2, p. 643)

names

1869 There are good & great men, no doubt, who put an initial for their first name & spell their second out in full—but the awful majority of men who do that, will lie, & swindle & steal, just from a natural instinct.

(Letter to Olivia Langdon, September 3, 1869, Ltrs-3, p. 332)

1897 Names are not always what they seem. The common Welsh name Bzjxxllwcp is pronounced Jackson.

—Pudd'nhead Wilson's New Calendar

(Foll. Equat., ch. 36, p. 324)

Naples, Italy

1906 When a teacher calls a boy by his entire name it means trouble.

(Autob/MTIE, p. 108)

Naples, Italy

1869 These Neapolitans always ask four times as much money as they intend to take, but if you give them what they first demand, they feel ashamed of themselves for aiming so low, and immediately ask more.

(Inn. Abroad, ch. 29, p. 312)

1869 "See Naples and die." Well, I do not know that one would necessarily die after merely seeing it, but to attempt to live there might turn out a little differently.

(Ibid., ch. 30, p. 315)

narrative

1892 Narrative is a difficult art; narrative should flow as flows the brook down through the hills and the leafy woodlands, its course changed by every bowlder it comes across and by every grass-clad gravelly spur that projects into its path; its surface broken, but its course not stayed by rocks and gravel on the bottom in the shoal places; a brook that never goes straight for a minute, but *goes*, and goes briskly, sometimes ungrammatically, and sometimes fetching a horseshoe three-quarters of a mile around, and at the end of the circuit flowing within a yard of the path it traversed an hour before; but always *going*, and always following at least one law, always loyal to that law, the law of *narrative*, which *has no law*. Nothing to do but make the trip; the how of it is not important, so that the trip is made.

(Autob/MTA, 1:237)

1896 Most people who have the narrative gift—that great and rare endowment—have with it the defect of telling their choice things over the same way every time, and this injures them and causes them to sound stale and wearisome after several repetitions . . .

(Joan of Arc, bk. 2, ch. 7, p. 116)

national symbol, American

1889 The Eagle, the scavenger bird, bird of prey—the proper symbol of royalty & nobility. But the unicorn Yank turned into a donkey to represent the people. But ours should be our native bird, the turkey. True, he *is* one of the biggest fools in featherdom, that is a merit—the majority of all peoples are fools.

(N&J-3, p. 525)

nationality

1885 The English. The arrogant nation. The Parisians, the adulterous nation. The Americans, the material nation. The Germans, the patient nation. The Russians, the unclassifiable nation. The several Roman Catholic countries, the ignorant nations. The French, the volatile nation. The Scotch, the get all you can & keep all you get thrifty nation. The Italians, the hot-blooded, kind-hearted nation. The Irish, the nation of chaste women . . .

(N&J-3, p. 173)

1898–99 There is but one first thing to do when a man is wounded & suffering: *relieve* him. If we have curiosity to know his nationality, that is a matter of no consequence & can wait.

(MTP, ts 42, p. 61; MTN, p. 344)

naturalists

1907 The professional who disputes another professional's facts damages the business and imperils his own statistics, there being no statistics connected with the business that are absolute and unassailable. The only wise and safe course is for all the naturalists to stand by each other and accept and endorse every discovery, or seeming discovery, that any one of them makes.

(Autob/MTIE, p. 23)

Nature's treacheries

1906 She is full of them; half the time she doesn't know which she likes best—to betray her child or protect it.

("Hunting the Deceitful Turkey," Mys. Stranger, p. 308)

necessity

1869 Necessity knows no law.

(Inn. Abroad, ch. 51, p. 542)

1872 Necessity is the mother of "taking chances."

(Rough. It, ch. 42, p. 274)

"neodamode"
(Greek word for a newly enfranchised Spartan helot)

1866 What a comfort these reporters do take in that graveyard word! They stick it at the head of an item, in all its native impenetrability, and then slash away cheerfully and finish the paragraph. It is too many for me—that word is, for all it is so handy. . . . It is the handiest heading I ever saw; it appears to fit any subject you please to tack to it to.

(Letter to Territorial Enterprise, *January 28, 1866,* MTSF, *pp. 200–201)*

Nevada

1861 Nevada Territory is fabulously rich in gold, silver, copper, lead, coal, iron, quicksilver, marble, granite, chalk, slate, plaster of Paris (gypsum,) thieves, murderers, desperadoes, ladies, children, lawyers, Christians, gamblers, Indians, Chinamen, Spaniards, sharpers, cuyotes, (pronounced ki-yo-ties,) preachers, poets and jackass-rabbits.

(Letter to mother, October 26, 1861, Ltrs-1, *p. 137)*

1862 Some people are malicious enough to think that if the devil were set at liberty and told to confine himself to Nevada Territory, that he would come here and loaf sadly around, awhile, and then get homesick and go back to hell again.

(Letter to mother and sister, February 8, 1862, Ltrs-1, *p. 159)*

1872 People accustomed to the monster mile-wide Mississippi, grow accustomed to associating the term "river" with a high degree of watery grandeur. Consequently, such people feel rather disappointed when they stand on the shores of the Humboldt or the Carson and find that a "river" in Nevada is a sickly rivulet which is just the counterpart of the Erie Canal in all respects save that the canal is twice as long and four times as deep. One of the pleasantest and most invigorating exercises one can contrive is to run and jump across the Humboldt river till he is overheated and then drink it dry.

(Rough. It, ch. 28, p. 184)

Nevada weather

1864 It has no character to speak of . . . and alas! in this respect it resembles many, ah, too many chambermaids in this wretched, wretched world. . . . It is mighty regular about not raining, though . . . It will start in here in November and rain about four, and sometimes as much as seven days on a stretch; after that, you may loan out your umbrella for twelve months, with the serene confidence which a Christian feels in four aces.

("Washoe.—'Information Wanted,'" ET&S-1, p. 368)

New England weather

1876 There is a sumptuous variety about the New England weather that compels the stranger's admiration—and regret. The weather is always doing something there . . . In the spring I have counted one hundred and thirty-six different kinds of weather inside of four and twenty hours. . . .

Yes, one of the brightest gems in the New England weather is the dazzling uncertainty of it.

(Speech in New York City, December 22, 1876, MT Speaking, pp. 100–101)

1876 Now, as to the *size* of the weather in New England—lengthways, I mean. It is utterly disproportioned to the size of that little country. Half the time, when it is packed as full as it can stick, you will see that New England weather sticking out beyond the edges and projecting around hundreds and hundreds of miles over the neighboring states. She can't hold a tenth part of her weather.

(Ibid., p. 102)

New Hampshire

1872 To be hanged in New Hampshire is happiness—it leaves an honored name behind a man, and introduces him at once into the best New Hampshire society in the other world.

("Lionizing Murderers," SN&O, p. 186)

New Year's resolutions

1863 Now is the accepted time to make your regular annual good resolutions. Next week you can begin paving hell with them as usual. . . . New Year's is a harmless annual institution, of no particular use to anybody save as a scapegoat for promiscuous drunks, and friendly calls, and humbug resolutions . . .

("New Year's Day," ET&S-1, p. 180)

1885 A new oath holds pretty well; but . . . when it is become old, and frayed out, and damaged by a dozen annual retyings of its remains, it ceases to be serviceable; any little strain will snap it.

(Speech in New York City, March 31, 1885, MT Speaking, p. 190)

New York City

1867 The only trouble about this town is, that it is too large. You cannot accomplish anything in the way of business, you cannot even pay a friendly call, without devoting a whole day to it—that is, what people call a whole day who do not get up early.

(Letter to Alta, February 2, 1867; MTTB, p. 82)

1885 A better name than the Empire City for New York would be the Ill-mannered City.

(N&J-3, p. 170)

1885 As long as American civilization lasts New York will last.

(Letter to New York Sun, July 27, 1885, Ltrs/Paine, 2:456)

New York police

1867 They are extremely useful—in fact, they present the anomaly of a police force that is an absolute necessity to the well-being of the city, and they earn every cent they get.

(Letter to Alta, February 18, 1867; MTTB, p. 91)

Newport, Rhode Island

1904 Holy Land of High Society, ineffable Domain of the American Aristocracy.

("The $30,000 Bequest," CT-2, p. 616; also in $30k Bequest)

1907 That breeding place—that stud farm, so to speak—of aristocracy; aristocracy of the American type; that auction mart where the English nobilities come to trade hereditary titles for American girls and cash.

(Autob/MTIE, p. 273)

newspapers

1864 Nothing in the world affords a newspaper reporter so much satisfaction as gathering up the details of a bloody and mysterious murder, and writing them up with aggravating circumstantiality.

("The Killing of Julius Caesar 'Localized,'" ET&S-2, p. 110)

1873 It seems to me that just in the ratio that our newspapers increase, our morals decay. The more newspapers the worse morals. Where we have one newspaper that does good, I think we have fifty that do harm.

(Paper delivered in Hartford, February 1873, Speeches/Paine, p. 47)

1880 A German daily is the slowest and saddest and dreariest of the inventions of man. Our own dailies infuriate the reader, pretty often; the German daily only stupefies him.

("German Journals," Tramp Abroad, pp. 626-627)

1894 As shy as a newspaper when referring to its own merits.

(MTP, ts 33, p. 55; MTN, p. 237)

1897 The old saw says, "Let a sleeping dog lie." Right. Still, when there is much at stake it is better to get a newspaper to do it.

—Pudd'nhead Wilson's New Calendar

(Foll. Equat., ch. 44, p. 400)

Niagara Falls

1897 I had to visit Niagara Falls fifteen times before I succeeded in getting my imaginary Falls gauged to the actuality and could begin to sanely and wholesomely wonder at them for what they were, and not what I had expected them to be.

(Foll. Equat., ch. 59, p. 574)

night work

1853 Incessant night work dulls one['s] ideas amazingly.

(Letter to Orion Clemens, November 28, 1853, Ltrs-1, p. 29)

1870 *I* would rather live on $100 a month & live like a human being, than have $8 more & live like an owl.

(Letter to Orion Clemens, November 11, 1870, Ltrs-4, p. 229)

nightingales

1897 The song of the nightingale is the deadliest known to ornithology. That demoniacal shriek can kill at thirty yards.

(Foll. Equat., ch. 56, p. 543)

nineteenth century

1892 "This century, the only century worth living in since time itself was invented . . ."   —Lecturer

(Amer. Claim., ch. 10, p. 101)

1904 "It was a stunning little century, for sure, that nineteenth! But it's a poor thing compared to what the twentieth is going to be."   —Satan

("Sold to Satan," E&E, pp. 330–331)

Noah's Ark

1893 The progress made in the great art of ship building since Noah's time is quite noticeable. Also, the looseness of the navigation laws in the time of Noah is in quite striking contrast with the strictness of the navigation laws of our time. It would not be possible for Noah to do in our day what he was permitted to do in his own. . . . Noah would not be allowed to sail from Bremen in our day. The inspectors would come and examine the Ark, and make all sorts of objections.

("About All Kinds of Ships," CT-2, p. 86)

c. 1896 Nobody but a farmer could have designed such a thing, for such a purpose.

(MTN, p. 266)

1908 It had no rudder, it had no sails, it had no compass, it had no pumps, it had no charts, no lead-lines, No anchors, no log, no light, no ventilation; and as for cargo-room—which was the main thing—the less said about that the better.

("Letters from the Earth," WIM&OPW, p. 420)

nobility

1888 What is the chiefest privilege remaining to nobility? That you shal[l] not laugh at it. No other class is exempt.

(N&J-3, p. 411)

1889 A nobleman is not valuable because he is a jackass. It is a mixture that is always ineffectual, and should never have been attempted in the first place. —[Hank Morgan]

(Conn. Yankee, ch. 15, p. 133)

1891 Only "birth" makes noble. So it follows indisputably that if Adam was noble, all are; & if he wasn't, none are.

(N&J-3, p. 606)

noise

1897 Noise proves nothing. Often a hen who has merely laid an egg cackles as if she had laid an asteroid.

—Pudd'nhead Wilson's New Calendar

(Foll. Equat., ch. 5, p. 77)

nomadism

1869 The nomadic instinct is a human instinct; it was born with Adam and transmitted through the patriarchs, and after thirty centuries of steady effort, civilization has not educated it entirely out of us yet.

(Inn. Abroad, ch. 55, p. 587)

nonsense

1879 It takes a heap of sense to write good nonsense[.]

(N&J-2, p. 303)

notoriety

1897 "Fame is a great and noble thing—and permanent. Notoriety is a noise—just a noise, and doesn't last." —James Carpenter

("Hellfire Hotchkiss," ch. 1, S&B, p. 184)

novels

1876 When one writes a novel about grown people, he knows exactly where to stop—that is, with a marriage; but when he writes of juveniles, he must stop where he best can.

(Tom Sawyer, Conclusion, p. 260)

1885 I can't stand George Eliot, & Hawthorne & those people; I see what they are at, a hundred years before they get to it, & they just tire me to death. And as for the Bostonians, I would rather be damned to John Bunyan's heaven than read that.

(Letter to W. D. Howells, July 21, 1885, Ltrs-Howells, 2:534)

1895 There is only one expert who is qualified to examine the souls and the life of a people and make a valuable report—the native novelist. This expert is so rare that the most populous country can never have fifteen conspicuously and confessedly competent ones in stock at one time. . . .

And when a thousand able novels have been written, *there* you have the soul of the people, the life of the people, the speech of the people; and not anywhere else can these be had. And the shadings of character, manners, feelings, ambitions, will be infinite.

("What Paul Bourget Thinks of Us," CT-2, pp. 167–168)

novelty

1889 Unquestionably, the popular thing in this world is novelty.

—[Hank Morgan]

(Conn. Yankee, ch. 39, p. 387)

1897 We take a natural interest in novelties, but it is against nature to take an interest in familiar things.

(Foll. Equat., ch. 18, p. 177)

obituaries

1902 An obituary is a thing which cannot be so judiciously edited by any hand as by that of the subject of it. In such a work it is not the Facts that are of chief importance, but the light which the obituarist shall throw upon them, the meanings which he shall dress them in, the conclusions which he shall draw from them, and the judgments which he shall deliver upon them. The Verdicts, you understand: that is the danger-line.

("Amended Obituaries," $30k Bequest, pp. 231-232)

obscurity

n.d. Obscurity and a competence. That is the life that is best worth living.

(MTN, p. 398)

Old Masters

1869 Any one who is acquainted with the old masters will comprehend how much the Last Supper is damaged when I say that the spectator can not really tell, now, whether the disciples are Hebrews or Italians. These ancient painters never succeeded in denationalizing themselves.

(Inn. Abroad, ch. 19, pp. 194-195)

COPYING FROM
OLD MASTERS

1880 When I wrote about the Old Masters before, I said the copies were better than the originals. That was a mistake of large dimensions. The Old

Masters were still unpleasing to me, but they were truly divine contrasted with the copies. The copy is to the original as the pallid, smart, inane new wax work group is to the vigorous, earnest, dignified group of living men and women whom it professes to duplicate.

(Tramp Abroad, ch. 48, p. 558)

opera

1878 Only the few are educated up to a point where high class music gives pleasure. I have never heard enough classic music to be able to enjoy it; & the simple truth is, I detest it. Not mildly, but with all my heart. To me an opera is the very climax & cap-stone of the absurd, the fantastic the unjustifiable. I hate the very name of opera—partly because of the nights of suffering I have endured in its presence, & partly because I want to love it and can't. I suppose one naturally hates the things he wants to love & can't. In America the opera is an affectation. The seeming love for [it] is a lie. Nine out of every ten of the males are bored by it, & 5 out of 10 women. Yet how they applaud, the ignorant liars!

(N&J-2, p. 139)

1880 The banging and slamming and booming and crashing [of *Lohengrin*] were something beyond belief. The racking and pitiless pain of it remains stored up in my memory alongside the memory of the time that I had my teeth fixed.

(Tramp Abroad, ch. 9, pp. 83–84)

1880 It deals so largely in pain that its scattered delights are prodigiously augmented by the contrasts. A pretty air in an opera is prettier there than it could be anywhere else, I suppose, just as an honest man in politics shines more than he would elsewhere.

(Ibid., pp. 86–87)

1891 The only operatic favorite I have ever had—an opera which has always driven me mad with ignorant delight whenever I have heard it— "Tannhäuser."

("At the Shrine of St. Wagner," WIM&OE, p. 216)

opinion

1884 Loyalty to petrified opinions never yet broke a chain or freed a human soul in *this* world—and never *will*.

(Paper delivered in Hartford, late 1884, Speeches/Paine, p. 130.
This quote is engraved on Mark Twain's bust at the national Hall of Fame.)

1894 It were not best that we should all think alike; it is difference of opinion that makes horse-races.   —Pudd'nhead Wilson's Calendar

(Pudd. Wilson, *ch. 19*, PW&TET, *p. 246*)

1900 "You tell me whar a man gits his corn-pone, en I'll tell you what his 'pinions is."   —Jerry

("Corn-pone Opinions," WIM&OPW, p. 92)

1905 Any man who's got anything worth while to say will be heard if he only says it often enough.

(Interview in New York Times, Nov. 26, 1905, MTSFH, p. 196)

1907 In disputed matters political and religious, one man's opinion is worth no more than his peer's, and hence it follows that no man's opinion possesses any real value.

("Christian Science," bk. 1, ch. 5, WIM&OPW, p. 237)

1908 I was in the common habit, in private conversation with friends, of revealing every private opinion I possessed relating to religion, politics, and men, but . . . I should never dream of *printing* one of them, because they are individually and collectively at war with almost everybody's public opinion, while at the same time they are in happy agreement with almost everybody's private opinion.

(Autob/MTIE, *p. 317*)

opportunity

1906 I was seldom able to see an opportunity until it had ceased to be one.

(Autob/MTIE, *p. 155*)

optimist

optimist

n.d. At 50 a man can be an ass without being an optimist but not an optimist without being an ass.

(More Max., p. 5)

ORATORICAL ENTHUSIASM

202

oratory, flights of

1908 A very dangerous thing, for often the wings which take one into clouds of oratorical enthusiasm are wax and melt up there, and down you come.

(Speech in New York City, May 14, 1908,
Speeches/Paine, p. 380)

Ornithorhyncus (duckbill platypus)

1897 That curious combination of bird, fish, amphibian, burrower, crawler, quadruped, and Christian called the Ornithorhyncus—grotesquest of animals, king of the animalculae of the world for versatility of character and make-up . . . "It is manifestly a kind of Christian, for it keeps the Sabbath when there is anybody around, and when there isn't, doesn't."

(Foll. Equat., ch. 8, pp. 102, 105)

osteopathy

1898–99 To ask a doctor's opinion of osteopathy is equivalent to going to Satan for information about [Chris]tianity.

(MTP, ts 42, p. 61; MTN, p. 344)

"out"

1897 It is easier to stay out than get out.

—Pudd'nhead Wilson's New Calendar
(Foll. Equat., ch. 18, p. 176)

Oxford University
(English university that awarded Mark Twain
an honorary degree in 1907)

1907 I am quite well aware—and so is America, and so is the rest of Christendom—that an Oxford decoration is a loftier distinction than is conferrable by any other university on either side of the ocean, and is worth twenty-five of any other, whether foreign or domestic.

(Autob/AMT, ch. 73, p. 349)

oysters

1869 When one comes to reflect upon the nature of an oyster, it seems plain that he does not care for scenery. An oyster has no taste for such things; he cares nothing for the beautiful. An oyster is of a retiring disposition, and not lively—not even cheerful above the average, and never enterprising.

(Inn. Abroad, ch. 39, p. 415)

Paige compositor
(typesetting machine on which Mark Twain lost a fortune)

1889 All the other wonderful inventions of the human brain sink pretty nearly into commonplaces contrasted with this awful mechanical miracle. Telephones, telegraphs, locomotives, cotton gins, sewing machines, Babbage calculators, Jacquard looms, perfecting presses, Arkwright's frames—all mere toys, simplicities! The Paige Compositor marches alone & far in the lead of human inventions.

(Letter to Orion Clemens, January 5, 1889, Ltrs/Paine, 2:508)

1893 That is unquestionably the boss machine of this world, but it is the toughest one on prophets, when it is in an incomplete state, that has ever seen the light.

(Letter to Fred J. Hall, August 6, 1893, Ltrs-Publs, *p. 357)*

Paige, James W. (inventor of the Paige compositor)

1890 Paige . . . is a most extraordinary compound of business thrift and commercial insanity; of cold calculation and jejune sentimentality; of veracity and falsehood; of fidelity and treachery; of nobility and baseness; of pluck and cowardice; of wasteful liberality and pitiful stinginess; of solid sense and weltering moonshine; of towering genius and trivial ambitions; of merciful bowels and a petrified heart; of colossal vanity and—But there the opposites stop. His vanity stands alone, sky-piercing, as sharp of outline as an Egyptian monolith. It is the only unpleasant feature in him that is not modified, softened, compensated by some converse characteristic. There is another point or two worth mentioning. He can persuade anybody, he can convince nobody.

(Autob/MTA, 1:72)

1890 Paige and I always meet on effusively affectionate terms, and yet he knows perfectly well that if I had him in a steel trap I would shut out all human succor and watch that trap till he died.

(Ibid., 1:78)

1893 What a talker he is. He could persuade a fish to come out and take a walk with him. Whe[n] he is present I always believe him—I cannot help it. When he is gone away all the belief evaporates. He is a most daring and majestic liar.

(MTN, p. 232)

pain

1891 It is believed by people generally . . . that the exquisitely sharp sensation which results from plunging the steel point [*of a dental drill*] is pain, but I think that this is doubtful. It is so vivid and sudden that one has no time to examine properly into its character. . . . I have every confidence that I can eventually prove to everyone's satisfaction that a nerve-stab produces pleasure; and not only that, but the most exquisite pleasure, the most perfect felicity which we are capable of feeling. I would not ask more than to be remembered hereafter as the man who conferred this priceless benefaction upon his race.

("Down the Rhône," E&E, *p. 163)*

1900 One can never get any but a loose and ignorant notion of such things except by experience.

("The Chronicle of Young Satan," ch. 7, Mys. Stranger Mss., *p. 131)*

Palestine

1869 The word Palestine always brought to my mind a vague suggestion of a country as large as the United States. I do not know why, but such was the case. I suppose it was because I could not conceive of a small country having so large a history.

(Inn. Abroad, ch. 46, p. 486)

"palladium"

1872 Trial by jury is the palladium of our liberties. I do not know what a palladium is, having never seen a palladium, but it is a good thing no doubt at any rate.

(Rough. It, ch. 49, p. 330)

palm tree

1897 Nature's imitation of an umbrella that has been out to see what a cyclone is like and is trying not to look disappointed.

(Foll. Equat., ch. 55, p. 524)

Paradise Lost
(epic poem by John Milton)

1900 I don't believe any of you have ever read *Paradise Lost*, and you don't want to. That's something that you just want to take on trust.

IMITATION UMBRELLA

parental instinct

It's a classic, just as Professor Winchester says, and it meets his definition of a classic—something that everybody wants to have read and
nobody wants to read.

(*Speech in New York City, November 20, 1900,* MT Speaking, *p. 359)*

parental instinct

1894 One must make allowances for a parental instinct that has been
starving for twenty-five or thirty years. It is famished, it is crazed with
hunger by that time, and will be entirely satisfied with anything that
comes handy; its taste is atrophied, it can't tell mud cat from shad. A
devil born to a young couple is measurably recognizable by them as a
devil before long, but a devil adopted by an old couple is an angel to
them, and remains so, through thick and thin.

(Ibid., ch. 19, pp. 247-248)

parentheses

1880 We have the Parenthesis disease in our literature, too . . . with us
it is the mark and sign of an unpractised writer or a cloudy intellect,
whereas with the Germans it is doubtless the mark and sign of a prac-
tised pen and of the presence of that sort of luminous intellectual fog
which stands for clearness among these people. . . . Parentheses in literature and dentistry are in bad taste.

("The Awful German Language," Tramp Abroad, *p. 604)*

Paris

1880 In Paris . . . the law says, in effect, "it is the business of the weak
to get out of the way of the strong." We fine a cabman if he runs over a
citizen; Paris fines the citizen for being run over.

*(*Tramp Abroad, *ch. 47, pp. 544-545)*

past

1876 I said there was but one solitary thing about the past worth
remembering, and that was the fact that it *is* the past—can't be restored.

(Letter to Jacob H. Burrough, November 1, 1876, Ltrs/Paine, *1:290)*

patent offices

1889 A country without a patent office and good patent laws was just a crab, and couldn't travel any way but sideways or backwards.

—[Hank Morgan]
(Conn. Yankee, ch. 9, p. 72)

pathos

1899 By some subtile law all tragic human experiences gain in pathos by the perspective of time.

("My Début As a Literary Person," MTCH&c, *p. 126)*

patriot

n.d. The person who can holler the loudest without knowing what he is hollering about.

(More Max., p. 12)

1897 A man can be a [Christ]ian *or* a patriot, but he can't legally be a [Christ]ian *and* a patriot—except in the usual way: one of the two with the mouth, the other with the heart.

(MTP, ts 41, p. 43; MTN, *p. 332)*

1906 "What is a Patriot, pray? One who grovels to the Family, and shouts for the Emperor and the Government, be they in the right or in the wrong,—and especially when they are in the wrong; that they call 'standing by the *Country*.' . . . Oh, it's a sweet thing, is Patriotism. Adam used to call it 'the last refuge of a scoundrel.'"

—Nanga Parbat *("The World in the Year 920 after Creation,"*
Lets. Earth, *p. 103)*

1909 Man is the only Patriot. He sets himself apart in his own country, under his own flag, and sneers at the other nations, and keeps multitudinous uniformed assassins on hand at heavy expense to grab slices of other people's countries.

("The Lowest Animal," Lets. Earth, *pp. 226-227)*

patriotism

1896 Talking of patriotism, what humbug it is; it is a word which always commemorates a robbery. There isn't a foot of land in the world which doesn't represent the ousting & re-ousting of a long line of successive "owners" who each in turn, as "patriots," with proud & swelling hearts defended it against the next gang of "robbers" who came to steal it & *did*—& became swelling-hearted patriots in *their* turn.

(MTP, ts 38, p. 34; MTN, pp. 295-296)

1897 Patriotism is Patriotism. Calling it Fanaticism cannot degrade it; nothing can degrade it.

(Foll. Equat., ch. 35, p. 321)

1905 To put it in rude, plain, unpalatable words—*true* patriotism, real patriotism: loyalty, not to a Family and a Fiction, but a loyalty to the Nation itself!

. . . "Remember this, take it to heart, live by it, die for it if necessary: that our patriotism is medieval, outworn, obsolete; that the modern patriotism, the true patriotism, the only rational patriotism, is *loyalty to the Nation* ALL *the time, loyalty to the Government when it deserves it.*"

—[Czar Nicholas II]

("The Czar's Soliloquy," CT-2, p. 645)

1908 Patriotism is usually the refuge of the scoundrel. He is the man who talks the loudest.

(Speech in New York City, May 14, 1908, Speeches/Paine, p. 378)

Paul, Saint (one of Christ's Apostles)

1869 He preached Christ so fearlessly in Damascus that the people sought to kill him, just as they would to-day for the same offense . . .

(Inn. Abroad, ch. 44, pp. 462-463)

pauses

n.d. The right word may be effective, but no word was ever as effective as a rightly timed pause.

(Speeches/Paine, Introduction, p. xi)

1905 That is the way to get the attention of a fussy and excited young crowd. Start to say something; then pause; they notice *that*, though they hadn't noticed your words—nor cared for them, either.

("Three Thousand Years among the Microbes," ch. 17, WWD&OSW, *p. 546)*

c. 1907 That impressive silence, that eloquent silence, that geometrically progressive silence which often achieves a desired effect where no combination of words howsoever felicitous could accomplish it.

(Autob/AMT, ch. 35, p. 181)

peace

1899 Peace by compulsion. That seems a better idea than the other. Peace by persuasion has a pleasant sound, but I think we should not be able to work it. We should have to tame the human race first, and history seems to show that that cannot be done.

(Letter to Wm. T. Stead, January 9, 1899, Ltrs/Paine, 2:672)

c. 1900–06 *"An inglorious peace is better than a dishonorable war."*
—Adam

("Passage from 'Glances at History,'" Fab. of Man, *p. 393)*

209

peasants

1896 Some day it will be found out that peasants are people. Yes, beings in a great many respects like ourselves. And I believe that some day *they* will find this out, too—and then! Well, then I think they will rise up and demand to be regarded as part of the race, and that by consequence there will be trouble.

(Joan of Arc, bk. 2, ch. 37, p. 290)

pen names

1907 It is a good idea to choose a name in advance, & then fit the literature onto it when the literature comes.

(Letter to Dorothy Quick, August 17-22, 1907, Ltrs-Angelfish, p. 53)

perfection

1880 None of us like mediocrity, but we all reverence perfection. This girl's music was perfection in its way; it was the worst music that had ever been achieved on our planet by a mere human being.

(Tramp Abroad, ch. 32, p. 342)

1880 One's admiration of a perfect thing always grows, never declines; and this is the surest evidence to him that it *is* perfect.

(Ibid., ch. 49, p. 567)

pessimists

c. 1902 The man who is a pessimist before 48, knows too much; if he is an optimist after it, he knows too little.

(MTP, ts 45, p. 43; MTN, p. 380;
see also letter to J. H. Twichell, March 14, 1905, Ltrs/Paine, 2:767)

1902 There is no sadder sight than a young pessimist. Except an old optimist.

(MTP, ts 45, p. 40; MTN, p. 385)

1905 Pessimists are born not made; optimists are born not made; but no man is born either pessimist wholly or optimist wholly; he is pessimistic along certain lines and optimistic along certain others. That is my case.

(Letter to L. M. Powers, November 9, 1905, Ltrs/Paine, 2:785)

Philippines

c. 1901 When the United States sent word to Spain that the Cuban atrocities must end she occupied the highest moral position ever taken by a nation since the Almighty made the earth. But when she snatched the Philippines she stained the flag.

(Quoted in MT:Biog, ch. 201, p. 1064)

phrasing

1905 Phrasing is everything, almost. Oh, yes, phrasing is a kind of photography: out of focus, a blurred picture; in focus, a sharp one. One must get the focus right—that is, frame the sentence with exactness and precision, in his mind—before he pulls the string.

("Three Thousand Years among the Microbes," ch. 7, WWD&OSW, p. 460)

phrenology

1901–02 I judged that the difference between a phrenologist drunk and a phrenologist sober was probably too small to materially influence results.

("The Secret History of Eddypus," bk. 2, ch. 2, Fab. of Man, p. 350)

"phthisis"

1906 We shall be rid of phthisis and phthisic and pneumonia and pneumatics, and diphtheria and pterodactyl, and all those other insane words which no man addicted to the simple Christian life can try to spell and not lose some of the bloom of his piety in the demoralizing attempt.

(Speech in New York City, September 19, 1906, Speeches/Paine, p. 316)

physicians

1882 The physician's is the highest & worthiest of all occupations—or would be, if human nature did not make superstitions & priests necessary.

(N&J-2, p. 500)

1891 A half-educated physician is not valuable. He thinks he can cure everything.

(MTP, ts 31, p. 12; MTN, p. 219)

1899 I don't believe a doctor can cure *any* really serious disease except by accident . . .

(Letter to H. H. Rogers, August 3, 1899, Ltrs-Rogers, p. 403)

1900 I am convinced that of all quackeries, the physician's is the grotesquest & the silliest. And they know they are shams & humbugs. They have taken the place of those augurs who couldn't look each other in the face without laughing.

(Letter to J. H. Twichell, January 8, 1900, Ltrs/Paine, 2:691)

1902 It seems a stupid idea to keep a student 4 years in a medical college to merely learn how to guess—and guess wrong. If ever I am deadly ill I hope you will stand by me and bar out the doctors and let me die a natural death.

(Letter to H. H. Rogers, September 18-19, 1902, Ltrs-Rogers, p. 506)

1908 Doctors do know so little and they do charge so much for it.

(Letter to Emilie Rogers, August 12, 1908, Ltrs-Rogers, p. 652)

Pilgrim's Progress, The (picaresque by John Bunyan)

1884 [*A book*] about a man that left his family it didn't say why.

—[Huck]

(Huck Finn, ch. 17, p. 137)

pirates

1884 Heathens don't amount to shucks alongside of pirates, to work a camp-meeting with. —[Huck]

(Huck Finn, ch. 20, p. 174)

1906 According to tradition, some of them [*my ancestors*] were pirates and slavers in Elizabeth's time. But this is no discredit to them, for so were Drake and Hawkins and the others. It was a respectable trade, then, and monarchs were partners in it. In my time I have had desires to be a pirate myself.

(NAR, September 7, 1906; Autob/NAR, p. 4)

CAMP-MEETING PIRATE

pity

1897 Pity is for the living, envy is for the dead.

—Pudd'nhead Wilson's New Calendar

(Foll. Equat., ch. 19, p. 184)

1902 The funeral of fame.

("The Five Boons of Life," WIM&OPW, ch. 3, p. 99)

place

1899 Have a place for everything & keep the thing somewhere else. This is not advice, it is merely custom.

(MTP, ts 42, p. 73; MTN, p. 347)

plagiarism

1897 Perhaps no poet is a conscious plagiarist; but there seems to be warrant for suspecting that there is no poet who is not at one time or another an unconscious one.

(Foll. Equat., ch. 8, p. 107)

1903 As if there was much of anything in any human utterance, oral or written, *except* plagiarism! The kernel, the soul—let us go further & say the substance, the bulk, the actual & valuable material of *all* human utterances—is plagiarism. For substantially all ideas are second-hand; consciously & unconsciously drawn from a million outside sources, & daily used by the garnerer with a pride & satisfaction born of the superstition that he originated them.

(Letter to Helen Keller, March 17, 1903, Ltrs/Paine, 2:731)

planets

1898 "There is much more interest attaching to the creation of a planet than attaches to the creation of a sun, on account of the life that is going to inhabit it."   —Boy

("Schoolhouse Hill," ch. 5, Mys. Stranger Mss., p. 214)

Platte River, Nebraska

1872 The shallow, yellow, muddy South Platte . . . a melancholy stream straggling through the centre of the enormous flat plain, and only saved from being impossible to find with the naked eye by its sentinel rank of scattering trees standing on either bank. The Platte was "up," they said—which made me wish I could see it when it was down, if it could look any sicker and sorrier.

(Rough. It, ch. 7, p. 41)

pledges

n.d. Taking the pledge will not make bad liquor good, but it will improve it.

(More Max., p. 13)

1897 To make a *pledge* of any kind is to declare war against nature; for a pledge is a chain that is always clanking and reminding the wearer of it that he is not a free man. . . .

I used to take pledges—and soon violate them. My will was not strong and I could not help it.

(Foll. Equat., ch. 1, pp. 29-30)

Pliny (ancient Roman historian)

1869 I have conceived a sort of unwarrantable unfriendliness toward Pliny and St. Paul, because it seems as if I can never ferret out a place that I can have to myself. It always and eternally transpires that St. Paul has been to that place, and Pliny has "mentioned" it.

(Inn. Abroad, ch. 49, p. 514)

Poe, Edgar Allan (American writer)

1909 To me his prose is unreadable—like Jane Austin's. No, there is a difference. I could read his prose on salary, but not Jane's.

(Letter to W. D. Howells, January 18, 1909, Ltrs-Howells, 2:841)

poetry

1862 When I wish to write a great poem, I just take a few lines from Tom, Dick and Harry, Shakspeare, and other poets, and by patching them together so as to make them rhyme occasionally, I have accomplished my object. Never mind the *sense*—sense, madam, has but little to do with poetry. By this wonderful method, any body can be a poet—or a bard—which sounds better, you know.

(Letter to mother, January 30, 1862, Ltrs-1, p. 146)

1865 My usual style of ciphering out the merits of poetry, which is to read a line or two near the top, a verse near the bottom and then strike an average . . .

("Answers to Correspondents," ET&S-2, p. 184)

1869 There are things which some people never attempt during their whole lives, but one of these is not poetry. Poetry attacks all human beings sooner or later, and, like the measles, is mild or violent according to the age of the sufferer.

(Column in Buffalo Express, August 18, 1869, MT:Bib, p. 179)

1906 What a lumbering poor vehicle prose is for the conveying of great thought! . . . Prose wanders around with a lantern & laboriously schedules & verifies the details & particulars of a valley & its frame of crags & peaks, then Poetry comes & lays bare the whole landscape with a single splendid flash.

(Letter to W. D. Howells, February 25, 1906, Ltrs-Howells, 2:800)

1906 Poetry is very difficult for me on account of its being outside the range of my great talents.

(Letter to Gertrude Natkin, March 2, 1906, Ltrs-Angelfish, p. 16)

poets

1883 War talk by men who have been in a war is always interesting; whereas moon talk by a poet who has not been in the moon is likely to be dull.

(Life on Miss., ch. 45, pp. 456-457)

1907 If poets when they get discouraged would blow their brains out, they could write very much better when they get well.

(Speech in Liverpool, July 10, 1907, Speeches/Paine, p. 580)

1908 No poet who isn't of the first class knows how to read, and so he is an affliction to everybody but himself when he tries it.

(Autob/MTIE, p. 302)

poi

1866 A villainous mixture it is, almost tasteless before it ferments and too sour for a luxury afterward.

(Ltrs-Hawaii, Letter 8, p. 68)

poker

1877 There are few things that are so unpardonably neglected in our country as poker. The upper class know very little about it. Now and then you find ambassadors who have a sort of general knowledge of the game, but the ignorance of the people is fearful. Why, I have known clergymen, good men, kind-hearted, liberal, sincere, and all that, who did not know the meaning of a "flush." It is enough to make one ashamed of one's species.

(Curtain call speech, quoted in MT:Bib, p. 140)

UNPARDONABLE NEGLECT

polecat (skunk)

1900 While a polecat is undoubtedly a comely and graceful animal to look at, none but an angel can get any real joy out of its company.

("The Chronicle of Young Satan," ch. 8, Mys. Stranger Mss., p. 140)

police

1855 Policemen are queer animals and have remarkably nice notions as to the great law of self-preservation. I doubt if the man is now living that ever caught one at a riot. To find "a needle in a hay stack" is a much easier matter than to scare up one of these gentry when he's wanted.

(Letter to Muscatine Tri-Weekly Journal, February 16, 1855, Ltrs-1, p. 47)

politeness

1882 The highest perfection of politeness is only a beautiful edifice, built, from the base to the dome, of graceful and gilded forms of charitable and unselfish lying.

("On the Decay of the Art of Lying," £1m Bank-note, pp. 220–221)

politics

n.d. *The New Political Gospel:* Public Office is private graft.

(More Max., p. 10)

1869 The more I thought of trying to transform myself into a political editor, the more incongruous & the more hazardous the thing looked. I always did hate politics.

(Letter to Mary Fairbanks, August 14, 1869, Ltrs-3, p. 298)

1906 "Politician and idiot are synonymous terms."

—Methuselah

("The World in the Year 920 after Creation," Lets. Earth, p. 95)

Polly, Aunt (character in *The Adventures of Tom Sawyer*)

1876 She was a subscriber for all the "Health" periodicals and phrenological frauds; and the solemn ignorance they were inflated with was breath to her nostrils. . . . and she never observed that her health-journals of the current month customarily upset everything they had recommended the month

AN EASY VICTIM

before. She was as simple-hearted and honest as the day was long, and she was an easy victim.

(Tom Sawyer, *ch. 12, pp. 92-93)*

polygamy, Mormon

1872 I was feverish to plunge in headlong and achieve a great reform here—until I saw the Mormon women. Then I was touched. My heart was wiser than my head. It warmed toward these poor, ungainly and pathetically "homely" creatures, and as I turned to hide the generous moisture in my eyes, I said, "No—the man that marries one of them has done an act of Christian charity which entitles him to the kindly applause of mankind, not their harsh censure—and the man that marries sixty of them has done a deed of open-handed generosity so sublime that the nations should stand uncovered in his presence and worship in silence."

(Rough. It, *ch. 14, pp. 97-98)*

pompanos

1883 The renowned fish called the pompano, delicious as the less criminal forms of sin.

(Life on Miss., *ch. 44, p. 445)*

popularity

1898 The best of us would rather be popular than right.

—[August Feldner]

(No. 44, *ch. 5, p. 26)*

porpoises

1897 The porpoise is the kitten of the sea; he never has a serious thought, he cares for nothing but fun and play.

(Foll. Equat., *ch. 9, p. 110; see also* MTN, *p. 267)*

portraits

1866 No photograph ever was good, yet, of anybody . . . If a man tries to look merely serious when he sits for his picture, the photograph makes him as solemn as an owl; if he smiles, the photograph smirks repulsively; if he tries to look pleasant, the photograph looks silly; if he makes the fatal mistake of attempting to seem pensive, the camera will surely write him down an ass. The sun never looks through the photographic instrument that it does not print a lie.

(Ltrs-Hawaii, Letter 17, pp. 185-186)

1867 Portraits should be accurate. We do not want feeling and intelligence smuggled into the pictured face of an idiot, and we do not want this glorified atmosphere smuggled into a portrait of the Yosemite, where it surely does not belong.

(Letter to Alta, June 2, 1867; MTTB, p. 251)

1898 I want to see *one* stunning portrait of myself before I get homely.

(Letter to H. H. Rogers, September 14, 1898, Ltrs-Rogers, p. 363)

posterity

1897 "I would rather be a dog's ancestor than a lieutenant governor's posterity."   —James Carpenter

("Hellfire Hotchkiss," ch. 1, S&B, p. 180)

poverty

1867 Honest poverty is a gem that even a King might feel proud to call his own, but I wish to sell out. I have sported that kind of jewelry long enough. I want some variety. I wish to become rich, so that I can instruct the people and glorify honest poverty a little, like those good, kindhearted, fat, benevolent people do.

(Letter to Alta, May 26, 1867; MTTB, p. 236)

1879 I admit also that I am not a friend of the poor man. I regard the poor man, in his present condition, as so much wasted raw material. Cut up and properly canned, he might be made useful to fatten the natives of the cannibal islands and to improve our export trade in that region.

(Article in New York Evening Post, June 9, 1879; MTSFH, p. 117)

1897–98 It is good to begin life poor; it is good to begin life rich— these are wholesome; but to begin it *prospectively* rich! The man who has not experienced it cannot imagine the curse of it.

(NAR, March 1, 1907; Autob/NAR, p. 111)

practical joker

1870 He is a pitiful creature indeed who will degrade the dignity of his humanity to the contriving of the witless inventions that go by that name.

("A Couple of Sad Experiences," CT-1, p. 388)

1906 When grown-up persons indulge in practical jokes, the fact gauges them. They have lived narrow, obscure, and ignorant lives, and at full manhood they still retain and cherish a job lot of left-over standards and ideals that would have been discarded with their boyhood if they had then moved out into the world and a broader life.

(Autob/MTA, 2:305)

praise

n.d. We are always more anxious to be distinguished for a talent which we do not possess, than to be praised for the fifteen which we do possess.

(More Max., p. 14)

1897 "Praise has a value—when it is earned. When it isn't earned, the male creature receiving it ought to despise it; and will, when there is a proper degree of manliness in him." —James Carpenter

("Hellfire Hotchkiss," ch. 1, S&B, p. 178)

WITLESS INVENTION

prayer

c. 1870 *Resolved*, That if the ordinary prayers of a nation were answered during a single day, the universal misery, misfortune, destruction and desolation which would ensue, would constitute a cataclysm which would take its place side by side with the deluge and so remain in history to the end of time.

("The Holy Children," Fab. of Man, p. 76)

1879 There is more than one way of praying and I like the butcher's way because the petitioner is so apt to be in earnest.

(Letter to J. H. Twichell, January 26, 1879, PortMT, p. 756)

YOU CAN'T PRAY A LIE.

1884 You can't pray a lie. —[Huck]

(Huck Finn, ch. 31, p. 269)

1906 I don't know of a single foreign product that enters this country untaxed except the answer to prayer.

(Speech in New York City, March 9, 1906, Speeches/Paine, p. 293)

preachers

1863 A man's profession has but little to do with his moral character. If we had as many preachers as lawyers, you would find it mixed as to which occupation could muster the most rascals.

(Letter to Territorial Enterprise, *February 6, 1863, MTOE, p. 60)*

1867 Preachers are always pleasant company when they are off duty.

(Letter to Alta, *April 30, 1867; MTTB, p. 166)*

precedents

1899 We realize that the edifice of public justice is built of precedents, from the ground upward; but we do not always realize that all the other details of our civilization are likewise built of precedents.

("Diplomatic Pay and Clothes," CT-2, *p. 344)*

"Presbyterian"

1904 My father was a St. Bernard, my mother was a collie, but I am a Presbyterian. This is what my mother told me, I do not know these nice distinctions myself. To me they are only fine large words meaning nothing. —[Aileen Mavourneen]

(Dog's Tale, ch. 1, p. 1)

"pretty much"

1880 "Pretty much" may not be elegant English, but it is high time it was. There is no elegant word or phrase which means just what it means.

(Tramp Abroad, ch. 38, p. 440n.)

pride

1897 Human pride is not worth while; there is always something lying in wait to take the wind out of it.

(Foll. Equat., Conclusion, p. 712)

Prince and the Pauper, The (1881 novel)

1880 If I knew it would never sell a copy my jubilant delight in writing it would not suffer any diminution.

(Letter to W. D. Howells, March 5, 1880, Ltrs-Howells, 1:290)

principles

n.d. We all live in the protection of certain cowardices which we call our principles.

(More Max., p. 14)

1900 Principles is another name for prejudices.

(Speech in London, May 2, 1900, MT Speaking, p. 337)

1901 Principles aren't of much account anyway, except at election time. After that you hang them up to let them season.

(Speech in New York City, January 4, 1901, Speeches/Paine, p. 220)

1904 Principles have no real force except when one is well fed.

—[Adam]

(Adam's Diary, p. 266)

printing

1898 "The printer's art . . . is the noblest and most puissant of all arts, and destined in the ages to come to promote the others and preserve them."   —Heinrich Stein

(No. 44, ch. 7, p. 33)

prisons

1864 Jail life must be very satisfactory, for those who have been compelled to spend a few days there come out of it completely satisfied. They don't want to go back, nor stay any longer than they can help, under the polite attentions of the man who carries the key.

(Article in Call, September 21, 1864; Cl. of Call, p. 264)

1870 I had long had an idea that Americans, being free, had no need of prisons, which are a contrivance of despots for keeping restless patriots out of mischief.

("Goldsmith's Friend Abroad Again," CT-1, p. 461)

1895 The fact that man invented imprisonment for debt, proves that man is an idiot & also that he is utterly vile & malignant. How can imprisonment pay a debt? Was the idea of it to pay the creditor in revenge?

(MTP, ts 34, p. 35; MTN, p. 257)

privacy

1887 I hate all public mention of my private history, anyway, It is none of the public's business.

(Letter to Orion Clemens, December 8, 1887, MT:Bus. Man, p. 389)

profanity

1867 I can't keep my temper in New York. The cars and carriages always come along and get in the way just as I want to cross a street, and if there is any thing that can make a man soar into flights of sublimity in the matter of profanity, it is that.

(Letter to Alta, June 5, 1867; MTTB, p. 261)

1897 "Profanity is better than flattery."　　　　—James Carpenter
("Hellfire Hotchkiss," ch. 1, S&B, p. 176)

professions, the

1869 I have worked there at all the different trades & professions known to the catalogue. I have been everything, from a newspaper editor down to cowcatcher on a locomotive, & I am encouraged to believe that if there had been a few more occupations to experiment on, I might have made a dazzling success at last, & found out what mysterious design Providence had in creating me.

(Letter to California Pioneers, October 11, 1869, Ltrs-3, p. 371)

1895 It is the loftiest of all human vocations—medicine & surgery. Relief from physical pain, physical distress. Next comes the pulpit, which solaces mental distress; soothes the sorrows of the soul. These two are the great professions, the noble professions. The gap between them & the rest is wide—an abyss.

(MTP, ts 35, p. 56; MTN, pp. 251-252)

promises

n.d. Better a broken promise than none at all.

(More Max., p. 6)

1869 I never could keep a promise. I do not blame myself for this weakness, because the fault must lie in my physical organization. It is likely that such a very liberal amount of space was given to the organ which enables me to *make* promises, that the organ which should enable me to keep them was crowded out. But I grieve not. I like no half-way things. I had rather have one faculty nobly developed than two faculties of mere ordinary capacity.

(Inn. Abroad, ch. 23, p. 239)

1876 To promise not to do a thing is the surest way in the world to make a body want to go and do that very thing.

(Tom Sawyer, ch. 22, p. 161)

proofreading

1884 I would not read the proof of one of my books for any fair & reasonable sum whatever, if I could get out of it. The proof-reading on the P & Pauper cost me the last rags of my religion.

(Letter to W. D. Howells, April 8, 1884, Ltrs-Howells, 2:483)

prophecy

1867 It is easy to prove a prophecy that promised destruction to a city—& it is impossible to prove one that promised *any* thing else—more particularly life & prosperity.

(N&J-1, p. 482)

1871 There are not books enough on earth to contain the record of the prophecies Indians and other unauthorized parties have made; but one may

FALSE PROPHET

223

proportions

carry in his overcoat-pockets the record of all the prophecies that have been fulfilled.

("A Burlesque Biography," $30k Bequest, *p. 204)*

1889 A prophet doesn't have to have any brains. They are good to have, of course, for the ordinary exigencies of life, but they are no use in professional work. It is the restfulest vocation there is. When the spirit of prophecy comes upon you, you merely take your intellect and lay it off in a cool place for a rest, and unship your jaw and leave it alone; it will work itself: the rest is Prophecy. —[Hank Morgan]

(Conn. Yankee, ch. 27, p. 269)

1896 Prophecies boldly uttered never fall barren on superstitious ears.

(Joan of Arc, bk. 2, ch. 4, p. 88)

1897–98 A man who goes around with a prophecy-gun ought never to get discouraged; if he will keep up his heart and fire at everything he sees, he is bound to hit something by and by.

(NAR, September 7, 1906; Autob/NAR, p. 8)

1906 Prophecies which promise valuable things, desirable things, good things, worthy things, never come true. Prophecies of this kind are like wars fought in a good cause—they are so rare that they don't count.

(Autob/MTA, 2:197)

1909 Prophesying was the only human art that couldn't be improved by practice.

("The International Lightning Trust," Fab. of Man, *p. 103)*

proportions

1894 Consider well the proportions of things. It is better to be a young June-bug than an old bird of paradise.

—Pudd'nhead Wilson's Calendar

(Pudd. Wilson, ch. 8, PW&TET, p. 93)

prosperity

n.d. When a man arrives at great prosperity God did it: when he falls into disaster, he did it himself.

(More Max., p. 14)

224

1867 Prosperity is the surest breeder of insolence I know of.

> *(Letter to* Alta, *February 23, 1867;*
> MTTB, *p. 110)*

1897 Prosperity is the best protector of principle.

> —Pudd'nhead Wilson's New Calendar
> *(Foll. Equat., ch. 38, p. 345)*

1897 Few of us can stand prosperity. Another man's, I mean.

> —Pudd'nhead Wilson's New Calendar
> *(Ibid., ch. 40, p. 369)*

1897 There is an old-time toast which is golden for its beauty. "When you ascend the hill of prosperity may you not meet a friend."

> —Pudd'nhead Wilson's New Calendar
> *(Ibid., ch. 41, p. 379)*

ARRIVING AT PROSPERITY

225

Providence

1872 "Prov'dence don't fire no blank ca'tridges, boys." —Jim Blaine

> *(Rough. It, ch. 53, p. 366)*

1877 Providence always makes it a point to find out what you are after, so as to see that you don't get it.

> *(Letter to Mary Fairbanks, October 31, 1877,* Ltrs-Fairbanks, *p. 211)*

1883 With my prejudices, I never count any prospective chickens when I know that Providence knows where the nest is.

> *(Letter to W. D. Howells, October 15, 1883,* Ltrs-Howells, *1:445)*

1894 I don't want to attract the attention of Providence. I always get along best when I am left alone.

> *(Letter to H. H. Rogers, October 13, 1894,* Ltrs-Rogers, *p. 85)*

1907 The proverb says that Providence protects children and idiots. This is really true. I know it because I have tested it.

> *(NAR, July 5, 1907;* Autob/NAR, *p. 185)*

public interest

1906 No public interest is anything other or nobler than a massed accumulation of private interests.

(Speech in New York City, September 19, 1906, Speeches/Paine, *p. 316)*

public men

1869 Public men get ample credit for all the sins they commit, & for a multitude of other sins they never were guilty of.

(Letter to Olivia L. (Mrs. Jervis) Langdon, February 13, 1869,
Ltrs-3, *pp. 90–91)*

public opinion

1873 That awful power, the public opinion of a nation, is created in America by a horde of ignorant, self-complacent simpletons who failed at ditching and shoemaking and fetched up in journalism on their way to the poorhouse. I am personally acquainted with hundreds of journalists, and the opinion of the majority of them would not be worth tuppence in private, but when they speak in print it is the *newspaper* that is talking (the pygmy scribe is not visible) and *then* their utterances shake the community like the thunders of prophecy.

(Paper delivered in Hartford, February 1873, Speeches/Paine, *p. 49)*

1900 It is held in reverence. It settles everything. Some think it the Voice of God.

("Corn-pone Opinions," WIM&OPW, *p. 97)*

public servants

n.d. Persons chosen by the people to distribute the graft.

*(*More Max., *p. 12)*

publishers

c. 1907 All publishers are Columbuses. The successful author is their America. The reflection that they—like Columbus—didn't discover what they expected to discover . . . doesn't trouble them. All they remember is that they discovered America; they forgot that they started out to discover some patch or corner of India.

(Autob/AMT, ch. 50, pp. 253–254)

Pudd'nhead Wilson (1894 novel)

1893 I have knocked out everything that delayed the march of the story—even the description of a Mississippi steamboat. There ain't any weather in [it], and there ain't any scenery—the story is stripped for flight!

(Letter to Fred J. Hall, July 30, 1893, Ltrs-Publs, p. 355)

pudd'nheads

1900 We do not guess, we know that 9 in 10 of the species are pudd'nheads.

(Letter to J. H. Twichell, January 8, 1900, Ltrs/Paine, 2:690)

pumpkins

1870 This berry is a favorite with the natives of the interior of New England, who prefer it to the gooseberry for the making of fruit-cake, and who likewise give it the preference over the raspberry for feeding cows, as being more filling and fully as satisfying. The pumpkin is the only esculent of the orange family that will thrive in the North, except the gourd and one or two varieties of the squash.

("How I Edited an Agricultural Paper Once," SN&O, p. 235)

punctuation

1880 One man can't punctuate another man's manuscript any more than one person can make the gestures for another person's speech.

(Anonymous article in Atlantic Monthly, *June 1880, LAIFI, p. 190;
see also N&J-1, p. 148)*

puns

1870 No circumstances, however dismal, will ever be considered a sufficient excuse for the admission of that last and saddest evidence of intellectual poverty, the Pun.

("Introductory to 'Memoranda,'" LAIFI, pp. 93-94)

1870 The fair record of my life has been tarnished by just one pun. My father overheard that, and he hunted me over four or five townships seeking to take my life.

("Wit Inspirations of the 'Two-Year-Olds,'" $30k Bequest, p. 213)

purity

1871 I only make them at funerals & places where I wish to feel sad.

(Letter to Pierre Reynolds, July 1871, Ltrs-4, p. 426)

purity

1900 To the pure all things are impure.

(MTP, ts 43, p. 6; MTN, p. 372)

pyjamas

1897 This foolish [*Indian*] night-dress consists of jacket and drawers. Sometimes they are made of silk, sometimes of a raspy, scratchy, slazy woolen material with a sandpaper surface. . . . Pyjamas are hot on a hot night and cold on a cold night—defects which a nightshirt is free from. . . . I was obliged to give them up, I couldn't stand them.

(Foll. Equat., ch. 49, p. 459)

quacks

1867 The surest sign of quack is picture of some ignorant stupid ass in horrible woodcut on a coarse lying, bragging handbill to be treasured by clowns & used in water closets by the rest of the world.

(N&J-1, pp. 336–337)

Quaker City
(ship on which Mark Twain sailed to Mediterranean in 1867)

1867 . . . the Quaker City's strange menagerie of ignorance, imbecility, bigotry & dotage . . .

(Letter to John Russell Young, November 22, 1867, Ltrs-2, p. 108)

1869 The pleasure ship was a synagogue, and the pleasure trip was a funeral excursion without a corpse.

(Inn. Abroad, ch. 61, p. 644)

quotations

1897 It is my belief that nearly any invented quotation, played with confidence, stands a good chance to deceive.

(Foll. Equat., ch. 5, p. 78)

1897 He made me better satisfied with myself than I had ever been before. It was plain that he had a deep fondness for humor . . . he made *me* laugh all along, and this was very trying—and very pleasant at the same time—for it was at quotations from my own books.

(Ibid., ch. 25, pp. 244–245)

race prejudice

1899 I am quite sure that (bar one) I have no race prejudices, and I think I have no color prejudices nor caste prejudices nor creed prejudices. Indeed, I know it. I can stand any society. All that I care to know is that a man is a human being—that is enough for me; he can't be any worse.

("Concerning the Jews," CT-2, p. 355)

racing

1883 Much the most enjoyable of all races is a steamboat race; but, next to that, I prefer the gay and joyous mule-rush. Two red-hot steamboats raging along, neck-and-neck, straining every nerve—that is to say, every rivet in the boilers—quaking and shaking and groaning from stem to stern, spouting white steam from the pipes, pouring black smoke from the chimneys, raining down sparks, parting the river into long breaks of hissing foam—this is sport that makes a body's very liver curl with enjoyment. A horse-race is pretty tame and colorless in comparison.

(Life on Miss., ch. 45, p. 464)

radicals

1899 The radical of one century is the conservative of the next.

The radical invents the views; when he has worn them out the conservative adopts them.

(MTP, ts 42, pp. 62–63; MTN, p. 344)

rafts

TRANQUIL PLEASURE

1867 For a tranquil pleasure excursion, there was nothing equal to a raft.

("The Facts Concerning the Recent Resignation," CT-1, p. 240)

1884 We said there warn't no home like a raft, after all. Other places do seem so cramped up and smothery, but a raft don't. You feel might free and easy and comfortable on a raft.

—[Huck]

(Huck Finn, ch. 18, p. 155)

railroad conductors

1869 [*In France*] you are in the hands of officials who zealously study your welfare and your interest, instead of turning their talents to the invention of new methods of discommoding and snubbing you, as is very often the main employment of that exceedingly self-satisfied monarch, the railroad conductor of America.

(Inn. Abroad, ch. 12, p. 106)

railroads

1867 A railroad is like a lie—you have to keep building to it to make it stand. A railroad is a ravenous destroyer of towns, unless those towns are put at the end of it and a sea beyond, so that you can't go further and find another terminus. And it is shaky trusting them, even then, for there is no telling what may be done with trestle-work.

(Letter to Alta, *April 16, 1867;* MTTB, *pp. 146–147)*

1869 It is hard to make railroading pleasant in any country. It is too tedious. Stage-coaching is infinitely more delightful.

(Inn. Abroad, ch. 12, p. 106)

rainbow

1880 We have not the reverent feeling for the rainbow that a savage has, because we know how it is made. We have lost as much as we gained by prying into that matter.

(Tramp Abroad, ch. 42, p. 503)

Raleigh, Sir Walter (16th–17th-century English explorer)

1876 The worshipful Sr Walter Ralegh, that browned, embattled, bloody swash-buckler . . .

(1601, p. 35)

"random"

1889 Random is a good word, and so is exegesis, for that matter, and so is holocaust, and defalcation, and usufruct, and a hundred others, but land! a body ought to discriminate . . .   —[Hank Morgan]

(Conn. Yankee, ch. 15, p. 131)

rank

1892 "It does rather look as if in a republic where all are free and equal, prosperity and position constitute *rank.*"   —Howard Tracy

(Amer. Claim., ch. 12, p. 129)

1902 When we understand rank, we always like to rub against it. When a man is conspicuous, we always want to see him.

("Does the Race of Man Love a Lord?," CT-2, p. 514)

1902 Emperors, kings, artisans, peasants, big people, little people—at bottom we are all alike and all the same; all just alike on the inside, and when our clothes are off, nobody can tell which of us is which.

(Ibid., p. 516)

reading

1877 One mustn't read when he has anything to do. It distracts. More than that—it burns intellectual fuel; then you have only a warm fire under your work when you could just as well have had a hot one.

(Letter to Mollie Fairbanks, August 6, 1877, Ltrs-Fairbanks, p. 206)

rebirth

1906 I have been born more times than anybody except Krishna, I suppose.

(Autob/MTIE, pp. 169–170)

redheads

1889 When red-headed people are above a certain social grade, their hair is auburn. —[Hank Morgan]

(Conn. Yankee, ch. 18, p. 169)

Redpath, James (Mark Twain's first lecture agent)

1906 The chief ingredients of Redpath's make-up were honesty, sincerity, kindliness, and pluck. He wasn't afraid.

(NAR, November 1907; Autob/NAR, p. 224)

references

1867 For my other references I chose men of bad character, in order that my mild virtues might shine luminously by contrast with their depravity.

(Letter to Alta, March 2, 1867; MTTB, p. 116)

refinement

1897 She was not quite what you would call refined. She was not quite what you would call unrefined. She was the kind of person that keeps a parrot. —Pudd'nhead Wilson's New Calendar

(Foll. Equat., ch. 57, p. 544)

1897 There are no people who are quite so vulgar as the over-refined ones. —Pudd'nhead Wilson's New Calendar

(Ibid., ch. 62, p. 609)

religion

n.d. The easy confidence with which I know another man's religion is folly teaches me to suspect that my own is also.

(Marginal note in Moncure D. Conway's Sacred Anthology,
quoted in MT:Biog, *ch. 295, p. 1584)*

1861 What a man wants with religion in these breadless times, surpasses my comprehension.

(Letter to Orion Clemens, March 18, 1861, Ltrs-1, p. 117)

1865 I have a religion—but you will call it blasphemy. It is that there is a God for the rich man but none for the poor.

(Letter to Orion and Mollie Clemens, October 19, 1865, Ltrs-1, p. 324)

1884 A but-little considered fact in human nature: that the religious folly you are born in you will *die* in, no matter what apparently reasonabler religious folly may seem to have taken its place meanwhile, & abolished & obliterated it.

(Letter to W. D. Howells, January 7, 1884, Ltrs-Howells, 2:461)

1888 I cannot see how a man of any large degree of humorous perception can ever be religious—except he purposely shut the eyes of his mind & keep them shut by force.

(N&J-3, p. 389)

1890 Religion had its share in the changes of civilization and national character, of course. What share? The lion's. In the history of the human race this has always been the case, will always be the case, to the end of time, no doubt; or at least until man by the slow process of evolution shall develop into something really fine and high—some billions of years hence, say.

("Bible Teaching and Religious Practice," WIM&OPW, p. 71)

1900 "No religion exists which is not littered with engaging and delightful comicalities, but the race never perceives them. Nothing can be more deliciously comical than hereditary royalties and aristocracies, but none except royal families and aristocrats are aware of it."   —Philip Traum

("The Chronicle of Young Satan," ch. 10,
Mys. Stranger Mss., *pp. 164–165)*

1909 Man is the Religious Animal. He is the only Religious Animal. He is the only animal that has the True Religion—several of them.

("The Lowest Animal," Lets. Earth, *p. 227)*

religious relics

1869 But isn't this relic matter a little overdone? We find a piece of the true cross in every old church we go into, and some of the nails that held it together. I would not like to be positive, but I think we have seen as much as a keg of these nails. Then there is the crown of thorns; they have part of one in Sainte Chapelle, in Paris, and part of one, also, in Notre Dame. And as for bones of St. Denis, I feel certain we have seen enough of them to duplicate him, if necessary.

(Inn. Abroad, ch. 17, p. 165)

remarks

234

1902 Often a quite assified remark becomes sanctified by use and petrified by custom; it is then a permanency, its term of activity a geologic period.

("Does the Race of Man Love a Lord?," CT-2, *p. 522)*

repentance

c. 1898 My repentances were very real, very earnest; and after each tragedy they happened every night for a long time. But as a rule they could not stand the daylight. They faded out and shredded away and disappeared in the glad splendor of the sun. They were the creatures of fear and darkness, and they could not live out of their own place.

(Autob/MTA, 1:134)

1908 Through want of reflection we associate it exclusively with Sin. We get the notion early, and keep it always, that we repent of bad deeds only; whereas we do a formidably large business in repenting of good deeds which we have done.

("Something About Repentance," Lets. Earth, *p. 167)*

repetition

1880 Repetition may be bad, but surely inexactness is worse.

("The Awful German Language," Tramp Abroad, *p. 616)*

c. 1907 Repetition is a mighty power in the domain of humor. If frequently used, nearly any precisely worded and unchanging formula will eventually compel laughter if it be gravely and earnestly repeated, at intervals, five or six times.

(Autob/AMT, ch. 28, pp. 143–144)

Republicans

1884 No one has ever seen a Republican mass meeting that was devoid of the perception of the ludicrous.

(Speech in Hartford, late October 1884, MT Speaking, p. 184)

1908 For fifty years our country has been a constitutional monarchy, with the Republican party sitting on the throne. Mr. Cleveland's couple of brief interruptions do not count . . . Ours is not only a monarchy but a hereditary monarchy—in the one political family.

(Autob/MTIE, pp. 2–3)

ASSOCIATED WITH SIN

235

reputation

c. 1886 A hall-mark: it can remove doubt from pure silver, & it can also make the plated article pass for pure.

(From "Unmailed letters," c. 1886, Ltrs/Paine, 2:472)

1904 A surface reputation, however great, is always mortal, and always killable if you go at it right—with pins and needles, and quiet slow poison, not with the club and tomahawk. But it is a different matter with the submerged reputation—down in the deep water; once a favorite there, always a favorite; once beloved, always beloved; once respected, always respected, honored, and believed in.

(NAR, September 21, 1906; Autob/NAR, p. 20)

respect

1897 When people do not respect us we are sharply offended; yet deep down in his private heart no man much respects himself.

—Pudd'nhead Wilson's New Calendar

(Foll. Equat., ch. 29, p. 279)

1906 "Respectability butters no parsnips . . ."   —Adam

("The World in the Year 920 after Creation," Lets. Earth, p. 93)

retorts

1896 A law of our nature—an irresistible law—to enjoy and applaud a spirited and promptly delivered retort, no matter who makes it.

(Joan of Arc, bk. 3, ch. 20, p. 431)

revenge

1869 Revenge is wicked, & unchristian & in every way unbecoming, & I am not the man to countenance it or show it any favor. (But it is powerful sweet, anyway).

(Letter to Olivia Langdon, December 27, 1869, Ltrs-3, p. 440)

1886 Therein lies the defect of revenge: it's all in the anticipation; the thing itself is a pain, not a pleasure; at least the pain is the biggest end of it.

(Letter to W. D. Howells, May 13, 1886, Ltrs-Howells, 2:562)

reverence

1892 "There's manifestly prodigious force in reverence. If you can get a man to reverence your ideals, he's your slave."　　—Howard Tracy

(Amer. Claim., ch. 10, p. 99)

1897 The ordinary reverence, the reverence defined and explained by the dictionary costs nothing. Reverence for one's own sacred things—parents, religion, flag, laws, and respect for one's own beliefs—these are feelings which we cannot even help. They come natural to us; they are involuntary, like breathing. There is no personal merit in breathing. But the reverence which is difficult, and which has personal merit in it, is the respect which you pay, without compulsion, to the political or religious attitude of a man whose beliefs are not yours.

(Foll. Equat., ch. 53, p. 514)

revolution

1889 No people in this world ever did achieve their freedom by goody-goody talk and moral suasion: it being immutable law that all revolutions that will succeed, must *begin* in blood, whatever may answer afterward. If history teaches anything, it teaches that.　　—[Hank Morgan]

(Conn. Yankee, ch. 20, p. 183)

1897 "It's where there ain't only nine-tenths of the people satisfied with the gov'ment, and the others is down on it and rises up full of patriotic devotion and knocks the props from under it and sets up a more different one. There's nearly about as much glory in a revolution as there is in a civil war, and ain't half the trouble and expense if you are on the right side, because you don't have to have so many men. It's the economicalest thing there is. Anybody can get up a revolution."

—Tom Sawyer

("Tom Sawyer's Conspiracy," HF&TS, ch. 1, p. 138)

Rhodes, Cecil
(British financier in Southern Africa)

1897 Whether Mr. Rhodes is the lofty and worshipful patriot and statesman that multitudes believe him to be, or Satan come again, as the rest of the world account him, he is still the most imposing figure in the British empire outside of England. . . . he is the only unroyal outsider whose arrival in London can compete for attention with an eclipse. . . .

I admire him, I frankly confess it; and when his time comes I shall buy a piece of the rope for a keepsake.

(Foll. Equat., ch. 69, pp. 708, 710)

Rhodesia
(African country—now Zimbabwe—occupied by
Cecil Rhodes's British South Africa Co.)

1897 A happy name for that land of piracy and pillage, and puts the right stain upon it.

(Foll. Equat., ch. 68, p. 691)

riddles

1894 I have damaged my intellect trying to imagine why a man should want to invent a repeating clock, and how another man could be found to lust after it and buy it. The man who can guess these riddles is far on the way to guess why the human race was invented—which is another riddle which tires me.

(Letter to H. H. Rogers, September 24, 1894, Ltrs-Rogers, p. 78)

237

ridicule

1888 No god & no religion can survive ridicule. no political church, no nobility, no royalty or other fraud, can face ridicule in a fair field, & live.

(N&J-3, p. 411)

1894 There is no character, howsoever good and fine, but it can be destroyed by ridicule, howsoever poor and witless.

(Pudd. Wilson, "A Whisper to the Reader," PW&TET, p. 15)

DOING RIGHT

righteousness

1901 Always do right. This will gratify some people & astonish the rest.

(Note to Young People's Society, February 16, 1901, Autob/MTIE, flyleaf)

1906 I prefer good taste to righteousness.

(Autob/MTIE, p. 86)

rights

c. 1894 Man has not a single right which is the product of anything but might.

(MTN, p. 394)

rising

1862 I get up as early as 8 o'clock, sometimes, on purpose to enjoy the gorgeous spectacle of Sunrise. After signifying my approbation, I go back to bed again. I have been practising this sort of thing for some, time, and I mean to keep it up, for I am already improving in health, and am convinced that early rising is the cause of it.

(Letter to William H. Clagett, February 28, 1862, Ltrs-1, p. 166)

1864 I have tried getting up early, and I have tried getting up late—and the latter agrees with me best.

(Article in Golden Era, July 3, 1864; ET&S-2, p. 24)

rivals

1896 Rivals become brothers when a common affliction assails them and a common enemy bears off the victory.

(Joan of Arc, bk. 2, ch. 15, p. 162)

rivers

1897 The difference between a river and the sea is, that the river looks fluid, the sea solid—usually looks as if you could step out and walk on it.

(Foll. Equat., ch. 62, p. 609)

robbers

1876 "They ain't anybody as polite as robbers—you'll see that in any book." —Tom

(Tom Sawyer, ch. 33, p. 244)

1876 "A robber is more high-toned than what a pirate is—as a general thing. In most countries they're awful high up in the nobility—dukes and such." —Tom Sawyer

(Ibid., ch. 35, p. 258)

Rogers, Henry Huttleston
(American financier and friend of Mark Twain)

1894 You have saved me and my family from ruin and humiliation. You have been to me the best friend that ever a man had, and yet you have never by any word made me feel the weight of this deep obligation. And Lord, how welcome is the sight of your face to me!

(Letter to H. H. Rogers, March, 4 1894, Ltrs-Rogers, p. 38)

1904 His commercial wisdom has protected my pocket ever since in those lucid intervals wherein I have been willing to listen to his counsels and abide by his advice—a thing which I do half the time and half the time I don't.

(Autob/MTA, 1:250)

1905 Jesus! but I had a narrow escape. Suppose you had gone into humor instead of oil—where would I be?

(Letter to H. H. Rogers, July 13, 1905, Ltrs-Rogers, p. 591)

1909 He is supposed to be a moon which has one side dark and the other bright. But the other side, though you don't see it, is not dark; it is bright, and its rays penetrate, and others do see it who are not God.

(Speech in Norfolk, Virginia, April 3, 1909, MT Speaking, p. 642)

Roman Catholic church

1869 I have been educated to enmity toward everything that is Catholic, and sometimes, in consequence of this, I find it much easier to discover Catholic faults than Catholic merits.

(Inn. Abroad, ch. 55, p. 599)

Rome, Italy

1878 Rome seems to be a great fair of shams, humbugs, & frauds. Religion is its commerce & its wealth, like dung in the Black Forest.

(N&J-2, p. 230)

Roosevelt, Theodore (president of the United States, 1901–09)

1905 Every time, in 25 years, that I have met Roosevelt the man, a wave of welcome has streaked through me with the hand-grip; but whenever (as a rule) I meet Roosevelt the statesman & politician, I find him destitute of morals & not respectworthy. It is plain that where his political self & his party self are concerned he has nothing resembling a conscience.

(Letter to J. H. Twichell, February 16, 1905, Ltrs/Paine, 2:766–767)

1906 Roosevelt is far and away the worst President we have ever had, and also the most admired and the most satisfactory.

(Ibid., p. 34)

1907 I think the President is clearly insane in several ways, and insanest upon war and its supreme glories. I think he longs for a big war wherein he can spectacularly perform as chief general and chief admiral and go down in history as the only monarch of modern times that has served both offices at the same time.

(Ibid., pp. 8–9)

1907 He was once a reasonably modest man, but his judgement has been out of focus so long now that he imagines that everything he does, little or big, is colossal.

(Ibid., p. 11)

1907 The Tom Sawyer of the political world of the twentieth century; always showing off; always hunting for a chance to show off . . . he would go to Halifax for half a chance to show off, and he would go to hell for a whole one.

(Ibid., p. 49)

Roughing It (1872 travel book)

1870 The "Innocents Abroad" will have to get up early to beat it. It will be a book that will jump right strait into a continental celebrity the first month it is issued.

(Letter to Elisha Bliss, September 4, 1870, Ltrs-4, p. 90)

1871 This is a better book than the Innocents, & *much* better written. If the subject were less hackneyed it would be a great success.

(Letter to Olivia Clemens, November 27, 1871, Ltrs-4, p. 499)

241

Roxy (character in *Pudd'nhead Wilson*)

1894 To all intents and purposes Roxy was as white as anybody, but the one sixteenth of her which was black outvoted the other fifteen parts and made her a negro. She was a slave, and salable as such. Her child was thirty-one parts white, and he, too, was a slave, and by a fiction of law and custom a negro.

(Pudd. Wilson, ch. 2, PW&TET, pp. 32–33)

1894 The heir of two centuries of unatoned insult and outrage . . .

(Ibid., ch. 8, p. 109)

AS WHITE AS ANYBODY

INSULT TO THE HUMAN RACE

royalty

1888 In a constitutional—figure-head—monarchy, a royal family of Chimpanzees would answer every purpose, be worshiped as abjectly by the nation, & be cheaper.

(N&J-3, p. 419)

1888 The institution of royalty, in any form, is an insult to the human race.

(Ibid., p. 424)

1889 A royal family of cats . . . would be as useful as any other royal family, they would know as much, they would have the same virtues and the same vices, the same fidelities and the same treacheries, the same disposition to get up shindies with other royal cats, they would be laughably vain and absurd and never know it, and they would be wholly inexpensive; finally, they would have as sound a divine right as any other royal house, and "Tom VII, or Tom XI, or Tom XIV by the grace of God King," would sound as well as it would when applied to the ordinary royal tomcat with tights on. —[Hank Morgan, paraphrasing Clarence]

(Conn. Yankee, ch. 40, p. 399)

1891 Once a prince always a prince—that is to say, an imitation god, and neither hard fortune nor an infamous character nor an addled brain nor the speech of an ass can undeify him.

("At the Shrine of St. Wagner," WIM&OE, pp. 219–220)

Russia

1890 What is the Czar of Russia but a house afire in the midst of a city of eighty millions of inhabitants? Yet instead of extinguishing him, together with his nest & system, the liberation-parties are all anxious to merely cool him down a little & keep him. . . . The properest way to demolish the Russian throne would be by revolution. But it is not possible to get up a revolution there; so the only thing left to do, apparently, is to keep the throne vacant by dynamite until a day when candidates shall decline with thanks. Then organize the Republic.

(Unpublished letter to editor of Free Russia, after July 1, 1890, Ltrs/Paine, 2:536–537)

1894 "It spreads all around and everywheres, and yet ain't no more important in this world than Rhode Island is, and hasn't got half as much in it that's worth saving."   —Tom

(Tom Sawyer Abrd., ch. 9, p. 68)

1906 We are accustomed now to speak of Russia as medieval and as standing still in the Middle Ages, but that is flattery. Russia is way back of the Middle Ages; the Middle Ages are a long way in front of her and she is not likely to catch up with them so long as the Czardom continues to exist.

(Autob/MTIE, p. 212)

Sabbath day

1866 The day of rest comes but once a week, and sorry I am that it does not come oftener. Man is so constituted that he can stand more rest than this. I often think regretfully that it would have been so easy to have two Sundays in a week, and yet it was not so ordained. The omnipotent Creator could have made the world in three days just as easily as he made it in six, and this would have doubled the Sundays.

("Reflections on the Sabbath," WIM&OPW, p. 39)

1895 Sunday on the Continent is a blessing. In England and America it is a curse and certainly ought to be abolished—no—stripped of its power to oppress.

(MTN, pp. 245–246)

1904 I believe I see what the week is for: it is to give time to rest up from the weariness of Sunday. It seems a good idea.   —[Adam]

(Adam's Diary, p. 29)

1908 To forty-nine men in fifty the Sabbath Day is a dreary, dreary bore.

("Letters from the Earth," WIM&OPW, p. 407)

Sacramento, California

1866 Going north on the [*Sacramento*] river gradually enfeebles one's mind, and accounts for the strange imbecility of legislators who leave here sensible men and become the reverse, to the astonishment of their constituents, by the time they reach their seats in the Capitol at Sacramento.

(Article in Territorial Enterprise, *c. March 1866;* MTSFH, *p. 30)*

saddles

1872 And now there can be no fitter occasion than the present to pronounce a left-handed blessing upon the man who invented the American saddle. There is no seat to speak of about it—one might as well sit in a shovel—and the stirrups are nothing but an ornamental nuisance. If I were to write down here all the abuse I expended on those stirrups, it would make a large book, even without pictures.

(Rough. It, ch. 64, p. 438)

244

sagebrush

1872 Sage-brush is very fair fuel, but as a vegetable it is a distinguished failure. Nothing can abide the taste of it but the jackass and his illegitimate child the mule.

(Ibid., ch. 3, pp. 14–15)

GHASTLY INFLICTION

sailors

1878 A common sailor's life is often a hell . . . there are probably more brutes in command of little ships than in any other occupation in life.

(N&J-2, p. 69)

Saint Louis, Missouri

1868 There is something in my deep hatred of St. Louis that will hardly let me appear cheery even at my mother's own fireside. Nobody knows what a ghastly infliction it is on me to visit St. Louis. I am afraid I do not always disguise it, either.

(Letter to Mary Fairbanks, September 24, 1868, Ltrs-2, p. 252)

saints

1899 It is an art apart. St. Francis of Assissi said all saints can do miracles, but few of them can keep hotel.

(MTP, ts 42, p. 70; MTN, *p. 346)*

Salt Lake City, Utah (center of Mormon Church)

1872 The stronghold of the prophets, the capital of the only absolute monarch in America—Great Salt Lake City.

(Rough. It, ch. 12, p. 87)

San Francisco, California

1865 San Francisco is a city of startling events. Happy is the man whose destiny it is to gather them up and record them in a daily newspaper!

(Letter to Territorial Enterprise, *December 23, 1865,* ET&S-2, *p. 416)*

1872 San Francisco, a truly fascinating city to live in, is stately and handsome at a fair distance, but close at hand one notes that the architecture is mostly old-fashioned, many streets are made up of decaying, smoke-grimed, wooden houses, and the barren sand-hills toward the outskirts obtrude themselves too prominently. Even the kindly climate is sometimes pleasanter when read about than personally experienced . . .

(Rough. It, ch. 56, p. 387)

c. 1905 I have done more for San Francisco than any other of its old residents. Since I left there it has increased in population fully 300,000. I could have done more—I could have gone earlier—it was suggested.

(Undated letter, quoted in MT:Biog, *ch. 235, p. 1248)*

San Francisco Call

(newspaper for which Mark Twain reported in 1864)

1880 That degraded "Morning Call," whose mission from hell & politics was to lick the boots of the Irish & throw brave mud at the Chinamen.

(Letter to W. D. Howells, September 3, 1880, Ltrs-Howells, *1:326)*

sand

1894 Sand is the comfortablest bed there is, and I don't see why people that can afford it don't have it more. —[Huck Finn]
(Tom Sawyer Abrd., ch. 11, p. 81)

Sandy (character in *Connecticut Yankee*)

1889 It may be that this girl had a fact in her somewhere, but I don't believe you could have sluiced it out with a hydraulic; nor got it with the earlier forms of blasting, even; it was a case for dynamite. Why, she was a perfect ass; and yet the king and his knights had listened to her as if she had been a leaf out of the gospel. —[Hank Morgan]
(Conn. Yankee, ch. 11, p. 93)

Satan

1898 All men speak in bitter disapproval of the Devil, but they do it reverently, not flippantly . . . —[August Feldner]
(No. 44, ch. 1, p. 9)

1899 A person who has for untold centuries maintained the imposing position of spiritual head of four-fifths of the human race, and political head of the whole of it, must be granted the possession of executive abilities of the loftiest order.
("Concerning the Jews," CT-2, p. 355)

1906 I have always felt friendly toward Satan. Of course that is ancestral; it must be in the blood.
(NAR, September 7, 1906; Autob/NAR, p. 5)

satire

1879 A man can't write successful satire except he be in a calm judicial good-humor—whereas I *hate* travel, & *hate* hotels, & I *hate* the opera, & I *hate* the Old Masters—in truth I don't ever seem to be in a good enough humor with ANYthing to *satirize* it; no, I want to stand up before it & *curse* it, & foam at the mouth,—or take a club & pound it to rags & pulp.
(Letter to W. D. Howells, January 30, 1879, Ltrs-Howells, 1:248–249)

savages

1897 There are many humorous things in the world; among them the white man's notion that he is less savage than the other savages.

(Foll. Equat., ch. 21, p. 214)

1904 The only very marked difference between the average civilized man & the average savage is, that the one is gilded, & the other painted.

(MTP, ts 47, p. 18; MTN, p. 392)

saving

1897 Simple rules for saving money: To save half, when you are fired by an eager impulse to contribute to a charity, wait, and count forty. To save three-quarters, count sixty. To save it all, count sixty-five.

—Pudd'nhead Wilson's New Calendar

(Foll. Equat., ch. 47, p. 437)

Sawyer, Tom (character in *The Adventures of Tom Sawyer*)

1875–76 "*Hang* your *books*. Nothing suits *you* unless it happens as it would in a *book*. . . . I don't care anything *about* the books."

—Aunt Polly to Tom

("Tom Sawyer: A Play," HH&T, p. 322)

1876 He was not the Model Boy of the village. He knew the model boy very well though—and loathed him.

(Tom Sawyer, ch. 1, p. 5)

1884 I never seen the like of that boy for just solid gobs of brains and level headedness.   —[Huck]

("Huck Finn and Tom Sawyer Among the Indians," HF&TS, ch. 9, p. 79)

NOT THE MODEL BOY

1897 "There's only one Tom Sawyer, and the mould's busted."

—Mr. Baxter

("Tom Sawyer's Conspiracy," HF&TS, ch. 4, p. 160)

247

scarlet fever

1884 The scarlet fever, once domesticated, is a permanent member of the family. Money may desert you, friends forsake you, enemies grow indifferent to you, but the scarlet fever will be true to you, through thick & thin, till you be all saved or damned, down to the last one.

(Letter to W. D. Howells, January 7, 1884, Ltrs-Howells, 2:460)

school boards

1897 In the first place God made idiots. This was for practice. Then He made School Boards.   —Pudd'nhead Wilson's New Calendar

(Foll. Equat., ch. 61, p. 597)

scientists

1880 A scientist will never show any kindness for a theory which he did not start himself.

(Tramp Abroad, ch. 43, p. 507)

1902 The scientist . . . will spend thirty years in building up a mountain range of facts with the intent to prove a certain theory; then he is so happy in his achievement that as a rule he overlooks the main chief fact of all—that his accumulation proves an entirely different thing. When you point out this miscarriage to him he does not answer your letters; when you call to convince him, the servant prevaricates and you do not get in. Scientists have odious manners, except when you prop up their theory; then you can borrow money off of them.

("The Bee," WIM&OE, p. 283)

scotch

1907 Scotch whisky to a Scotchman is as innocent as milk is to the rest of the human race.

(NAR, December 1907; Autob/NAR, p. 238)

Scott, Sir Walter (early-19th-century Scottish novelist)

1883 The South has not yet recovered from the debilitating influence of his books.

(Life on Miss., ch. 40, p. 416)

1883 He did measureless harm; more real and lasting harm, perhaps, than any other individual that ever wrote. . . . But for the Sir Walter disease, the character of the Southerner . . . would be wholly modern, in place of modern and mediaeval mixed, and the South would be fully a generation further advanced than it is. It was Sir Walter that made every gentleman in the South a Major or a Colonel, or a General or a Judge, before the war; and it was he, also, that made these gentlemen value these bogus decorations. For it was he that created rank and caste down there, and also reverence for rank and caste, and pride and pleasure in them. . . .

Sir Walter had so large a hand in making Southern character, as it existed before the war, that he is in great measure responsible for the war.

(Ibid., ch. 46, pp. 467–469)

1900 You've got to be one of two ages to appreciate Scott. When you're eighteen you can read *Ivanhoe,* and you want to wait until you are ninety to read some of the rest.

(Speech in New York City, November 20, 1900, MT Speaking, p. 359)

sea, the

1893 One thing is gone, to return no more forever—the romance of the sea. Soft sentimentality about the sea has retired from the activities of this life, and is but a memory of the past, already remote and much faded.

("About All Kinds of Ships," CT-2, p. 94)

1897 That pitiless ruffian, the sea.

(Foll. Equat., ch. 9, p. 110)

seasickness

1869 If there is one thing in the world that will make a man peculiarly and insufferably self-conceited, it is to have his stomach behave itself, the first day at sea, when nearly all his comrades are seasick.

(Inn. Abroad, ch. 3, p. 33)

secrecy

1897 Secrecy is the natural refuge of people who are doubtful about their conduct.

("Which Was the Dream?," WWD&OSW, p. 54)

seduction

1903 The law is stern with the assassin, but gentle with the seducer; stern with the murderer of the body, but gentle with the murderer of all that can make life worth the living—honor, self-respect, the esteem of friends, the adoring worship of the sacred home circle, father, mother, and the cradle-mates of the earlier and innocent years.

(Article in Harper's Weekly, May 2, 1903; MTSFH, p. 181)

self-evaluation

1902 In prayer we call ourselves "worms of the dust," but it is only on a sort of tacit understanding that the remark shall not be taken at par. *We*—worms of the dust! Oh, no, we are not that. Except in fact; and we do not deal much in fact when we are contemplating ourselves.

("Does the Race of Man Love a Lord?," CT-2, p. 522)

selfishness

1901 When I search myself away down deep, I find this out. Whatever a man feels or thinks or does, there is never any but one reason for it— & that is a selfish one.

(Letter to J. H. Twichell, January 29, 1901, Ltrs/Paine, 2:705)

"self-sacrifice"

1906 We have smuggled a word into the dictionary which ought not to be there at all—Self-Sacrifice. It describes a thing which does not exist.

—Old Man

("What Is Man?," ch. 2, WIM&OPW, p. 147)

Sellers, Colonel

(character in *The Gilded Age* and *The American Claimant*)

1874 The Colonel's tongue was a magician's wand that turned dried apples into figs and water into wine as easily as it could change a hovel into a palace and present poverty into imminent future riches.

(Gilded Age, ch. 8, p. 83)

1897–98 Many persons regarded "Colonel Sellers" as a fiction, an invention, an extravagant impossibility, and did me the honor to call him a "creation"; but they were mistaken. I merely put him on paper as he was; he was not a person who could be exaggerated. . . .

The real Colonel Sellers, as I knew him in James Lampton, was a pathetic and beautiful spirit, a manly man . . .

(NAR, September 7, 1906; Autob/NAR, p. 8)

251

senators

n.d. Persons who makes laws in Washington when not doing time.

(More Max., p. 12)

1874 A United States Senator was a sort of god in the understanding of these people who never had seen any creature mightier than a county judge. To them a United States Senator was a vast, vague colossus, an awe-inspiring unreality.

(Gilded Age, ch. 53, p. 478)

1907 There are many Senators whom I hold in a certain respect and would not think of declining to meet socially, if I believed it was the will of God.

(Autob/MTIE, p. 71)

SORT OF A GOD

sense of humor

1901–02 The sense of humor may be called the mind's measuring-rod, also its focussing-adjustment. Without it, even the finest mind can make mistakes as to the *proportions* of things; also, as to the *relations* of things to each other . . .

("The Secret History of Eddypus," bk. 2, ch. 1, Fab. of Man, p. 339)

sentimentality

1876 There is one thing which I can't stand, & *won't* stand, from many people. That is, sham sentimentality—the kind a school-girl puts into her graduating composition; the sort that makes up the Original Poetry column of a country newspaper; the rot that deals in "the happy days of yore," "the sweet yet melancholy past," with its "blighted hopes" and its "vanished dreams"—and all that sort of drivel.

(Letter to Jacob H. Burrough, November 1, 1876, Ltrs/Paine, 1:290)

serenading

1865 Don't go serenading at all—it is a wicked, unhappy and seditious practice, and a calamity to all souls that are weary and desire to slumber and be at rest.

("Answers to Correspondents," ET&S-2, p. 183)

sexual intercourse

1908 He [*man*] has imagined a heaven, and has left entirely out of it the supremest of all his delights, the one ecstasy that stands first and foremost in the heart of every individual of his race—and of ours—sexual intercourse!

("Letters from the Earth," WIM&OPW, p. 407)

Shah of Persia

1873 The only way whereby you may pronounce the Shah's title correctly is by taking a pinch of snuff. The result will be "t-Shah!"

("O'Shah," E&E, p. 86)

Shakespeare, William

1906 Shakspeare created nothing. He correctly observed, and he marvelously painted. He exactly portrayed people whom *God* had created; but he created none himself. . . . *He was a machine, and machines do not create.* —Old Man

("What Is Man?," ch. 1, WIM&OPW, p. 130)

1909 How curious and interesting is the parallel—as far as poverty of biographical details is concerned—between Satan and Shakespeare. It is wonderful, it is unique, it stands quite alone . . . How sublime is their position, and how overtopping, how sky-reaching, how supreme—the two Great Unknowns, the two Illustrious Conjecturabilities! They are the best-known unknown persons that have ever drawn breath upon the planet.

(ISD, ch. 3, p. 27)

1909 Shall I set down the Conjectures which constitute the giant Biography of William Shakespeare? It would strain the Unabridged Dictionary to hold them. He is a Brontosaur: nine bones and six hundred barrels of plaster of Paris.

(Ibid., ch. 4, p. 49)

shaving

1906 Shaving was always a trying ordeal for me, and I could seldom carry it through to a finish without verbal helps.

(NAR, November 2, 1906; Autob/NAR, p. 46)

Sheridan, Philip (Union general during the Civil War)

1879 By all odds the superbest figure of a soldier *I* ever looked upon.

(Letter to W. D. Howells, November 17, 1879, Ltrs-Howells, 1:280)

ships

1867 A ship is precisely a little village, where gossips abound, & where every man's business is his neighbor's.

(N&J-1, p. 270)

INSEPARABLE COMPANIONS

Siamese twins

1868 Even as children they were inseparable companions . . . They nearly always played together; and, so accustomed was their mother to this peculiarity, that, whenever both of them chanced to be lost, she usually only hunted for one of them—satisfied that when she found that one she would find his brother somewhere in the immediate neighborhood.

("The Siamese Twins," CT-1, p. 296)

1869 The wonderful two-headed girl is still on exhibition in New England. She sings duets by herself. She has a great advantage over the rest of her sex, for she never has to stop talking to eat, and when she is not eating, she keeps both tongues going at once.

(Column in Buffalo Express, September 2, 1869, MT:Bib, p. 184)

1894 A stupefying apparition—a double-headed human creature with four arms, one body, and a single pair of legs!

("Those Extraordinary Twins," ch. 1, PW&TET, p. 320)

sin

1875 One could . . . say that God is the personage who should shoulder the blame for the sin that is in the world (& suffer the punishment) because He made sin attractive & put it in the reach of the sinner.

(Letter to Pamela A. Moffett, July 23, 1875, MT:Bus. Man, p. 133)

1883 He [*Adam*] invented sin—not that I think that that was much. Anybody here—that I am acquainted with—could have done it, I reckon. Could have done it myself. *Have* invented *some* kinds.

He invented sin—he was the author of sin—& I wish he had taken out an international copyright on it.

(N&J-3, p. 15)

1899 A sin takes on new and real terrors when there seems a chance that it is going to be found out.

("The Man That Corrupted Hadleyburg," CT-2, p. 434; also in MTCH&c)

singing

1866 That choir sang everything they ought not to have sung except one, and I trembled to think the surroundings would yet suggest it. I

254

refer to the song called "Roll On, Silver Moon." If they had attempted that outrage I would have scuttled the ship. I can stand a good deal, but I cannot stand everything. I would rather perish than lose my reason.

(Letter to Alta, *December 23, 1866;* MTTB, *p. 29)*

1878 Congregational singing reminds one of nothing but the dental chair[.]

(N&J-2, p. 57)

1891 Singing is one of the most entrancing and bewitching and moving and eloquent of all the vehicles invented by man for the conveying of feeling; but it seems to me that the chief virtue in song is melody, air, tune, rhythm, or what you please to call it, and that when this feature is absent what remains is a picture with the color left out.

("At the Shrine of St. Wagner," WIM&OE, *p. 214)*

1601 (scatological sketch written in 1876)

1906 The piece is a supposititious conversation which takes place in Queen Elizabeth's closet in that year . . . The object was only a serious attempt to reveal to Rev. Joe Twichell the picturesqueness of parlor conversation in Elizabeth's time; therefore if there is a decent or delicate word findable in it, it is because I overlooked it.

(Letter to Charles Orr, July 30, 1906, in Autob/MTIE, *p. 205)*

1906 A letter which I wrote to Twichell, about 1897, from my study at Quarry Farm one summer day when I ought to have been better employed. . . . It is years since I have seen a copy of *1601*. I wonder if it would be as funny to me now as it was in those comparatively youthful days when I wrote it.

(Ibid., pp. 206–207)

skin color

1897 Nearly all black and brown skins are beautiful, but a beautiful white skin is rare. . . . Where dark complexions are massed, they make the whites look bleached-out, unwholesome, and sometimes frankly ghastly. . . . The splendid black satin skin of the South African Zulus of Durban seemed to me to come very close to perfection.

(Foll. Equat., ch. 41, p. 381)

slander

1897 It takes your enemy and your friend, working together, to hurt you to the heart; the one to slander you and the other to get the news to you.
—Pudd'nhead Wilson's New Calendar
(Foll. Equat., ch. 45, p. 410)

1906 Few slanders can stand the wear of silence.
(NAR, May 3, 1907; Autob/NAR, p. 158)

slang

n.d. Slang in a woman's mouth is not obscene, it only sounds so.
(More Max., p. 12)

1910 The First Man introduced slang into the world, & thus tacitly, by his high authority, made its use legitimate forever.
(Letter to Helen Allen, c. 1910, Ltrs-Angelfish, p. 270)

slavery

1890 Slavery was a bald, grotesque and unwarrantable usurpation.
("Jane Lampton Clemens," HF&TS, p. 87)

1890 To be a slave by meek consent is baser than to be a slave by compulsion . . .
(Ibid., p. 88)

1890 It is commonly believed that an infallible effect of slavery was to make such as lived in its midst hardhearted. I think it had no such effect . . . I think it stupefied everybody's humanity, as regarded the slave, but stopped there.
(Ibid., p. 89)

1897–98 In my schoolboy days I had no aversion to slavery. I was not aware that there was anything wrong about it. No one arraigned it in my hearing; the local papers said nothing against it; the local pulpit taught us that God approved it, that it was a holy thing and that the doubter need only look in the Bible

THE ONLY ANIMAL WHO ENSLAVES

if he wished to settle his mind—and then the texts were read aloud to us to make the matter sure . . .

(Autob/MTA, 1:101)

1899 It would not be possible for a humane and intelligent person to invent a rational excuse for slavery.

("My First Lie, and How I Got Out of It," CT-2, p. 440)

1904 The skin of every human being contains a slave.

(MTP, ts 47, p. 18; MTN, p. 393)

1909 Man is the only Slave. And he is the only animal who enslaves.

("The Lowest Animal," Lets. Earth, p. 226)

sleep

1869 That vast mysterious void which men call sleep.

(Inn. Abroad, ch. 12, p. 117)

1880 I hate a man who goes to sleep at once; there is a sort of indefinable something about it which is not exactly an insult, and yet is an insolence; and one which is hard to bear, too.

(Tramp Abroad, ch. 13, p. 114)

1894 The sleep of the unjust, which is serener and sounder than the other kind, as we know by the hanging-eve history of a million rascals.

(Pudd. Wilson, ch. 15, PW&TET, p. 213)

smells

1892 [The] aggressive stench of bygone cabbage and kindred smells; smells which are to be found nowhere but in a cheap private boarding house; smells which once encountered can never be forgotten; smells which encountered generations later are instantly recognizable, but never recognizable with pleasure.

(Amer. Claim., ch. 12, p. 118)

1900 He [*Satan*] said that unpleasant smells were an invention of Civilization—like modesty, and indecency. . . . To the pure all smells were sweet, to the decent all things were decent.

("The Chronicle of Young Satan," ch. 8, Mys. Stranger Mss., p. 139)

Smiley, Jim (character in the jumping frog story)

1865 He was the curiosest man about always betting on anything that turned up you ever see, if he could get anybody to bet on the other side, and if he couldn't he'd change sides—any way that suited the other man would suit *him*—any way just so's he got a bet, *he* was satisfied. But still, he was lucky—uncommon lucky; he most always come out winner. He was always ready and laying for a chance; there couldn't be no solitry thing mentioned but that feller'd offer to bet on it—and take any side you please . . .

("Jim Smiley and His Jumping Frog," ET&S-2, *p. 283)*

smoking

1870 Now there are *no* arguments that can convince me that *moderate* smoking is deleterious to me. I cannot attach any weight to either the arguments or the evidence of those who know nothing about the matter personally & so must simply theorize. Theorizing has no effect on me. I have smoked habitually for 26 of my 34 years, & I am the only healthy member our family has.

(Letter to Olivia L. Langdon, January 13, 1870, Ltrs-4, *p. 21)*

1876 This majestic vice . . .

*(*Tom Sawyer, *ch. 13, p. 104)*

1906 I had been a smoker from my ninth year—a private one during the first two years, but a public one after that—that is to say, after my father's death.

*(*Autob/MTA, *2:100)*

snorers

1894 There ain't no way to find out why a snorer can't hear himself snore. —[Huck Finn]

*(*Tom Sawyer Abrd., *ch. 10, p. 73)*

snow

1869 Snow never falls otherwise than in flakes. When it falls in icy pellets it is hail—in homeopathic pills, it is sleet—in globules of water, it is rain. Such is snow.

("L'Homme Qui Rit," ch. 1, S&B, *p. 43)*

1870 Albeit snow is very beautiful when falling, its loveliness passes away very shortly afterward. The grand unpoetical result is merely chilblains & slush.

(Letter to in-laws, March 27, 1870, Ltrs-4, p. 98)

sobriety

c. 1895 What marriage is to morality, a properly conducted licensed liquor traffic is to sobriety.

(MTN, p. 257)

soldiering

1896 Soldiering makes few saints.

(Joan of Arc, bk. 2, ch. 34, p. 268)

solitude

1900 Of all the hard things to bear, to be cut by your neighbors and left in contemptuous solitude is maybe the hardest.

("The Chronicle of Young Satan," ch. 4, Mys. Stranger Mss., p. 81)

Solomon
(Old Testament figure who had hundreds of wives)

1884 "Yit dey say Sollermun de wises' man dat ever live'. I doan' take no stock in dat. Bekase why: would a wise man want to live in de mids' er sich a blimblammin' all de time? No—'deed he would-n't. A wise man 'ud take en buil' a biler-factry; en den he could shet *down* de biler-factry when he want to res'." —Jim

(Huck Finn, ch. 14, p. 94)

THE WISEST MAN

Sophia, Mosque of Saint (former basilica in Istanbul)

1869 It is the rustiest old barn in heathendom.

(Inn. Abroad, ch. 33, p. 362)

soul

1896 A great soul, with a great purpose, can make a weak body strong and keep it so . . .

(Joan of Arc, bk. 2, ch. 4, p. 87)

1897 Be careless in your dress if you must, but keep a tidy soul.
—Pudd'nhead Wilson's New Calendar
(Foll. Equat., ch. 23, p. 223)

Southerners

1883 A Southerner talks music. . . . The educated Southerner has no use for an *r* except at the beginning of a word. He says "honah," and "dinnah," and "Gove'nuh," and "befo' the waw," and so on.

(Life on Miss., ch. 44, pp. 448–449)

Spain

1870 The reason arable land is so scarce in Spain is because the people squander so much of it on their persons, and then when they die it is improvidently buried with them.

("A Royal Compliment," p. 451)

Spanish-American War

1898 I have never enjoyed a war—even in written history—as I am enjoying this one. For this is the worthiest one that was ever fought, so far as my knowledge goes. It is a worthy thing to fight for one's freedom; it is another sight finer to fight for another man's. And I think this is the first time it has been done.

(Letter to J. H. Twichell, June 17, 1898, Ltrs/Paine, 2:663)

1900 Apparently we are not proposing to set the Filipinos free & give their islands to them; & apparently we are not proposing to hang the priests & confiscate their property. If these things are so, the war out there has no interest for me.

(Letter to J. H. Twichell, January 27, 1900, Ltrs/Paine, 2:694)

spectacles

1873 If a spectacle is going to be particularly imposing I prefer to see it through somebody else's eyes, because that man will always exaggerate. Then I can exaggerate his exaggeration, and my own account of the thing will be the most impressive.

("O'Shah," E&E, p. 53)

speculation

1888 There are two times in a man's life when he should not speculate: when he can afford it, and when he can't.

(N&J-3, p. 433; also in Foll. Equat., *ch. 56, p. 535)*

1894 October. This is one of the peculiarly dangerous months to speculate in stocks in. The others are July, January, September, April, November, May, March, June, December, August, and February.

—Pudd'nhead Wilson's Calendar

(Pudd. Wilson, Conclusion, PW&TET, p. 300)

speech, human

1866 That deadly enemy of a man, his own tongue . . .

(Ltrs-Hawaii, Letter 16, p. 171)

1879 Lord, what an organ is human speech when it is played by a master!

(Letter to Olivia Clemens, November 14, 1879, Ltrs/Paine, 1:371)

1907 Written things are not for speech; their form is literary; they are stiff, inflexible, and will not lend themselves to happy and effective delivery with the tongue.

(Autob/MTIE, p. 216)

speeches

1885 The best and most telling speech is not the actual impromptu one, but the counterfeit of it . . . that speech is most worth listening to which has been carefully prepared in private and tried on a plaster cast, or an

spelling

empty chair, or any other appreciative object that will keep quiet, until the speaker has got his matter and his delivery limbered up so that they will seem impromptu to an audience.

(Speech in New York City, March 31, 1885, MT Speaking, *p. 191)*

1906 I love to hear myself talk, because I get so much instruction and moral upheaval out of it, but I lose the bulk of this joy when I charge for it.

(Letter to Maj. Gen. F. D. Grant, March 1906, Ltrs/Paine, *2:791)*

spelling

1866 I see, now, stronger than ever before, the absurdity of our still retaining the crude, uncouth, inefficient, distressing orthography invented for us by our ancestors in a rude, ignorant, uncultivated age of the world. We have discarded their coarseness & obscenity of conversation; their groping & groveling superstitions; their slow methods of locomotion & transmission of intelligence—*why* should we retain their ugly & aggravating orthography?

(N&J-1, p. 155)

1906 The ability to learn to spell correctly is a gift . . . it is born in a person, and is a sign of intellectual inferiority. By parity of reasoning, its absence is a sign of great mental power.

("Extract from Eve's Autobiography," Lets. Earth, *p. 87)*

1906 I never had any large respect for good spelling. That is my feeling yet. Before the spelling-book came with its arbitrary forms, men unconsciously revealed shades of their characters, and also added enlightening shades of expression to what they wrote by their spelling, and so it is possible that the spelling-book has been a doubtful benevolence to us.

(Autob/MTA, 2:68)

1906 I have had an aversion to good spelling for sixty years and more, merely for the reason that when I was a boy there was not a thing I could do creditably except spell according to the book. It was a poor and mean distinction, and I learned to disenjoy it.

(Ibid., 2:257)

1906 I shall soon be where they won't care how I spell so long as I keep the Sabbath.

> *(Speech in New York City, September 19, 1906, Speeches/Paine, p. 321)*

1907 Simplified spelling is all right, but, like chastity, you can carry it too far.

> *(Speech in New York City, December 9, 1907, Speeches/Paine, p. 367)*

"sphere of influence"

1897 That is a courteous modern phrase which means robbing your neighbor—for your neighbor's benefit; and the great theater of its benevolences is Africa.

> *(Foll. Equat., ch. 3, p. 48)*

Sphinx

1869 The great face was so sad, so earnest, so longing, so patient. There was a dignity not of earth in its mien, and in its countenance a benignity such as never any thing human wore. It was stone, but it seemed sentient. If ever image of stone thought, it was thinking.

> *(Inn. Abroad, ch. 58, pp. 628–629)*

263

spirit

1904 Spirit . . . has fifty times the strength and staying-power of brawn and muscle.

> *("Saint Joan of Arc," CT-2, p. 595)*

stage fright

1906 If there is an awful, horrible malady in the world, it is stage-fright—and seasickness. They are a pair.

> *(Speech in Norfolk, Connecticut, October 5, 1906, Speeches/Paine, p. 303)*

stagecoaches

1874 The stage-coach is but a poor, plodding, vulgar thing in the solitudes of the highway.

> *(Gilded Age, ch. 7, pp. 75–76)*

AWFUL, HORRIBLE MALADY

Stanley, Henry M. (British-American explorer)

1886 When you come to regard the achievements of these two men, Columbus and Stanley, from the standpoint of the difficulties they encountered, the advantage is with Stanley and against Columbus.

(Speech in Boston, December 9, 1886, MT Speaking, *p. 214)*

statesmanship

n.d. If we had less statesmanship we could get along with fewer battleships.

(More Max., p. 9)

1889 The true statesman does not despise any wisdom, howsoever lowly may be its origin . . . —[Hank Morgan]

(Conn. Yankee, ch. 26, p. 255)

1897 In statesmanship get the formalities right, never mind about the moralities. —Pudd'nhead Wilson's New Calendar

(Foll. Equat., ch. 65, p. 644)

statistics

1880 A man can't prove anything without statistics; no man can. . . . why statistics are more precious and useful than any other one thing in this world, except whisky—I mean hymnbooks.

(Speech in Hartford, October 26, 1880, MT Speaking, *p. 140)*

1904 Figures often beguile me, particularly when I have the arranging of them myself; in which case the remark attributed to Disraeli would often apply with justice and force:

"There are three kinds of lies: lies, damned lies, and statistics."

(NAR, July 5, 1907; Autob/NAR, p. 185)

Statue of Liberty

1883 What do we care for a statue of liberty when we've got the thing itself in its wildest sublimity? What you want of a monument is to keep you in mind of something you haven't got—something you've lost.

(Article in New York Times, *December 4, 1883;* MTSFH, *p. 135)*

stealing

n.d. It is better to take what does not belong to you than to let it lie around neglected.

(More Max., p. 9)

1876 There was no getting around the stubborn fact that taking sweetmeats was only "hooking," while taking bacon and hams and such valuables was plain simple *stealing*—and there was a command against that in the Bible.

(Tom Sawyer, ch. 13, p. 85)

1884 Pap always said it warn't no harm to borrow things, if you was meaning to pay them back, sometime; but the widow said it warn't anything but a soft name for stealing . . .

—[Huck]
(Huck Finn, ch. 12, p. 80)

1901 Morally, there are no degrees in stealing. The Commandment merely says, "Thou shalt not *steal*," and stops there.

("To My Missionary Critics," E&E, p. 289)

NO MORAL DEGREES

steamboat piloting

1866 I wish I was back there piloting up & down the river again. Verily, all is vanity and little worth—save piloting.

(Letter to mother and sister, October 19–20, 1865, Ltrs-1, p. 327)

1883 Your true pilot cares nothing about anything on earth but the river, and his pride in his occupation surpasses the pride of kings.

(Life on Miss., ch. 7, p. 92)

1883 I loved the profession far better than any I have followed since, and I took a measureless pride in it. The reason is plain: A pilot, in those days, was the only unfettered and entirely independent human being that lived in the earth. . . . In truth, every man and woman and child has a master, and worries and frets in servitude; but, in the day I write of, the

Mississippi pilot had *none*. . . . So here was the novelty of a king without a keeper, an absolute monarch who was absolute in sober truth and not by a fiction of words.

(Ibid., ch. 14, pp. 166–167)

ONE PERMANENT AMBITION

steamboating

1883 When I was a boy, there was but one permanent ambition among my comrades in our village on the west bank of the Mississippi River. That was, to be a steamboatman. We had transient ambitions of other sorts, but they were only transient. . . . the ambition to be a steamboatman always remained.

(Life on Miss., ch. 4, pp. 62–63)

1894 If there was anything better in this world than steamboating, it was the glory to be got by telling about it.

(Pudd. Wilson, ch. 8, PW&TET, p. 97)

stillness

c. 1907 Stillness and solemnity have a subduing power of their own, let the occasion be what it may.

(Autob/MTIE, p. 343)

stories

1892 I conceive that the right way to write a story for boys is to write so that it will not only interest boys but will also strongly interest any man *who has ever been a boy*. That immensely *enlarges the audience.*

(Letter to Fred J. Hall, August 10, 1892, Ltrs-Publs, p. 314)

1895 There are several kinds of stories, but only one difficult kind— the humorous. . . . The humorous story is American, the comic story is English, the witty story is French. The humorous story depends for its effect upon the *manner* of the telling; the comic story and the witty story upon the *matter.*

("How to Tell a Story," CT-2, p. 201; also in How to Tell a Story*)*

1906 There is only one right form for a story, and if you fail to find that form the story will not tell itself.

(Autob/MTIE, p. 199)

1907 I like a good story well told. That is the reason I am sometimes forced to tell them myself.

(Speech in Annapolis, Maryland, May 10, 1907, MT Speaking, p. 551)

Stormfield, Admiral Abner

(character modeled on Edgar Wakeman)

1905–06 "He is a fine and bluff old sailor, honest, unworldly, simple, innocent as a child—but doesn't know it, of course—knows not a thing outside of his profession, but *thinks* he knows a lot . . . and he *does* know his Bible, (just well enough to misquote it with confidence,) and frankly thinks he can beat the band at explaining it, whereas his explanations simply make the listener dizzy, they are so astronomically wide of the mark . . ."

—David

("The Refuge of the Derelicts," ch. 1, Fab. of Man, p. 166)

storms

1867 Storms always rise in certain conditions of the atmosphere.

They are caused by certain forces operating against certain other forces which are called by certain names and are well known by persons who are familiar with them.

("A Novel: Who Was He?," S&B, p. 27)

story telling

1899 If you wish to lower yourself in a person's favor, one good way is to tell his story over again the way *you* heard it.

(MTP, ts 42, p. 64; MTN, p. 345)

strangers

1875 Experience has taught me that strangers never call upon a man with any other desire than to sell him a lightning-rod.

(Letter to Hartford Courant, c. October 1, 1875, MTSFH, p. 98)

street commissioners

1869 Is it not the inborn nature of Street commissioners to avoid their duty whenever they get a chance? I wish I knew the name of the last one that held office in Pompeii so that I could give him a blast. I speak with feeling on this subject, because I caught my foot in one of those ruts, and the sadness that came over me when I saw the first poor skeleton, with ashes and lava sticking to it, was tempered by the reflection that may be that party was the Street Commissioner.

(Inn. Abroad, ch. 31, pp. 328–329)

stupidity

1873 Stupid people—who constitute the grand overwhelming majority of this and all other nations—*do* believe and *are* moulded . . . by what they get out of a newspaper.

(Paper delivered in Hartford, February 1873, Speeches/Paine, *p. 48)*

1889 Don't you know, there are some things that can beat smartness and foresight? Awkwardness and stupidity can. The best swordsman in the world doesn't need to fear the second best swordsman in the world; no, the person for him to be afraid of is some ignorant antagonist who has never had a sword in his hand before; he doesn't do the thing he ought to do, and so the expert isn't prepared for him; he does the thing he ought not to do: and often it catches the expert out, and ends him on the spot. —[Hank Morgan]

(Conn. Yankee, ch. 34, pp. 341–342)

style, writing

c. 1894 Style may be likened to an army, the author to its general, the book to the campaign.

("Cooper's Prose Style," Lets. Earth, *p. 139)*

subjunctive

1896 DAMN the subjunctive. It brings all our writers to shame.

(MTP, ts 38, p. 73; MTN, p. 303)

suggestion

c. 1909 There is conscious suggestion & there is unconscious suggestion—both come from outside—whence all ideas come.

(Memorandum, quoted in MT:Biog, *ch. 267, p. 1514)*

suicide

1878 "A suicide's a prime thing in its way, but it don't begin with 'n' assassination. You've got to be mighty reserved and respectful about a suicide, or you'll have the surviving relatives in your hair. You can't spread, you know—family won't stand it. You've got to cramp your item down to a short quarter of a column—and you've always got to say it's t('k!)emporary aber*ration*. Temporary aberration!—and half these suicides haven't got anything to aberrate! . . . But you let a man be assassinated once, and you can string him out to five columns. . . .

A PRIME THING

"Yes, a suicide's a kind of lean stuff for literature . . ."

—Tom Hooker

("Simon Wheeler, Detective," ch. 6, S&B, *pp. 392–393)*

1897 Unfortunately none of us can see far ahead; prophecy is not for us. Hence the paucity of suicides.

("Which Was the Dream?," WWD&OSW, *p. 51)*

1901 Would-be suicides are very changeable and hard to hold to their purpose.

(Speech in New York City, February 2, 1901, Speeches/Paine, *p. 226)*

sun spots

1892 "At present they merely make trouble and do harm in the evoking of cyclones and other kinds of electric storms; but once under humane and intelligent control this will cease and they will become a boon to man."   —Colonel Sellers

(Amer. Claim., ch. 25, p. 272)

Sunday school

1876 Sunday-school—a place that Tom hated with his whole heart . . .

(Tom Sawyer, ch. 4, p. 25)

sunsets

1883 All the Upper Mississippi region has these extraordinary sunsets as a familiar spectacle. It is the true Sunset Land . . . The sunrises are also said to be exceedingly fine. I do not know.

(Life on Miss., ch. 57, p. 563)

1899 I shall never see another sunset to begin with it this side of heaven. Venice? land, what a poor interest that is! This [*Sanna, Sweden*] is the place to be. I have seen about 60 sunsets here; & a good 40 of them were clear & away beyond anything I had ever imagined before for dainty & exquisite & marvelous beauty & infinite change & variety. America? Italy? the tropics? They have no notion of what a sunset ought to be. And this one—this unspeakable wonder! It discounts all the rest. It brings the tears, it is so unutterably beautiful.

(Letter to J. H. Twichell, September 6, 1899, Ltrs/Paine, 2:683)

superstition

1897 Let me make the superstitions of a nation and I care not who makes its laws or its songs either.

—Pudd'nhead Wilson's New Calendar
(Foll. Equat., ch. 51, p. 484)

1908 When the human race has once acquired a superstition nothing short of death is ever likely to remove it.

(Autob/AMT, ch. 78, p. 370)

supposing

c. 1907 An old and wise and stern maxim of mine, to wit: "Supposing is good, but finding out is better."

(Autob/MTIE, p. 324)

swearing

1885 What a lie it is to call this a free country where none but the unworthy and undeserving may swear.

(Speech in New York City, March 31, 1885, MT Speaking, p. 193)

1888 Don't imagine that I have lost my temper, because I swear. I swear all day, but I do not lose my temper.

(Letter to Orion Clemens, November 29, 1888, Ltrs/Paine, 2:503)

1897 The spirit of wrath—not the words—is the sin; and the spirit of wrath is cursing. We begin to swear before we can talk.

—Pudd'nhead Wilson's New Calendar

(Foll. Equat., ch. 31, p. 290)

1899 Let us swear while we may, for in heaven it will not be allowed.

(MTP, ts 42, p. 64; MTN, p. 344)

1899 "Swearing is like any other music . . . If it is not done well, if it is not done with a fine and discriminating art, and vitalized with gracious and heartborn feeling, it lacks beauty, it lacks charm, it lacks expression, it lacks nobleness, it lacks majesty . . ."

—David Gridley

("Indiantown," WWD&OSW, p. 173)

1904 The existing phrase-books are inadequate. They are well enough as far as they go, but when you fall down and skin your leg they don't tell you what to say.

("Italian Without a Master," CT-2, p. 583)

1906 The idea that no gentleman ever swears is all wrong; he can swear and still be a gentleman if he does it in a nice and benevolent and affectionate way.

(Speech in New York City, January 22, 1906, Speeches/Paine, p. 279)

LIKE ANY OTHER MUSIC

271

Switzerland

1880 Switzerland is simply a large, humpy, solid rock, with a thin skin of grass stretched over it.

(Tramp Abroad, ch. 42, p. 483)

sympathy

1892 After trying the political atmosphere of the neighboring monarchies, it is healing and refreshing to breathe in air that has known no taint of slavery for six hundred years, and to come among a people whose political history is great and fine, and worthy to be taught in all schools and studied by all races and peoples.

("Switzerland, The Cradle of Liberty," WIM&OE, p. 194)

sympathy

1868 One should not bring sympathy to a sick man. It is always kindly meant, & of course it has to be taken—but it isn't much of an improvement on castor oil. One who has a sick man's true interest at heart will forbear spoken sympathy, & bring him surreptitious soup, & fried oysters & other trifles that the doctor has tabooed.

(Letter to Mary Fairbanks, February 20, 1868, Ltrs-2, p. 190)

tabus

1897 The tabu was the most ingenious and effective of all the inventions that has ever been devised for keeping a people's privileges satisfactorily restricted.

(Foll. Equat., ch. 3, p. 52)

Tahoe, Lake (California-Nevada lake)

1863 No foul disease may hope to live in the presence of such beauty as that.

(Letter to mother and sister, February 16, 1863, Ltrs-1, p. 245)

1863 It is the masterpiece of the Creator.

(Letter to mother and sister, August 19, 1863, Ltrs-1, p. 264)

1864 The fish in Lake Tahoe are not troublesome; they will let a man rest there till he rots, and never inflict upon him the fatigue of putting on a fresh bait.

(Article in Call, *September 4, 1864;* ET&S-2, *p. 470)*

1869 I measure all lakes by Tahoe, partly because I am far more familiar with it than with any other, and partly because I have such a high admiration for it and such a world of pleasant recollections of it, that it is very nearly impossible for me to speak of lakes and not mention it.

(Ibid., ch. 48, p. 507n.)

1872 Three months of camp life on Lake Tahoe would restore an Egyptian mummy to his pristine vigor, and give him an appetite like an alligator. I do not mean the oldest and driest mummies, of course, but the fresher ones. The air up there in the clouds is very pure and fine, bracing and delicious. And why shouldn't it be?—it is the same the angels breathe.

(Rough. It, ch. 22, p. 149)

Taj Mahal (mausoleum in India)

1897 By all my senses, all my faculties, I know that the ice-storm is Nature's supremest achievement in the domain of the superb and the beautiful; and by my reason, at least, I know that the Taj is man's icestorm.

(Foll. Equat., ch. 59, p. 580)

tamarinds

1872 I thought tamarinds were made to eat, but that was probably not the idea. I ate several, and it seemed to me that they were rather sour that year. They pursed my lips, till they resembled the stem-end of a tomato, and I had to take my sustenance through a quill for twenty-four hours.

(Rough. It, ch. 63, p. 435)

NOT FOR EATING

Tangier, Morocco

1869 Tangier is a foreign land if ever there was one; and the true spirit of it can never be found in any book save the Arabian Nights.

(Inn. Abroad, ch. 8, p. 76)

273

tarantulas

1869 Tangier is full of interest for one day, but after that it is a weary prison. The Consul-General has been here five years, and has got enough of it to do him for a century . . . It is the completest exile that I can conceive of. I would seriously recommend to the Government of the United States that when a man commits a crime so heinous that the law provides no adequate punishment for it, they make him Consul-General to Tangier.

(Ibid., ch. 9, pp. 88–89)

tarantulas

OFFENDED DIGNITY

1872 When their feelings were hurt, or their dignity offended, they were the wickedest-looking desperadoes the animal world can furnish. . . . Starchy?—proud? Indeed, they would take up a straw and pick their teeth like a member of Congress.

(Rough. It, ch. 21, p. 144)

taste

1880 Foreigners cannot enjoy our food, I suppose, any more than we can enjoy theirs. It is not strange; for tastes are made, not born. I might glorify my bill of fare until I was tired; but after all, the Scotchman would shake his head and say, "Where's your haggis?" and the Fijian would sigh and say, "Where's your missionary?"

(Tramp Abroad, ch. 49, p. 575)

1895 There *are* no standards—of taste, in wines, cigars, poetry, prose, &c. Each man's own taste is the standard, & a majority vote cannot decide for him, or in any slightest degree affect the supremacy of his own standard.

(MTP, ts 35, p. 16; MTN, p. 245)

tautology

1902 To create man was a fine & original idea; but to add the sheep was tautology.

(MTP, ts 45, p. 40; MTN, p. 379)

taxidermists

1902 What is the difference between a taxidermist & a tax-collector? The taxidermist takes only your skin.

(MTP, ts 45, p. 39; MTN, *p. 379)*

teaching

1906 If I have a passion for anything, it is for teaching. It is noble to teach oneself; it is still nobler to teacher others—and less trouble.

(Speech, c. February–March 1906, Speeches/Paine, *p. 296; corrected date is supplied by* MT Speaking, *p. 487)*

teeth

1883 Never lend your teeth.

(N&J-3, p. 34)

teetotalling

1885 How I do hate those enemies of the human race who go around enslaving God's free people with PLEDGES—to quit drinking, instead of to quit *wanting* to drink.

(Letter to Henry Ward Beecher, September 11, 1885, Ltrs/Paine, *2:459)*

telegrams

1886 People ALWAYS read a telegram first, & *then* look to see who it is addressed to. In the 41 years that the telegraph service has existed there has been no instance of an exception to this rule.

(Letter to W. D. Howells, May 13, 1886, Ltrs-Howells, *2:560)*

telephones

1889 "Confound a telephone, anyway. It is the very demon for conveying similarities of sound that are miracles of divergence from similarity of sense."

—Hank Morgan

(Conn. Yankee, ch. 24, p. 230)

1897 It is a time-saving, profanity-breeding, useful invention, and in America is to be found in all houses except parsonages.

("Letters to Satan," E&E, *p. 216)*

1906 When I lived up in Hartford, I was the very first man, in that part of New England at least, to put in a telephone, but it was constantly getting me into trouble because of the things I said carelessly.

(Interview in New York Times, *December 23, 1906, MTSFH, p. 219)*

temperament

1894 It takes me a long time to lose my temper, but once lost I could not find it with a dog.

(MTN, p. 240)

c. 1907 It is my conviction that a person's temperament is a law, an iron law, and has to be obeyed, no matter who disapproves . . .

(Autob/AMT, ch. 63, p. 306)

1910 Circumstance is powerful, but it cannot work alone; it has to have a partner. Its partner is man's *temperament*—his natural disposition. His temperament is not his invention, it is *born* in him, and he has no authority over it, neither is he responsible for its acts. He cannot change it, nothing can change it, nothing can modify it—except temporarily.

("The Turning-Point of My Life," WIM&OPW, *p. 460)*

temperance

1896 Temperate temperance is best. Intemperate temperance injures the cause of temperance, while temperate temperance helps it in its fight against intemperate intemperance.

(MTP, ts 39, p. 29; MTN, p. 310)

temptation

1897 There are several good protections against temptations, but the surest is cowardice.　　　　　—Pudd'nhead Wilson's New Calendar

(Foll. Equat., ch. 36, p. 324)

Thanksgiving Day

1894 Let all give humble, hearty, and sincere thanks, now, but the turkeys. In the island of Fiji they do not use turkeys; they use plumbers. It does not become you and me to sneer at Fiji.

　　　　　—Pudd'nhead Wilson's Calendar

(Pudd. Wilson, ch. 18, PW&TET, p. 225)

Thatcher, Becky

(character in *The Adventures of Tom Sawyer*)

1876 A lovely little blue-eyed creature with yellow hair plaited into two long tails, white summer frock and embroidered pantalettes. The fresh-crowned hero [*Tom Sawyer*] fell without firing a shot.

(Tom Sawyer, ch. 3, pp. 19–20)

theory

1889 How empty is theory in presence of fact!
—[Hank Morgan]
(Conn. Yankee, ch. 43, p. 481)

1894 Tom . . . said the trouble about arguments is, they ain't nothing but *theories*, after all, and theories don't prove nothing, they only give you a place to rest on, a spell, when you are tuckered out butting around and around trying to find out something there ain't no way *to* find out. And he says—

"There's another trouble about theories: there's always a hole in them somewheres, sure, if you look close enough."

(Tom Sawyer Abrd., ch. 9, p. 67)

thought

1898 "A man *originates* nothing in his head, he merely observes exterior things, and *combines* them in his head—puts several things together and draws a conclusion. His mind is merely a machine, that is all—an *automatic* one, and he has no control over it; it cannot conceive of a *new* thing, an original thing, it can only gather material from the outside and combine it into new *forms* and patterns. But it always has to have the *materials* from the *outside*, for it can't make them itself. That is to say, a man's mind cannot *create*—a god's can, and my race can. That is the difference. We need no contributed materials, we *create* them—out of thought. All things that exist were made out of thought—and out of nothing else." —44

(No. 44, ch. 22, pp. 114–115)

1906 *None but gods have ever had a thought which did not come from the outside.* —Old Man

("What Is Man?," ch. 1, WIM&OPW, p. 129)

BECKY THATCHER

Tilden, Samuel (Democratic candidate for president in 1876)

1876 If Tilden is elected I think the entire country will go pretty straight to Mrs. Howells's bad place.

(Letter to W. D. Howells, August 9, 1876, Ltrs-Howells, 1:143)

time

n.d. Geological time is not money.

(More Max., p. 7)

1867 Time and hash wait for no man.

(Letter to Alta, September 1867; TWIA, p. 242)

1905 Let us adopt geological time. Then—time being money—there will be no more poverty.

(MTP, ts 48, p. 5; MTN, p. 393)

timidity

1897 The timid man yearns for full value and asks for a tenth. The bold man strikes for double value and compromises on par.

—Pudd'nhead Wilson's New Calendar

(Foll. Equat., ch. 13, p. 137)

titles

1874 Titles never die in America, although we *do* take a republican pride in poking fun at such trifles . . .

(Gilded Age, ch. 33, p. 304)

1877 You give an American a hand in creating a title which he may bear himself some day, and you may let him alone to make that title pompous enough.

("Autobiography of a Damned Fool," S&B, ch. 4, p. 149)

1878 To call a butcher a gentleman is as absurd as it would be to call an English Earl a prince. These titles signify station, not worthiness or manly excellence.

(N&J-2, p. 118)

1879 I couldn't gird at the English love for titles while our own love for titles was still more open to sarcasm. Take our "Hon.," for instance. Unless my memory has gone wholly astray, no man in America has any right to stick that word before his name; to do it is a sham, and a very poor sham at that.

(Interview in New York World, *c. May 1879, MTSFH, p. 112)*

1906 Titles of honor and dignity once acquired in a democracy, even by accident and properly usable for only forty-eight hours, are as permanent here as eternity is in heaven. You can never take away those titles. Once a justice of the peace for a week, always "judge" afterward. Once a major of militia for a campaign on the Fourth of July, always a major. To be called colonel, purely by mistake and without intention, confers that dignity on a man for the rest of his life. We adore titles and heredities in our hearts, and ridicule them with our mouths. This is our democratic privilege.

(Autob/MTA, 2:350)

toadstools

1894 Remark of Dr. [William] Baldwin's, concerning upstarts: We don't care to eat toadstools that think they are truffles.

—Pudd'nhead Wilson's Calendar

(Pudd. Wilson, ch. 5, PW&TET, p. 67)

Tom Sawyer, The Adventures of (1876 novel)

1875 It is *not* a boy's book at all. It will only be read by adults. It is only written for adults.

(Letter to W. D. Howells, July 5, 1875, Ltrs-Howells, 1:91)

1887 That is a book, dear sir, which cannot be dramatized. One might as well try to dramatize any other hymn. Tom Sawyer is simply a hymn, put into prose form to give it a worldly air.

(Unmailed letter to W. R. Ward, September 8, 1887, Ltrs/Paine, 2:477)

tomorrow

n.d. Do not put off till tomorrow what can be put off till day-after-tomorrow just as well.

(More Max., p. 7)

279

1904 The tomorrows have nothing for us. Too many times they have breathed the word of promise to our ear & broken it to our hope. We take no to-morrow's word any more.

(Letter to J. H. Twichell, May 11, 1904, Ltrs/Paine, *2:753)*

tom-tom drums

1866 The wretchedest of all wretched musical abortions, the tom-tom.

(Ltrs-Hawaii, Letter 16, p. 170)

A WELL-DEFINED OFFICE

town drunkard

1906 An exceedingly well-defined and unofficial office of those days.

(NAR, August 2, 1907; Autob/NAR, *p. 191)*

training

1879 Talent is useless without training . . .

(Letter to Mary Fairbanks, September 23, 1879, Ltrs-Fairbanks, *p. 234)*

c. 1901 There is nothing that training cannot do. Nothing is above its reach or below it. It can turn bad morals to good, good morals to bad; it can destroy principles, it can re-create them; it can debase angels to men and lift men to angelship. And it can do any one of these miracles in a year—even in six months.

("As Regards Patriotism," E&E, *p. 303)*

1906 *Training* is potent. Training toward higher, and higher, and ever higher ideals is worth any man's thought and labor and diligence.

—Old Man

("What Is Man?," ch. 3, WIM&OPW, *p. 156)*

traitors

1889 The citizen who thinks he sees that the commonwealth's political clothes are worn out, and yet holds his peace and does not agitate for a new suit, is disloyal; he is a traitor. That he may be the only one who thinks he sees this decay, does not excuse him: it is his duty to agi-

280

tate anyway, and it is the duty of others to vote him down if they do not see the matter as he does. —[Hank Morgan]

(Conn. Yankee, ch. 13, pp. 113–114)

Tramp Abroad, A (1880 travel book)

1879 A gossipy volume of travel . . . It talks about anything and every-thing, and always drops a subject the moment my interest in it begins to slacken. It is as discursive as a conversation; it has no more restraints or limitations than a fireside talk has. I have been drifting around on an idle, easy-going tramp—so to speak—for a year, stopping when I pleased, moving on when I got ready. In a word, it is a book written by one loafer for a brother loafer to read.

(Interview in New York World, *May 11, 1879; quoted in* N&J-2, *p. 4)*

1879 I want to make a book which people will *read*,—& I shall make it profitable reading in spots—in spots merely *because* there's not much material for a larger amount.

(Letter to W. D. Howells, January 30, 1879, Ltrs-Howells, 1:250)

"translate"

1897 I knowed all about that word, becuz the Widow told me; I knowed you can translate a book, but you can't translate a boy, becuz translat-ing means turning a thing out of one language into another, and you can't do that with a boy. —[Huck Finn]

("Tom Sawyer's Conspiracy," HF&TS, ch. 3, p. 153)

translations

1880 I have a prejudice against people who print things in a foreign lan-guage and add no translation. When I am the reader, and the author con-siders me able to do the translating myself, he pays me quite a nice compliment—but if he would do the translating for me, I would try to get along without the compliment.

(Tramp Abroad, ch. 16, p. 146)

1882 Translations always reverse a thing, and bring an entirely new side of it into view, thus doubling the property and making two things out of what was only one thing before.

(Speech in Holyoke, Massachusetts, January 31, 1882,
MT Speaking, p. 167)

travel

1867 There is no unhappiness like the misery of sighting land (& work) again after a cheerful, careless voyage.

(Letter to William Bowen, June 7, 1867, Ltrs-2, p. 54)

1869 A long sea-voyage not only brings out all the mean traits one has, and exaggerates them, but raises up others which he never suspected he possessed, and even creates new ones. A twelve months' voyage at sea would make an ordinary man a very miracle of meanness.

(Inn. Abroad, Conclusion, p. 648)

1869 Travel is fatal to prejudice, bigotry and narrow-mindedness, and many of our people need it sorely on these accounts. Broad, wholesome, charitable views of men and things can not be acquired by vegetating in one little corner of the earth all one's lifetime.

(Ibid., p. 650)

282

1870 Tastes differ, & 200 miles mule-back in company is the next best thing to a sea-voyage to bring a man's worst points to the surface.

(Letter to A. Francis Judd, December 20, 1870, Ltrs-4, p. 278)

1891 Travel has no longer any charm for me. I have seen all the foreign countries I want to see except heaven & hell, & I have only a vague curiosity as concerns one of those.

(Letter to W. D. Howells, May 20, 1891, Ltrs-Howells, 2:645)

1894 There ain't no surer way to find out whether you like people or hate them than to travel with them . . .   —[Huck Finn]

(Tom Sawyer Abrd., ch. 11, p. 78)

CHARMS OF TRAVEL

troubles

1871 I know very well that each individual's troubles are stately from *his* point of view.

(Letter to Orion Clemens, March 15, 1871, Ltrs-4, p. 363)

1897 We all like to see people in trouble, if it doesn't cost us anything.

(Foll. Equat., ch. 48, p. 448)

troy weight and avoirdupois

1897 Nobody knows what they mean. When you buy a pound of a drug and the man asks you which you want, troy or avoirdupois, it is best to say "Yes," and shift the subject.

(Foll. Equat., ch. 23, p. 225)

truth

n.d. Never tell the truth to people who are not worthy of it.

(More Max., p. 11)

1880 Only rigid cultivation can enable a man to find truth in a lie.

(Tramp Abroad, ch. 24, p. 238)

1888 The best part of a story; or indeed of any other thing. Even liars have to admit that, if they are intelligent liars.

(Letter to Louis Pendleton, August 4, 1888, Ltrs/Paine, 2:497)

1894 Tell the truth or trump—but get the trick.

—Pudd'nhead Wilson's Calendar

(Pudd. Wilson, ch. 1, PW&TET, p. 17)

1894 If you tell the truth you don't have to remember anything.

(MTP, ts 33, p. 59; MTN, p. 240)

1897 When in doubt, tell the truth.

—Pudd'nhead Wilson's New Calendar

(Foll. Equat., ch. 2, p. 35)

1897 Truth is the most valuable thing we have. Let us economize it.

—Pudd'nhead Wilson's New Calendar

(Ibid., ch. 7, p. 56)

1897 Truth is stranger than fiction—to some people, but I am measurably familiar with it.

Truth *is* stranger than fiction, but it is because Fiction is obliged to stick to possibilities; Truth isn't.

—Pudd'nhead Wilson's New Calendar

(Ibid., ch. 15, p. 156)

1897 Often, the surest way to convey misinformation is tell the strict truth. —Pudd'nhead Wilson's New Calendar

(Ibid., ch. 59, p. 567)

1899 Truth is mighty & will prevail. There is nothing the matter with this except that it ain't so.

(MTP, ts 42, p. 67; MTN, p. 345)

1902 "There's a good many Truths with a capital T running at large and dressed as gentlemen, that would lose their liberty if they were arrested and sharply cross-questioned." —Sol Bailey

("Which Was It?," ch. 13, WWD&OSW, p. 306)

1906 That maxim ["*When in doubt, tell the truth*"] I did invent, but never expected it to be applied to me. I meant to say, "When *you* are in doubt"; when I am in doubt myself, I use more sagacity.

(Speech in New York City, March 9, 1906, Speeches/Paine, p. 292)

1906 It is not worth while to strain one's self to tell the truth to people who habitually discount everything you tell them, whether it is true or isn't.

(Autob/MTIE, p. 116)

1907 It was ever thus, all through my life: whenever I have diverged from custom and principle and uttered a truth, the rule has been that the hearer hadn't strength of mind enough to believe it.

(NAR, July 5, 1907; Autob/NAR, p. 186)

Malignant swindle

Turkish baths

1869 It is a malignant swindle. The man who enjoys it is qualified to enjoy anything that is repulsive to sight or sense, and he that can invest it with a charm of poetry is able to do the same with any thing else in the world that is tedious, and wretched, and dismal, and nasty.

(Inn. Abroad, ch. 34, p. 380)

turnips

1870 "Turnips should never be pulled—it injures them. It is much better to send a boy up and let him shake the tree."

("How I Edited an Agricultural Paper Once," CT-1, *p. 413)*

Twichell, Joseph A.
(close friend and traveling companion of Mark Twain)

1877 A good man, one of the best of men, although a clergyman.

("Some Rambling Notes of an Idle Excursion," part 1, SWE, *p. 36)*

typewriters

1905 I will now claim—until dispossessed—that I was the first person in the world to *apply the typewriter to literature.* That book must have been *The Adventures of Tom Sawyer.*

("The First Writing-Machines," $30k Bequest, *p. 169)*

undertaking

1883 "Undertaking?—why it's the dead-surest business in Christendom, and the nobbiest."   —New Orleans undertaker

(Life on Miss., ch. 43, p. 438)

usurpation

1891 The so-called usurpations with which history is littered are the most excusable misdemeanors which men have committed. To usurp a usurpation—that is all it amounts to, isn't it?

("At the Shrine of St. Wagner," WIM&OE, *p. 220)*

V

valedictories

1869 If there is anything more uncalled for than a "salutatory," it is one of those tearful, blubbering, long-winded "valedictories"—wherein a man who has been annoying the public for ten years cannot take leave of them without sitting down to cry a column and a half.

*("Salutatory," Editorial introducing himself
in* Buffalo Express, E&E, *p. 16)*

vanity

1899 There are no grades of vanity, there are only grades of ability in concealing it.

(MTP, ts 42, p. 64; MTN, p. 345)

1899 "Vanity—the place where feeble and foolish people are most vulnerable." —The Stranger

("The Man That Corrupted Hadleyburg," CT-2, p. 426; also in MTCH&c)

Venice, Italy

1869 Her glory is departed, and with her crumbling grandeur of wharves and palaces about her she sits among her stagnant lagoons, forlorn and beggared, forgotten of the world.

(Inn. Abroad, ch. 22, p. 217)

1869 It must be a paradise for cripples, for verily a man has no use for legs here.

(Ibid., p. 221)

Venus

n.d. An occultation of Venus is not half so difficult as an eclipse of the Sun, but because it comes seldom the world thinks it's a grand thing.

(More Max., p. 11)

verbs

1900 Now a verb has a hard time enough of it in this world when it's all together. It's downright inhuman to split it up. But that's just what those Germans do. They take part of a verb and put it down here, like a stake, and they take the other part of it and put it away over yonder like another stake, and between these two limits they just shovel in German.

(Speech in New York City, November 20, 1900, MT Speaking, *p. 358)*

vices

1865 Now I don't approve of dissipation, and I don't indulge in it, either, but I haven't a particle of confidence in a man who has no redeeming petty vices whatever . . .

("Answers to Correspondents," ET&S-2, *p. 190)*

Victoria, Queen

1908 As a woman the Queen was all that the most exacting standards could require. As a far-reaching and effective beneficent moral force she had no peer in her time among either monarchs or commoners. As a monarch she was without reproach in her great office. We may not venture, perhaps, to say so sweeping a thing as this in cold blood about any monarch that preceded her upon either her own throne or upon any other. It is a colossal eulogy, but it is justified.

(Speech in New York City, May 25, 1908, Speeches/Paine, *pp. 387–388)*

virtue

1899 "The weakest of all weak things is a virtue which has not been tested in the fire."   —The Stranger

("The Man That Corrupted Hadleyburg," CT-2, *p. 426; also in* MTCH&c)

1902 "There is nothing teaches like a fall. The man that gets a fall *realizes* things. . . . He recognizes that he was moral in theory before; he is likely to be moral in *fact* after that rude experience. He was walking on precept and sentiment before—he is likely to walk on the ground afterward. . . . Until a man falls, once or twice, he isn't safe, I tell you! His virtues have not been tested in the fire; until they have been hardened in the fire they are not to be depended on."   —Andrew Harrison

("Which Was It?," ch. 11, WWD&OSW, *p. 282)*

vivisection

1899 I believe I am not interested to know whether Vivisection produces results that are profitable to the human race or doesn't. To know that the results are profitable to the race would not remove my hostility to it. The pain which it inflicts upon unconsenting animals is the basis of my enmity towards it, and it is to me sufficient justification of the enmity without looking further.

(Letter to secretary of London Anti-Vivisection Society,
May 26, 1899, LAIFI, *p. 238)*

vote, the

n.d. The only commodity that is peddleable without a license.

(More Max., p. 13)

vows

1899 There is no pleasure comparable to making a vow in the presence of one who appreciates that vow, in the presence of men who honor and appreciate you for making the vow, and men who admire you for making the vow.

There is only one pleasure higher than that, and that is to get outside and break the vow.

(Speech in London, June 16, 1899,
MT Speaking, *p. 325)*

INCOMPARABLE PLEASURE

Wagner, Richard (19th-century German composer)

1891 Nothing can make a Wagner opera absolutely perfect and satisfactory to the untutored but to leave out the vocal parts. I wish I could see a Wagner opera done in pantomime once.

("At the Shrine of St. Wagner," WIM&OE, p. 213)

1906 The late Bill Nye once said, "I have been told that Wagner's music is better than it sounds." That felicitous description of a something which so many people have tried to describe, and couldn't, does seem to fit the general's manner of speech exactly. His talk is much better than it is. No, that is not the idea—there seems to be a lack there somewhere. Maybe it is another case of the sort just quoted. Maybe Nye would say that "it is better than it sounds." I think that is it. His talk does *not* sound entertaining, but it *is* distinctly entertaining.

(Autob/MTA, 1:338)

1906 I have witnessed, and greatly enjoyed, the first act of everything which Wagner created, but the effect on me has always been so powerful that one act was quite sufficient; whenever I have witnessed two acts I have gone away physically exhausted; and whenever I have ventured an entire opera the result has been the next thing to suicide.

(NAR, June 7, 1907; Autob/NAR, p. 175)

waiters

1869 The strangest curiosity yet—a really polite hotel waiter who isn't an idiot.

(Inn. Abroad, ch. 11, p. 98)

Wakeman, Edgar (sea captain whom Mark Twain used as a model for Captain Stormfield and other characters)

1866 I have been listening to some of Captain Waxman's [*Mark Twain's pseudonym for Wakeman*] stunning forecastle yarns, and I will do him the credit to say he knows how to tell them. With his strong, cheery voice, animated countenance, quaint phraseology, defiance of grammar and extraordinary vim in the matter of gesture and emphasis, he makes a most effective story out of very unpromising materials. There is a contagion about his whole-souled jollity that the chief mourner at a funeral could not resist. He is fifty years old, and as rough as a bear in voice and action, and yet as kind-hearted and tender as a woman. He is a burly, hairy, sun-burned, stormy-voiced old salt, who mixes strange oaths with incomprehensible sailor phraseology and the gentlest and most touching pathos, and is tattooed from head to foot like a Feejee Islander. His tongue is forever going when he has got no business on his hands, and though he knows nothing of policy or the ways of the world, he can cheer up any company of passengers that ever travelled in a ship, and keep them cheered up. He never drinks a drop, never gambles, and never swears where a lady or child may chance to hear him—but with all things consonant with the occasion he sometimes soars into flights of fancy swearing that fill the listener with admiration.

(Letter to Alta, December 20, 1866; MTTB, p. 22)

1906 He was full of human nature, and the best kind of human nature. He was as hearty and sympathetic and loyal and loving a soul as I have found anywhere and when his temper was up he performed all the functions of an earthquake, without the noise.

(Autob/MTIE, p. 244)

walking

FRIGHTFUL VELOCITY

1880 Now, the true charm of pedestrianism does not lie in the walking, or in the scenery, but in the talking.

(Tramp Abroad, ch. 23, p. 221)

waltz, the

1862 I was exceedingly delighted with the waltz, and also with the polka. These differ in name, but there the difference ceases—the dances are precisely the same. You have only to spin around with frightful velocity and steer clear of the furniture. . . . The waltz and the polka are very exhilarating—to use a mild term—amazingly exhilarating.

(Letter to Territorial Enterprise, December 12, 1862, MTOE, p. 40)

war

1897 To me, the military problems of the situation are of more interest than the political ones, because by disposition I have always been especially fond of war. No, I mean fond of discussing war; and fond of giving military advice.

(Foll. Equat., ch. 67, p. 669)

1900 "There has never been a just one, never an honorable one—on the part of the instigator of the war. I can see a million years ahead, and this rule will never change in so many as half a dozen instances. The loud little handful—as usual—will shout for the war. The pulpit will—warily and cautiously—object—at first; the great, big dull bulk of the nation will rub its sleepy eyes and try to make out why there should be a war, and will say, earnestly and indignantly, 'It is unjust and dishonorable, and there is no necessity for it.' Then the handful will shout louder."

—Philip Traum
("Chronicle of Young Satan," ch. 9, p. 155)

1906 War is a rude friend, but a kind one. It keeps us down to sixty billion and saves the hard-grubbing world alive.

("Extract from Eve's Autobiography," Lets. Earth, p. 92)

1909 Man is the only animal that deals in that atrocity of atrocities, War.

("The Lowest Animal," Lets. Earth, p. 226)

Ward, Artemus (19th-century American humorist)

1880 One of the kindest and gentlest men in the world . . . I think his lecture on the "Babes in the Wood" was the funniest thing I ever listened to.

(Letter to Knoxville Tribune, c. January 2, 1880, MTSFH, p. 124)

Warner, Charles Dudley (writer and friend of Mark Twain)

1892 If my market value is below Charley Warner's, it is a case of Since When? I should multiply it by two or three if required to testify.

(Letter to Fred J. Hall, August 10, 1892, Ltrs-Publs, p. 315)

1906 It is not the privilege of the most of us to have many intimate friends—a dozen is our aggregate—but I think he could count his by the score. It is seldom that a man is so beloved by both sexes and all ages as Warner was. There was a charm about his spirit, and his ways, and his words, that won all that came within the sphere of its influence.

(NAR, November 1907; Autob/NAR, p. 222)

Washington, Booker T. (African American educationist)

1908 A man worth a hundred [*Theodore*] Roosevelts, a man whose shoe-latchets Mr. Roosevelt is not worthy to untie.

(Autob/MTIE, p. 30)

Washington, D.C.

1874 There is something good and motherly about Washington, the grand old benevolent National Asylum for the Helpless.

(Gilded Age, ch. 24, p. 225)

1892 "When a man comes to Washington . . . it's because he *wants* something. And I know that as a rule he's not going to get it; that he'll stay and try for another thing and won't get that; the same luck with the next and the next and the next; and keeps on till he strikes bottom, and is too poor and ashamed to go back . . . and at last his heart breaks and they take up a collection and bury him."   —Colonel Sellers

(Amer. Claim., ch. 2, pp. 30–31)

Washington, George (first president of the United States)

1868 A boy that could not tell a lie—*could not tell a lie*! But he *never had any chance*. It might have been different if he had belonged to the Washington Newspaper Correspondents Club.

(Speech in Washington, D.C., January 11, 1868, MT Speaking, p. 21)

1871 I am different from Washington; I have a higher and grander standard of principle. Washington could not lie. I *can* lie, but I *won't*.

("Roughing It" lecture, 1871–72 season; MT Speaking, p. 60)

Washington Monument

1874 The Monument to the Father of his Country towers out of the mud—sacred soil is the customary term. It has the aspect of a factory chimney with the top broken off. . . . The Monument is to be finished, some day, and at that time our Washington will have risen still higher in the nation's veneration, and will be known as the Great-Great-Grand-father of his Country.

(Gilded Age, ch. 24, pp. 221–222)

Washoe zephyr (powerful wind in Nevada)

1872 A Washoe wind is by no means a trifling matter. It blows flimsy houses down, lifts shingle roofs occasionally, rolls up tin ones like sheet music, now and then blows a stage-coach over and spills the passengers; and tradition says the reason there are so many bald people there, is, that the wind blows the hair off their heads while they are looking sky-ward after their hats.

(Rough. It, ch. 21, p. 139)

watches

1870 A correct average is only a mild virtue in a watch . . .

("My Watch," CT-1, p. 498)

1870 My uncle William (now deceased, alas!) used to say that a good horse was a good horse until it had run away once, and that a good watch was a good watch until the repairers got a chance at it.

(Ibid., p. 499)

1897 When your watch gets out of order you have choice of two things to do: throw it in the fire or take it to the watch-tinker. The former is the quickest. —Pudd'nhead Wilson's New Calendar

(Foll. Equat., ch. 64, p. 630)

1910 I see no great difference between a man and a watch, except that the man is conscious and the watch isn't, and the man *tries* to plan things and the watch doesn't.

("The Turning-Point of My Life," WIM&OPW, p. 463)

REPAIRER GETS HIS CHANCE

water

1880 Europeans say ice-water impairs digestion. How do they know?—they never drink any.

(Tramp Abroad, ch. 28, p. 290)

1880 In Europe everywhere except in the mountains, the water is flat and insipid beyond the power of words to describe. It is served lukewarm; but no matter, ice could not help it; it is incurably flat, incurably insipid. It is only good to wash with; I wonder it doesn't occur to the average inhabitant to try it for that.

(Ibid., ch. 46, p. 536)

ACQUIRED BY ART

watermelons

1894 The true Southern watermelon is a boon apart, and not to be mentioned with commoner things. It is chief of this world's luxuries, king by the grace of God over all the fruits of the earth. When one has tasted it, he knows what the angels eat. It was not a Southern watermelon that Eve took; we know it because she repented.

—Pudd'nhead Wilson's Calendar
(Pudd. Wilson, ch. 14, PW&TET, p. 179)

1897–98 I know the taste of the watermelon which has been honestly come by, and I know the taste of the watermelon which has been acquired by art. Both taste good, but the experienced know which tastes best.

(NAR, March 1, 1907; Autob/NAR, p. 121)

wealth

1869 It isn't what a man has that constitutes wealth. No—it is to be *satisfied* with what one has; that is wealth.

("Open Letter to Commodore Vanderbilt," LAIFI, p. 40)

1904 Vast wealth has temptations which fatally and surely undermine the moral structure of persons not habituated to its possession. . . . Vast wealth, to the person unaccustomed to it, is a bane; it eats into the flesh and bone of his morals.

("The $30,000 Bequest," CT-2, pp. 615, 616; also in $30k Bequest)

weather

n.d. It is best to read the weather forecast before we pray for rain.

(More Max., p. 8)

1892 Weather is necessary to a narrative of human experience. That is conceded. But it ought to be put where it will not be in the way; where it will not interrupt the flow of the narrative. And it ought to be the ablest weather that can be had, not ignorant, poor-quality, amateur weather. Weather is a literary specialty, and no untrained hand can turn out a good article of it.

(Amer. Claim., Prefatory note, p. ix)

1897 When a person is accustomed to 138 in the shade, his ideas about cold weather are not valuable. . . . I believe that in India "cold weather" is merely a conventional phrase and has come into use through the necessity of having some way to distinguish between weather which will melt a brass door-knob and weather which will only make it mushy.

(Foll. Equat., ch. 54, p. 523)

Webster, Charles L. (nephew by marriage of Mark Twain and head of the latter's publishing company)

1881 I consider that you are not any more capable of a selfish or unjust act toward me than your aunt Livy is.

(Letter to Charles L. Webster, October 28, 1881, MT:Bus. Man, p. 174)

1889 I have never hated any creature with a hundred thousandth fraction of the hatred which I bear that human louse, Webster.

(Letter to Orion Clemens, July 1, 1889, Ltrs-Publs, p. 1)

1906 His ignorance covered the whole earth like a blanket and there was hardly a hole in it anywhere.

(Autob/MTIE, p. 180)

1906 In his obscure days his hat was number six and a quarter; in these latter days he was not able to get his head into a barrel.

(Ibid., p. 186)

What Is Man?
(Socratic dialogue by Mark Twain published anonymously in 1906)

1899 Since I wrote my Bible, (last year) which Mrs. Clemens loathes, & shudders over, & will not listen to the last half nor allow me to print any part of it, Man is not to me the respect-worthy person he was before; & so I have lost my pride in him & can't write gaily nor praisefully about him any more.

(Letter to W. D. Howells, April 2–13, 1899, Ltrs-Howells, 2:689)

1906 It is a desolating doctrine; it is not inspiring, enthusing, uplifting. It takes the glory out of man, it takes the pride out of him, it takes the heroism out of him, it denies him all personal credit, all applause; it not only degrades him to a machine, but allows him no control over the machine; makes a mere coffee-mill of him, and neither permits him to supply the coffee nor turn the crank; his sole and piteously humble function being to grind coarse or fine, according to his make, outside impulse doing all the rest.   —Young Man

("What Is Man?," ch. 6, WIM&OPW, pp. 208–209)

1907 Many a time in the past eight or nine years I have been strongly moved to publish that little book, but the doubtfulness of the wisdom of doing it has always been a little stronger than the desire to do it.

(Autob/MTIE, p. 239)

whiskey

1883 How solemn and beautiful is the thought, that the earliest pioneer of civilization, the van-leader of civilization, is never the steamboat, never the railroad, never the newspaper, never the Sabbath-school, never the missionary—but always whiskey! . . . Westward the Jug of Empire takes its way.

(Life on Miss., ch. 60, pp. 586–587)

1895 Separately, foreign marriages and whisky are bad; mixed, they are fatal.

(Letter to Olivia Clemens, June 3, 1895, Ltrs-Love, p. 261)

White House
(official residence of the president of the United States)

1874 A fine large white barn, with wide unhandsome grounds about it. The President lives there. It is ugly enough outside, but that is nothing to what it is inside. Dreariness, flimsiness, bad taste reduced to mathematical completeness is what the inside offers to the eye, if it remains yet what it always has been.

(Gilded Age, ch. 24, p. 222)

Wilhelm II, Emperor (ruler of Germany)

1906 The Emperor did most of the talking, and he talked well, and in faultless English. In both of these conspicuousnesses I was gratified to recognize a resemblance to myself—a very exact resemblance; no, almost exact, but not quite that—a modified exactness, with the advantage in favor of the Emperor. My English, like his, is nearly faultless; like him I talk well; and when I have guests at dinner I prefer to do all the talking myself.

(NAR, March 15, 1907; Autob/NAR, p. 125)

wills

1891 Wills made when you are expecting to be drowned at sea should be made with a *pencil*.

(N&J-3, p. 637)

Wilson, David
(title character of *Pudd'nhead Wilson*)

1894 He was a homely, freckled, sandy-haired young fellow, with an intelligent blue eye that had frankness and comradeship in it and a covert twinkle of a pleasant sort. But for an unfortunate remark of his, he would no doubt have entered at once upon a successful career at Dawson's Landing.

(Pudd. Wilson, ch. 1, PW&TET, p. 23)

1894 I have never thought of Pudd'nhead as a *character*, but only as a piece of machinery—a button or a crank or a lever, with a useful function to perform in a machine, but with no dignity above that.

(Letter to Olivia Clemens, January 12, 1894, Ltrs-Love, p. 291)

wine

1878 All Rhine wines are disguised vinegar.

(N&J-2, p. 132)

AN UNFORTUNATE REMARK

wisdom

1864 As far as becoming wiser is concerned, you might put all the wisdom I acquired in these experiments in your eye, without obstructing your vision any to speak of.

(Article in Golden Era, *July 3, 1864; ET&S-2, p. 25)*

1866 A man *nev[e]r* reaches that dizzy height of wisdom when he can no longer be led by the nose.

(N&J-1, p. 172)

1899 Of the demonstrably wise there are but two: those who commit suicide, & those who keep their reasoning faculties atrophied with drink.

(MTP, ts 42, p. 62; MTN, p. 344)

wit

1885 Wit & Humor—if any difference, it is in *duration*—lightning & electric light. Same material, apparently; but one is vivid, brief & can do damage—tother fools along & enjoys elaboration.

(N&J-3, p. 162)

1885 Somebody [*Sidney Smith*] has said, "Wit is the sudden marriage of ideas which before their union were not perceived to have any relation."

(Ibid., p. 172)

1888 There is no difference between Wit & humor, except that Wit can succeed without any pretence of being unconscious, but humor can't.

(Ibid., pp. 449–450)

EXTRAVAGANT PROPOSITIONS

witnesses

1864 If there is anything more absurd than the general average of Police Court testimony, we do not know what it is. Witnesses stand up here, every day, and swear to the most extravagant propositions with an easy indifference to consequences in the next world that is altogether refreshing.

(Article in Call, *July 12, 1864; Cl. of Call, p. 214)*

1864 That a thing cannot be all black and all white at the same time, is as self evident as that two objects cannot occupy the same space at the same time, and when a man makes a statement under the solemn sanction of an oath, the implication is that what he utters is a fact, the verity of which is not to be questioned. Notwithstanding witnesses are so often warned of the nature of an oath, and the consequences of perjury, yet it is a daily occurrence in the Police Court for men and women to mount the witness stand and swear to statements diametrically opposite.

(Article in Call, *September 9, 1864; ET&S-2, p. 473)*

women

1868 I love the sex. I love *all* the women, sir, irrespective, of age or color.

(Speech in Washington, D.C., January 11, 1868, MT Speaking, p. 20)

1873 I am proud, indeed, of the distinction of being chosen to respond to this especial toast, to "The Ladies," or to women if you please, for that is the preferable term, perhaps; it is certainly the older, and therefore the more entitled to reverence.

(Speech in London, November 8, 1873, SN&O, p. 213)

1882 Some civilized women would lose half their charm without dress; and some would lose all of it.

(Speech to New England Society of New York,
December 22, 1882, MT Speaking, p. 174)

1892 The average American girl possesses the valuable qualities of naturalness, honesty, and inoffensive straightforwardness; she is nearly barren of troublesome conventions and artificialities, consequently her presence and her ways are unembarrassing, and one is acquainted with her and on the pleasantest terms with her before he knows how it came about.

(Amer. Claim., ch. 20, pp. 204–205)

1906 There is nothing comparable to the endurance of a woman. In military life she would tire out any army of men, either in camp or on the march.

(Autob/MTA, 2:116)

women lecturers

1871 The idea of a *woman* reading a *humorous* lecture is perhaps the ghastliest conception to which the human mind has yet given birth.

(Letter to James Redpath, June 15, 1871, Ltrs-4, p. 408)

women's rights

1895 We easily perceive that the peoples furthest from civilization are the ones where equality between man & woman is furthest apart—& we consider this one of the *signs* of savagery. But we are so stupid that we can't see that we thus plainly admit that no civiliz[ation] can be perfect until exact equality between man & woman is included.

(MTP, ts 34, p. 32; MTN, p. 256)

1898 By-and-by ladies will form a part of the membership of all the legislatures in the world; as soon as they can prove competency they will be admitted.

("Stirring Times in Austria," part 3, MTCH&c, p. 326)

1901 For twenty-five years I've been a woman's rights man. . . . I should like to see the time come when women shall help to make the laws.

(Speech in New York City, January 20, 1901, Speeches/Paine, p. 223)

wonders

1897 I find that, as a rule, when a thing is a wonder to us it is not because of what *we* see in it, but because of what *others* have seen in it. We get almost all our wonders at second hand.

(Foll. Equat., ch. 53, p. 507)

words

1888 The difference between the *almost*-right word & the *right* word is really a large matter—it's the difference between the lightning-bug & the lightning.

*(Letter to George Bainton, October 15, 1888, photocopy of manuscript at
Mark Twain Project; also quoted in George Bainton, ed.,
The Art of Authorship [New York: Appleton, 1890], pp. 87–88)*

1889 Words are only painted fire; a look is the fire itself.

—[Hank Morgan]
(Conn. Yankee, ch. 35, p. 357)

1906 That elusive and shifty grain of gold, the *right word*. . . . A powerful agent is the right word: it lights the reader's way and makes it plain; a close approximation to it will answer, and much traveling is done in a well-enough fashion by its help, but we do not welcome it and applaud it and rejoice in it as we do when *the* right one blazes out on us. Whenever we come upon one of those intensely right words in a book or a newspaper the resulting effect is physical as well as spiritual and electrically prompt: it tingles exquisitely around through the walls of the mouth and tastes as tart and crisp and good as the autumn-butter that creams the sumac-berry. One has no time to examine the word and vote upon its rank and standing, the automatic recognition of its supremacy is so immediate.

("William Dean Howells," WIM&OE, p. 229)

1907 Size is the main thing about a word . . .

(Horse's Tale, ch. 1, p. 6)

work

n.d. Work and play are words used to describe the same thing under differing conditions.

(More Max., p. 14)

1859 I love to work. Why, sir, when I have a piece of work to perform, I go away to myself, sit down in the shade and muse over the coming enjoyment. Sometimes I am so industrious that I muse too long.

(Letter to John T. Moore, July 6, 1859, Ltrs-1, p. 92)

1866 I took a tranquil delight in that kind of labor which is such a luxury to the enlightened Christian—to wit, the labor of other people.

(Ltrs-Hawaii, Letter 1, p. 5)

1876 He [*Tom Sawyer*] had discovered a great law of human action, without knowing it—namely, that in order to make a man or a boy covet a thing, it is only necessary to make the thing difficult to attain. If he had been a great and wise philosopher, like the writer of this book, he would now have comprehended that Work consists of whatever a body is *obliged* to do, and that Play consists of whatever a body is not obliged to do.

(Tom Sawyer, ch. 2, p. 16)

A GREAT LAW OF
HUMAN ACTION

1889 Intellectual "work" is misnamed; it is a pleasure, a dissipation, and is its own highest reward. The poorest paid architect, engineer, general, author, sculptor, painter, lecturer, advocate, legislator, actor, preacher, singer, is constructively in heaven when he is at work . . . The law of work does seem utterly unfair—but there it is, and nothing can change it: the higher the pay in enjoyment the worker gets out of it, the higher shall be his pay in cash, also.   —[Hank Morgan]

(Conn. Yankee, ch. 28, p. 279)

1891 I do not like work even when another person does it.

("The Lost Napoleon," E&E, p. 172)

1896 Experience has convinced me that when one wishes to set a hard-worked man at something which he mightn't prefer to be bothered with, it is best to move upon him behind his wife. If she can't convince him it isn't worth while for other people to try.

(Letter to Emilie Rogers, November 26, 1896, Ltrs-Rogers, p. 253)

1908 Piloting on the Mississippi River was not work to me; it was play—delightful play, vigorous play, adventurous play—and I loved it; silver mining in the Humboldt Mountains was play, only play, because I did not do any of the work . . . The writing of books and magazine matter was always play, not work. I enjoyed it; it was merely billiards to me.

(Autob/MTIE, pp. 304–305)

worms

n.d. You can straighten a worm, but the crook is in him and only waiting.

(More Max., p. 14)

worship

1907 Worship does not question nor criticise, it obeys.

("Christian Science," bk. 2, ch. 13, WIM&OPW, p. 354)

wrinkles

1897 Wrinkles should merely indicate where smiles have been.

—Pudd'nhead Wilson's New Calendar

(Foll. Equat., ch. 52, p. 496)

writing

1871 Fools who never wrote a book are always giving me their infernal advice about how to write a book . . .

(Letter to Orion Clemens, June 29, 1871, Ltrs-4, p. 423)

1874 My interest in my work dies a sudden & violent death when the work is done.

(Letter to Dr. John Brown, September 4, 1874, Ltrs/Paine, 1:225)

1879 Apprentice-lawyers, doctors & preachers have to *pay* for their training: ours is the only reputable trade where the apprentice impudently demands compliments & wages right in the start. No ink is black enough to paint my detestation of these devils.

(Letter to Mary Fairbanks, September 23, 1879, Ltrs-Fairbanks, p. 233)

1884 If I'd a knowed what a trouble it was to make a book I wouldn't a tackled it and ain't agoing to no more.　　　　—[Huck]

(Huck Finn, Chapter the Last, p. 362)

1902 The time to begin writing an article is when you have finished it to your satisfaction. By that time you begin to clearly & logically perceive what it is that you really want to say.

(MTP, ts 45, p. 42; MTN, p. 380)

1906 I shall never finish my five or six unfinished books, for the reason that by forty years of slavery to the pen I have earned my freedom. I detest the pen and I wouldn't use it again to sign the death warrant of my dearest enemy.

(NAR, August 2, 1907; Autob/NAR, p. 190)

WHAT A TROUBLE TO MAKE A BOOK!

c. 1907 I made the great discovery that when the tank runs dry you've only to leave it alone and it will fill up again in time, while you are asleep—also while you are at work at other things and are quite unaware that this unconscious and profitable cerebration is going on.

(Autob/AMT, ch. 53, p. 265)

Young, Brigham (president of the Mormon church)

1872 "There is a batch of governors, and judges, and other officials here, shipped from Washington, and they maintain the semblance of a republican form of government—but the petrified truth is that Utah is an absolute monarchy and Brigham Young is king!"

—Mr. [James] Street
(Rough. It, ch. 14, p. 96)

youth

1897 The only thing that was worth giving to the race.

(Letter to W. D. Howells, February 23, 1897,
Ltrs-Howells, 2:665)

SHOWING OFF

1906 I was fourteen or fifteen years old—the age at which a boy is willing to endure all things, suffer all things, short of death by fire, if thereby he may be conspicuous and show off before the public . . .

(NAR, January 4, 1907; Autob/NAR, p. 81)

c. 1907 Sixteen . . . that dearest and sweetest of all ages.

(Autob/MTIE, p. 325)

"Youth"

1906 That word "Youth," as the reader has per-haps already guessed, was my wife's pet name for me. It was gently satirical, but also affectionate. I had certain mental and material peculiarities and cus-toms proper to a much younger person than I was.

(NAR, October 19, 1906; Autob/NAR, p. 44)

Zola, Emile

(French writer imprisoned for defending Alfred Dreyfus)

1898 The manliest man in France[.]

("A Word of Encouragement for Our Blushing Exiles," E&E, p. 223)

Bibliography

*I*n common with many other aspects of Mark Twain's complex life, his bibliography is a vast tangle. Scarcely one of his many books fails to pose some kind of bibliographical riddle. As for his shorter works—their publishing histories are so perplexing that no one has yet undertaken to compile a comprehensive bibliography. His early sketches are especially confusing; many appeared in more than a dozen different newspapers and magazines, with no two versions exactly alike. Throughout his life, many of his stories and sketches were collected in more than one book, occasionally under different titles. Moreover, ostensibly identical texts often differed slightly. Countless complications such as these have scared off bibliographers, making it difficult for everyone to locate texts and nearly impossible to know which versions are the most trustworthy.

Happily, all this confusion is gradually being cleared up by the publications of the Mark Twain Project at the University of California in Berkeley. The Project's long-term goal is to republish each of Mark Twain's significant works—whether or not he himself collected them—in a form that comes as close as possible to what the author intended to publish, thus removing the interference of editors, typists, typesetters, proofreaders, and chance itself. The Project's goal is more ambitious than casual observers might imagine—and more important than even some scholars understand—but it is the only possible solution to giving order to the vast riches of the author who is arguably America's greatest.

That said, it should now be clear that these notes are no attempt at a comprehensive bibliography of Mark Twain's writings. Their purpose is simply to identify the specific sources from which quotations in this book are taken. I assume—indeed hope—that many readers will want to see the full texts from which the quotations come. To aid such endeavors, source citations following quotes use abbreviated references that are fully defined at the end of this section.

Literally thousands of editions of Mark Twain's works have been published, and almost all of them are paginated differently. However, while the page references given in *The Quotable Mark Twain*'s citations will not apply to editions other than those cited, their chapter numbers generally will. With the exception of some foreign editions and two-volume American editions (which are discussed in the following pages), chapter numbers are consistent among different editions.

Wording, spelling, capitalization, and punctuation in the quotes in *The Quotable Mark Twain* follow their cited sources closely but will frequently be found to differ from texts in other editions. Most differences are comparatively minor, such as the spelling out of "and" for ampersands, or the thinning out of commas. Occasionally, however, the differences are substantial enough to change meanings, so it is important to consider the authority of the editions that one consults. (By "authority" I mean the strength of the claim that an edition can make to being a faithful rendition of Mark Twain's original texts.)

To get as close as possible to what Mark Twain actually wrote or said, *The Quotable Mark Twain* draws on the most authoritative published texts available, while also allowing that many readers will prefer to see references to books that are reasonably accessible over manuscripts or scarce books and periodicals. Readers who wish to carry their inquiries beyond the published texts that are cited will find substantial bibliographical help in Mark Twain Project publications, in the afterwords to the Oxford Mark Twain (OMT) volumes, and in the *Collected Tales, Sketches, Speeches, & Essays* (*CT*) volumes.

My first reference choices for citations are books edited by the Mark Twain Project—all of which are listed in this bibliography. The Project's publications include first editions of previously unpublished manuscripts and meticulously corrected new editions of previously published works. The first group of books—containing such material as notebooks, letters, and unfinished stories—is formally known as the "Mark Twain Papers." The latter books have been issued in two overlapping series: the "Works of Mark Twain" (the scholarly hardcover edition, originally known as the Iowa-California edition) and the "Mark Twain Library" (issued in both hard- and softcovers). "Works" editions contain elaborate editorial apparatuses with extensive notes; their "Mark Twain Library" counterparts have identical texts, often with minor corrections of the Works texts, but always with simpler editorial apparatuses. Where choices need to be made between the two series, Mark Twain Library editions are cited here because they have wider circulations and more fully corrected texts. In the most recently published Works and Library editions, corresponding titles have the same page numbers, so a reference to one will serve as a reference to the other. However, this is not true of earlier titles. The listed entries explain how page numbers among matched pairs of Library and Works titles are related.

In cases of long works not yet available in Mark Twain Project editions (such as *Life on the Mississippi*), I draw on first editions. Reprints of virtually all of these books became available in late 1996, when the Oxford Mark Twain edition (OMT), edited by Shelley Fisher Fishkin, was published. This 29-volume set contains facsimile reprints of all but a few of Mark Twain's first American editions. These reprints retain the page numbers of the originals, giving them the same reference utility.

For short works not yet published in Mark Twain Project editions such as *ET&S*, the most authoritative published collections are the two volumes of *Collected Tales, Sketches, Speeches, & Essays* (*CT-1* and *CT-2*) edited by Louis J. Budd. Most items in *CT-1* use texts corrected by the Mark Twain Project (including many for still-unpublished *ET&S* volumes). Other texts in *CT-1* and *CT-2* are taken directly from their earliest published forms, which were typically in magazines.

Most of the short writings cited in *The Quotable Mark Twain* appear in one or more of the collections reprinted in the OMT. Several points should be noted about collections such as *Sketches, New and Old* (*SN&O*) and *The Man That Corrupted Hadleyburg and Other Stories and Essays* (*MTCH&c*). First, I do not cite texts in these volumes that are also in either Mark Twain Project editions or the *CT* volumes, even if such texts are the title stories for collections, such as "The Man That Corrupted Hadleyburg," because the other editions have greater authority. Second, be aware that collections with the same—or very similar—titles in later uniform sets (such as the "Author's National Edition") are *not* identical to these first-edition namesakes. A prime example of the kind of confusion found in all these editions is *A Double-Barrelled Detective Story*. That novella was first published in book form by itself (see *DBDS* in the listings); it was also collected in the first edition of *The $30,000 Bequest and Other Stories* (*$30k Bequest*); however, in Harper & Brothers uniform editions it appears in *The Man That Corrupted Hadleyburg and Other Essays and Stories*.

Another category of material on which I have drawn is books published after Mark Twain's lifetime. These include new collections of previously published and unpublished stories and essays and collections of his early journalism and travel letters. Some book titles in the first group, such as *What Is Man? and Other Essays* (*WIM&OE*), are titles in one or more uniform sets. Readers should be aware that pagination of volumes in different sets varies somewhat—even among volumes with identical titles and copyright information.

One final bibliographical complication merits a general comment. Many books on Mark Twain cite two-volume editions of his longest works (*Innocents Abroad, Roughing It, The Gilded Age, A Tramp Abroad, Joan of Arc,* and *Following the Equator*); all or most of these editions were published in uniform sets. (Foreign editions aside, Mark Twain published no two-volume books during his lifetime.) The multivolume editions add yet another level of confusion by numbering their chapters separately in each of their two volumes. For example, chapter 60 of the first edition of *Innocents Abroad* becomes chapter 33 of volume 2 in later editions. The notes on individual titles that follow explain how to convert chapter numbers in one- and two-volume editions.

Although considerable confusion reigns in Mark Twain bibliography, patience and attention to bibliographical details will help one to win through. Be patient. It is, after all, Mark Twain's words—not dreary bibliographical facts—that matter.

The abbreviated titles used to cite individual books are designed to strike a reasonable balance between brevity and recognizability. Many of these abbreviations are commonly used in Mark Twain scholarship, but I have also introduced some innovations to group closely related books together. For example, abbreviations for all the autobiography editions begin with "*Autob/*" followed by acronyms, such as "*AMT*," for the books' actual titles. Abbreviations for collections of letters begin with "*Ltrs-,*" followed by either a Mark Twain Project series number, a correspondent's name, or a key word. (An exception is "*Ltrs/Paine,*" which uses a slash instead of a hyphen because Paine is the name of the editor, not a correspondent.) Other collections of travel letters, journalism, sketches, stories, and essays are generally entered under acronyms of titles, such as "*MTTB*," for *Mark Twain's Travels with Mr. Brown*. The system is doubtless imperfect, but it should be serviceable.

All the books prepared by the Mark Twain Project are published by the University of California Press. Every title listed for which this press is the publisher is an official Project edition—with the exceptions of *Cl. of Call* and *MTOE*, both of which were prepared with the help of the Project. All titles listed for which the term "1st ed." is asterisked (*) are available in OMT editions, whose page numbers match those of the first editions.

Adam's Diary   *Extracts from Adam's Diary* (1st ed.* New York: Harper & Brothers, 1904). Extended sketch narrated by the biblical Adam.

Amer. Claim.   *The American Claimant* (1st ed.* New York: Charles L. Webster, 1892). Novel. This edition contains only the novel. Around 1917 Harper & Brothers began publishing a collection in its uniform sets that was variously titled *The American Claimant* and *The American Claimant and Other Stories*. This later edition—and its successors—contain the novel (paginated differently) and most of the original contents of *Merry Tales*.

Autob/AMT   *The Autobiography of Mark Twain, Including Chapters Now Published for the First Time* ed. Charles Neider (1st ed. New York: Harper & Row, 1959). This fourth published version of Mark Twain's autobiographical writings duplicates much of the material from earlier versions, adds some previously unpublished material, and arranges the whole to follow the chronology of Mark Twain's life. Note that the dates that *The Quotable Mark Twain* assigns to quotations taken from the various autobiography editions indicate when the passages were written or dictated, so far as such dates can be determined.

Autob/MTA   *Mark Twain's Autobiography* ed. Albert Bigelow Paine (1st ed. 2 vols., New York: Harper & Brothers, 1924). Selection of autobiographical writings and dictations prepared by Mark Twain's literary executor and first editor of the Mark Twain Papers. Includes much of the material previously published in the *North American Review* (see *Autob/NAR*), often arranged quite differently. Each volume is separately paginated and indexed.

Autob/MTIE   *Mark Twain in Eruption: Hitherto Unpublished Pages About Men and Events* ed. Bernard DeVoto (1st ed. New York: Harper & Brothers, 1940). Autobiographical material not used in *Autob/MTA*. The pagination of this first edition was retained by the later Capricorn paperback reprint editions.

Autob/NAR   *Mark Twain's Own Autobiography: The Chapters from the North American Review* ed. Michael J. Kiskis (1st ed. Madison: University of Wisconsin Press, 1990). First book publication of articles that were originally published in a magazine under Mark Twain's supervision in 1906–07. Much of this material also appears in the other autobiography editions that precede this listing. Citations following quotes give both the date of the original *North American Review* (*NAR*) publication and the *Autob/NAR* page reference. The *NAR* citations can be used to find the passages in the OMT volume titled *Chapters from My Autobiography*. It contains facsimile reprints of the original *NAR* pages, including their original page numbers.

Cl. of Call   *Clemens of the Call: Mark Twain in San Francisco* ed. Edgar M. Branch (1st ed. Berkeley: University of California Press, 1969). Selected articles that Mark Twain wrote, but did not sign, for the *San Francisco Call* in 1864.

Conn. Yankee   *A Connecticut Yankee in King Arthur's Court* ed. Bernard Stein (Berkeley: University of California Press, Mark Twain Library, 1983). First published in 1889, this novel is structured as a frame story, most of whose narrative is in the voice of the title character, Hank Morgan. Page numbers of this Mark Twain Library edition are consistently 46 pages lower than their counterparts in the 1979 Works edition, and its text corrects minor flaws that were detected in the Works edition.

CT-1   *Collected Tales, Sketches, Speeches, & Essays, 1852–1890* ed. Louis J. Budd (New York: Library of America, 1992). The two volumes in this set contain the broadest and most authoritative collection of Mark Twain's short works yet published. Most texts in *CT-1* were edited by the Mark Twain Project for the five-volume *ET&S* series (only two volumes of which have been published to date). Most remaining items in *CT-1* and *CT-2* are taken directly from the first magazines and books in which they appeared. Contains substantial bibliographical notes.

CT-2   *Collected Tales, Sketches, Speeches, & Essays, 1891–1910* ed. Louis J. Budd (New York: Library of America, 1992). See *CT-1*.

DBDS *A Double-Barrelled Detective Story* (1st ed.* New York: Harper & Brothers, 1902). Novella. The first edition is divided into two parts, each with chapters numbered 1–5. Later printings, in *$30k Bequest* (1st ed. only) and other collections, number all the chapters 1–10.

Dog's Tale *A Dog's Tale* (1st ed. New York: Harper & Brothers, 1904). Novella narrated by a dog. Reprinted in *$30k Bequest*.

E&E *Europe and Elsewhere* ed. Albert Bigelow Paine (New York: Harper & Brothers, 1923). Posthumous collection of previously unpublished and published essays.

ET&S-1 *Early Tales & Sketches, vol. 1, 1851–1864* ed. Edgar Marquess Branch and Robert H. Hirst (Berkeley: University of California Press, 1979). These volumes contain carefully corrected texts of Mark Twain's early short works with extensive bibliographical notes. Many texts prepared for forthcoming volumes 3–5 are in *CT-1*.

ET&S-2 *Early Tales & Sketches, vol. 2, 1864–1865* ed. Edgar Marquess Branch and Robert H. Hirst (Berkeley: University of California Press, 1981). See *ET&S-1*.

Eve's Diary *Eve's Diary* (1st ed.* New York: Harper & Brothers, 1906). Extended sketch narrated by the biblical Eve, with an afterword by Adam.

Fab. of Man *Mark Twain's Fables of Man* ed. John S. Tuckey (1st ed. Berkeley: University of California Press, 1972). Collection of previously unpublished, and mostly unfinished, stories. Some of these texts are reprinted in Tuckey's *The Devil's Race-Track: Mark Twain's Great Dark Writings* (1984).

Foll. Equat. *Following the Equator: A Journey Around the World* (1st ed.* Hartford, Connecticut: American Publishing Co., 1897). Travel book. The first volumes of later two-volume editions have 36 chapters; the second volumes renumber the remaining chapters, with chapter 37 of the first edition becoming volume 2, chapter 1, and so on. (See also *More Tramps*.)

Gilded Age *The Gilded Age: A Tale of To-day* (1st ed.* Hartford, Connecticut: American Publishing Co., 1874). Novel coauthored by Charles Dudley Warner. Quotations in *The Quotable Mark Twain* are taken only from chapters known to have been written primarily by Mark Twain. The second volumes of later two-volume editions begin renumbering the chapters at the first edition's chapter 32—which thus becomes volume 2, chapter 1.

HF&TS *Huck Finn and Tom Sawyer Among the Indians and Other Unfinished Stories* ed. Dahlia Armon, Walter Blair, et al. (1st ed. Berkeley: University of California Press, Mark Twain Library, 1989). Most of its texts are reprinted from *HH&T*, with some minor corrections from manuscripts.

HH&T *Hannibal, Huck & Tom* ed. Walter Blair (1st ed. Berkeley: University of California Press, 1969). Collection of previously unpublished and mostly unfinished manuscripts. Most of its texts are reprinted in *HF&TS*.

Horse's Tale *A Horse's Tale* (1st ed. New York: Harper & Brothers, 1907). Novella, each chapter of which has a different narrator. Reprinted in *Mys. Stranger*.

How to Tell a Story *How to Tell a Story and Other Essays* (1st ed. New York: Harper & Brothers, 1897). Collection of previously published material, including some pieces printed in other collections.

Huck Finn *Adventures of Huckleberry Finn* (Berkeley: University of California Press, Mark Twain Library, 1985). Novel narrated by Huck Finn. First published in England in 1884 and in the United States in 1885. The pagination, layout, and main text of this Mark Twain Library edition are identical to those of the Works edition, which was published later.

Inn. Abroad *The Innocents Abroad, or The New Pilgrims' Progress* (1st ed.* Hartford, Connecticut: American Publishing Co., 1869). Travel book. The second volumes of later two-volume editions begin renumbering the chapters at chapter 28. Most of the chapters in *Innocents Abroad* are adapted from letters that Mark Twain wrote to the San Francisco *Alta California* and other newspapers; the original letters are reprinted in *TWIA*.

ISD *Is Shakespeare Dead? From My Autobiography* (1st ed.* New York: Harper & Brothers, 1909). Extended essay and memoir. Reprinted in *WIM&OE*.

Joan of Arc *Personal Recollections of Joan of Arc* (1st ed.* New York: Harper & Brothers, 1896). Novel first published anonymously and attributed to its fictitious narrator, Sieur Louis de Conte.

313

Later two-volume editions are paginated differently from the first edition, but they retain the same "book" and "chapter" numbers.

LAIFI   *Life As I Find It* ed. Charles Neider (New York: Perennial Library, 1977). Selection of previously uncollected short published works, many of which were originally published in the magazine *Galaxy* in the early 1870s. Pagination of this paperback edition differs from that of the first edition.

Lets. Earth   *Letters from the Earth* ed. Bernard DeVoto (1st ed. New York: Harper & Row, 1962). Collection of material not previously published at the time the book was originally prepared in 1940. A corrected text of the title piece, "Letters from the Earth," appears in *WIM&OPW*, which is the source of quotations in *The Quotable Mark Twain*. Pagination of later paperback editions differs from that of the first edition.

Life on Miss.   *Life on the Mississippi* (1st ed.* Boston: James R. Osgood, 1883). Travel book. Combines a revised version of "Old Times on the Mississippi" and an account of Mark Twain's return to the river in 1882.

Ltrs-1   *Mark Twain's Letters, vol. 1, 1853–1866* ed. Edgar Marquess Branch, Michael B. Frank, and Kenneth M. Sanderson (1st ed. Berkeley: University of California Press, 1988). Prepared by the Mark Twain Project at Berkeley, these nearly definitive collections of Mark Twain's letters will eventually supersede all previously published letter collections, including the Project's own *Ltrs-Publs* and *Ltrs-Rogers*.

Ltrs-2   *Mark Twain's Letters, vol. 2, 1867–1868* ed. Harriet Elinor Smith, Richard Bucci, and Lin Salamo (1st ed. Berkeley: University of California Press, 1990). See *Ltrs-1*.

Ltrs-3   *Mark Twain's Letters, vol. 3, 1869* ed. Victor Fischer, Michael B. Frank, and Dahlia Armon (1st ed. Berkeley: University of California Press, 1992). See *Ltrs-1*.

Ltrs-4   *Mark Twain's Letters, vol. 4, 1870–1871* ed. Victor Fischer, Michael B. Frank, and Lin Salamo (1st ed. Berkeley: University of California Press, 1995). See *Ltrs-1*.

Ltrs-5   *Mark Twain's Letters, vol. 5, 1872–1873* ed. Harriet Elinor Smith and Lin Salamo (1st ed. Berkeley: University of California Press, 1997). See *Ltrs-1*.

Ltrs-Angelfish   *Mark Twain's Aquarium: The Samuel Clemens Angelfish Correspondence, 1905–1910* ed. John Cooley (1st ed. Athens: University of Georgia Press, 1991). Previously unpublished letters to young girls whom Mark Twain called his "Angelfish."

Ltrs-Cable   *Twins of Genius* ed. Guy Cardwell (London: Neville Spearman, 1962). Small collection of Mark Twain's correspondence with George Washington Cable.

Ltrs-Fairbanks   *Mark Twain to Mrs. Fairbanks* ed. Dixon Wecter (1st ed. San Marino, California: Huntington Library, 1949). Letters to a friend whom Mark Twain met on the *Quaker City* voyage in 1867.

Ltrs-Hawaii   *Mark Twain's Letters from Hawaii* ed. A. Grove Day (Honolulu: University of Hawaii Press, 1979). One of several editions of letters that Mark Twain wrote to the *Sacramento Union* in 1866. The letter numbers it uses are also used in other editions of these letters.

Ltrs-Howells   *Mark Twain–Howells Letters: The Correspondence of Samuel L. Clemens and William D. Howells* ed. Henry Nash Smith and William M. Gibson (1st ed. 2 vols., Cambridge, Massachusetts: Harvard University Press, 1960). Letters exchanged by Mark Twain, William Dean Howells, and their wives. About half of this material is published in *Selected Mark Twain–Howells Letters, 1872–1910* (1968), which contains two letters not in the larger collection.

Ltrs-Love   *The Love Letters of Mark Twain* ed. Dixon Wecter (1st ed. New York: Harper & Brothers, 1949). Selected letters of Mark Twain to his wife, Livy, and other family members, from late 1868 to 1903.

Ltrs-Mary   *Mark Twain's Letters to Mary* ed. Lewis Leary (New York: Columbia University Press, 1963). Letters to the daughter-in-law of H. H. Rogers.

Ltrs/Paine   *Mark Twain's Letters* ed. Albert Bigelow Paine (1st ed. 2 vols., New York: Harper & Brothers, 1917). First published collection of Mark Twain's letters, selected and edited by his biographer. Since Paine often altered texts, quotations taken from this collection have been checked and silently corrected against manuscripts in the Mark Twain Papers collection.

Paine's edition is cited for the convenience of readers who wish to see the quotes in their fuller contexts.

Ltrs-Publs *Mark Twain's Letters to His Publishers, 1867–1894* ed. Hamlin Hill (1st ed. Berkeley: University of California Press, 1967). Collection of mostly business correspondence.

Ltrs-Rogers *Mark Twain's Correspondence with Henry Huttleston Rogers, 1893–1909* ed. Lewis Leary (1st ed. Berkeley: University of California Press, 1969). Collection of business and personal correspondence with Mark Twain's close friend and business consultant. Succeeds *Ltrs-Publs*.

Merry Tales *Merry Tales* (1st ed.* New York: Charles L. Webster, 1892). Collection of sketches. Most of the material in *Merry Tales* was later incorporated in a collection titled *The American Claimant* (see *Amer. Claim.*).

£1m Bank-note *£1,000,000 Bank-note and Other New Stories* (1st ed.* New York: Charles L. Webster, 1893). Nine previously published stories and essays. These stories are scattered among the volumes of later uniform editions.

More Max. *More Maxims of Mark* ed. Merle Johnson ([n.p.]: [privately published], 1927). Maxims extracted from Mark Twain's journals and miscellaneous memoranda. Reprinted in *CT-2*.

More Tramps *More Tramps Abroad* (3d ed. London: Chatto & Windus, 1898). English version of *Following the Equator*. Lacks the American book's illustrations, but has some additional text. Pagination and most chapter numbers differ from *Following the Equator*.

MT:Bib *Mark Twain: A Bibliography* Merle Johnson (New York: Harper & Brothers, 1935). Still the fullest bibliography of Mark Twain's first editions, this volume includes extracts from Mark Twain's speeches and minor writings that have apparently not been published elsewhere.

MT:Biog *Mark Twain: A Biography* Albert Bigelow Paine (1st ed. 3 vols., New York: Harper & Brothers, 1912). Paine's authorized biography includes hundreds of excerpts from Mark Twain's writings, some of which have not yet been published elsewhere. Paine rarely specifies the manuscript sources of his quotes, but those quotes that can be matched against manuscripts suggest that Paine's renderings of the remainder are probably at least as reliable as his letter transcriptions (see *Ltrs/Paine*) and other books. *MT:Biog* citations do not require volume numbers; pagination is sequential, with both chapter and page numbers remaining the same in two-, three-, and four-volume editions.

MT:Bus. Man   *Mark Twain, Business Man* ed. Samuel Charles Webster (Boston: Little, Brown, 1946). Collection of Mark Twain's business correspondence assembled by the son of Charles L. Webster, his nephew by marriage and first president of his publishing house.

MTCH&c   *The Man That Corrupted Hadleyburg and Other Stories and Essays* (1st ed.* New York: Harper & Brothers, 1900). Collection of previously published material. The contents of the first edition differ from those of a later Harper edition titled *The Man That Corrupted Hadleyburg and Other Essays and Stories* (note slightly altered title).

MTN   *Mark Twain's Notebook* ed. Albert Bigelow Paine (1st ed. New York: Harper & Brothers, 1935). Extracts from journals that Mark Twain kept throughout his adult life. *MTN* is being superseded by *N&J*. Most of the *MTN* quotations in *The Quotable Mark Twain* have been checked and corrected against Mark Twain's original manuscripts at the Mark Twain Project. Corrected texts are referenced to "MTP," followed by specific document citations and *MTN* page references.

MTOE   *Mark Twain of the Enterprise: Newspaper Articles & Other Documents, 1862–1864* ed. Henry Nash Smith (1st ed. Berkeley: University of California Press, 1957). Selection of Mark Twain's journalism in the Virginia City, Nevada, *Territorial Enterprise*. Corrected texts of the most important items are in *ET&S-1*.

MTP   Mark Twain Papers. See under *MTN*.

MTSF   *Mark Twain's San Francisco* ed. Bernard Taper (1st ed. New York: McGraw-Hill, 1963). Selections from Mark Twain's early western journalism. Much of this material appears in other books.

MTSFH   *Mark Twain Speaks for Himself* ed. Paul Fatout (1st ed. West Lafayette, Indiana: Purdue University Press, 1978). Collection of speeches, letters, and early journalism.

MT Speaking   *Mark Twain Speaking* ed. Paul Fatout (1st ed. Iowa City: University of Iowa Press, 1976). Collection of 200 speeches and lectures. Includes some texts from original manuscript sources; however, many speeches are taken directly from *Speeches/Paine* or are "composites" that Fatout assembled from more than one source. Many speeches—particularly formal lectures—are difficult to date precisely because Mark Twain delivered them multiple times. Speech titles are generally omitted in *The Quotable Mark Twain* citations because most of them were added by editors.

MTTB   *Mark Twain's Travels with Mr. Brown* ed. Franklin Walker and G. Ezra Dane (1st ed. New York: Alfred A. Knopf, 1940). Travel letters that Mark Twain wrote for the *San Francisco Alta California* from late December 1866 to early June 1867. Dates given for quotes from these letters are of composition, not original publication.

Mys. Stranger   *The Mysterious Stranger* ed. Albert Bigelow Paine (New York: Harper & Brothers, 1922). Collection of previously uncollected material, including the title story, "The Mysterious Stranger" (published as a book with the same title in 1916)—Paine's bowdlerized version of "The Chronicle of Young Satan." The only authentic text of the latter is in *Mys. Stranger Mss.*

Mys. Stranger Mss.   *Mark Twain's Mysterious Stranger Manuscripts* ed. William M. Gibson (1st ed. Berkeley: University of California Press, 1969). Includes "The Chronicle of Young Satan," "Schoolhouse Hill," and "No. 44, The Mysterious Stranger" (see *No. 44*). These texts are the *only* authoritative versions of "The Mysterious Stranger."

N&J-1   *Mark Twain's Notebooks & Journals. Vol. 1: 1855–1873* ed. Frederick Anderson, Michael B. Frank, and Kenneth M. Sanderson (1st ed. Berkeley: University of California Press, 1975). The first three volumes in this Mark Twain Project series supersede the first part of *MTN* through the year 1891.

N&J-2   *Mark Twain's Notebooks & Journals. Vol. 2: 1877–1883* ed. Frederick Anderson, Lin Salamo, and Bernard L. Stein (1st ed. Berkeley: University of California Press, 1975). See *N&J-1*.

N&J-3   *Mark Twain's Notebooks & Journals. Vol. 3: 1883–1891* ed.

Robert Pack Browning, Michael B. Frank, and Lin Salamo (1st ed. Berkeley: University of California Press, 1979). See *N&J-1*.

No. 44 *No. 44, The Mysterious Stranger* ed. John S. Tuckey and William M. Gibson (Berkeley: University of California Press, Mark Twain Library, 1982). Unfinished novel narrated by August Feldner. First published in *Mys. Stranger Mss.* in 1969, this story is not the same as *The Mysterious Stranger* (1916), which Paine and a Harpers editor cobbled together and partly rewrote from unpublished manuscripts, freely departing from Mark Twain's words and his final intention for the text.

OMT Oxford Mark Twain (New York: Oxford University Press, 1996). Twenty-nine-volume set of facsimile reprints of American first editions published during Mark Twain's lifetime. Most volume titles match those of the first editions, but a few volumes are composites. For example, a single volume combines *SWE*, *DBDS*, and *Tom Sawyer Det.* The facsimile pages of all OMT volumes retain the original page numbers of the first editions that they duplicate.

Pen Warmed Up *A Pen Warmed-up in Hell: Mark Twain in Protest* ed. Frederick Anderson (New York: Harper & Row, 1979). Collection prepared by a chief editor of the Mark Twain Papers that includes freshly edited versions of "The War Prayer" and "The Dervish and the Offensive Stranger."

PortMT *The Portable Mark Twain* ed. Bernard DeVoto (15th printing, New York: Viking, 1961). Diverse collection of texts that were first published in 1946, when DeVoto was editor of the Mark Twain Papers. Includes some letters not published in any other book.

Prince & Pauper *The Prince and the Pauper: A Tale for Young People of All Ages* (Berkeley: University of California Press, Mark Twain Library, 1983). Novel first published in 1881. Page numbers in this edition are consistently 44 pages lower than their counterparts in the 1979 Works edition, whose layout is otherwise identical. Its text corrects minor flaws that were detected in the Works edition.

Pudd. Wilson See *PW&TET*.

PW&TET *Pudd'nhead Wilson and Those Extraordinary Twins* (1st ed.* Hartford, Connecticut: American Publishing Co., 1894). This illustrated first edition of the novel *Pudd'nhead Wilson* also includes "Those Extraordinary Twins" as an appendix. Pagination of later editions is completely different.

Rough. It   *Roughing It* (Berkeley: University of California Press, Mark Twain Library, 1995). Travel book first published in 1872. The pagination, layout, and main text of this Mark Twain Library edition are identical to those of the 1993 Works edition. (These editions supersede the Mark Twain Project's 1972 edition.)

1601   *Mark Twain's [Date, 1601.] Conversation As It Was by the Social Fireside in the Time of the Tudors* ed. Franklin J. Meine (New York: Lyle Stuart, n.d.). Sketch written in 1876, privately printed in 1882, and published in many editions in later years. Punctuation and spelling vary greatly among editions. A facsimile of the first printing is part of the OMT volume that includes *ISD*.

S&B   *Mark Twain's Satires & Burlesques* ed. Franklin R. Rogers (1st ed. Berkeley: University of California Press, 1967). Collection of previously unpublished material, most of which Mark Twain left unfinished.

SN&O   *Sketches, New and Old* (1st ed.* Hartford, Connecticut: American Publishing Co., 1875). Illustrated collection of early sketches. Contents, pagination, and sketch titles used in this edition differ greatly from their counterparts in later uniform set editions of this same title. Corrected texts of many sketches published in *SN&O* also appear in *ET&S-1*, *ET&S-2* and *CT-2*.

Speeches/Paine   *Mark Twain's Speeches* ed. Albert Bigelow Paine (New York: Harper & Brothers, 1923). Revised edition of a collection of speeches that Mark Twain's literary executor first published in 1910. Speech titles are generally omitted in *The Quotable Mark Twain* citations because most of them were added by editors. (See also *MT Speaking*.)

Stormfield   *Extract from Captain Stormfield's Visit to Heaven* (1st ed.* New York: Harper & Brothers, 1909). Unfinished novella narrated by the title character.

SWE   *The Stolen White Elephant, Etc.* (1st ed.* Boston: James R. Osgood, 1882). Collection of sketches, essays, speeches, and stories, some of which (including the title story) were not previously published. Much of the material in *SWE* was reprinted in *Tom Sawyer Abroad, Tom Sawyer, Detective and Other Stories, etc., etc.* (New York: Harper & Brothers, 1896) and later editions of the same title.

$30k Bequest   *The $30,000 Bequest and Other Stories* (1st ed.* New York: Harper & Brothers, 1906). Collection of previously published material, including the title story. The contents of this edition differ from later editions of the same title.

Tom Sawyer   *The Adventures of Tom Sawyer* (Berkeley: University of California Press, Mark Twain Library, 1982). Novel first published in 1876. The Mark Twain Library edition contains all the original illustrations. Aside from minor additional corrections, its text is identical to the Mark Twain Project's unillustrated 1980 Works edition, *The Adventures of Tom Sawyer; Tom Sawyer Abroad; Tom Sawyer, Detective*, whose layout and pagination are completely different.

Tom Sawyer Abrd.   *Tom Sawyer Abroad; Tom Sawyer, Detective* (Berkeley: University of California Press, Mark Twain Library, 1982). *Tom Sawyer Abroad* is a novella first published in a bowdlerized version in both magazine and book forms in 1894. *Tom Sawyer, Detective* is a novella first published in 1896; unlike the former story, it was not published as a book by itself. Both stories were first combined in a single volume in 1896; afterward they were usually published together. The 1980 Works edition—the first to correct the original edition—includes both stories, along with *Tom Sawyer*.

Tom Sawyer Det.   See *Tom Sawyer Abrd.*

Tramp Abroad   *A Tramp Abroad* (1st ed.* Hartford, Connecticut: American Publishing Co., 1880). Travel book. The second volumes of later two-volume editions begin renumbering the chapters at chapter 30.

TWIA   *Traveling with the Innocents Abroad: Mark Twain's Original Reports from Europe and the Holy Land* ed. Daniel Morley McKeithan (1st ed. Norman: University of Oklahoma Press, 1958). Collection of Mark Twain's original newspaper letters from the 1867 *Quaker City* voyage. McKeithan's notes point out differences between these texts and their corresponding chapters in *Innocents Abroad*.

UCCL   *Union Catalog of Clemens Letters* ed. Paul Machlis (1st ed.

Berkeley: University of California Press, 1986). Index to all known letters written by Mark Twain and members of his immediate family. *UCCL* corrects the dates of many letters published in *Ltrs/Paine* and other books.

WIM&OE   *What Is Man? and Other Essays* ed. Albert Bigelow Paine (New York: Harper & Brothers, 1917). Collection of previously published writings. Many quotations extracted from essays appearing in *The Quotable Mark Twain*—including "What Is Man?" itself—are taken from more authoritative editions, such as *WIM&OPW*.

WIM&OPW   *What Is Man? and Other Philosophical Writings* ed. Paul Baender (1st ed. Berkeley: University of California Press, 1973). Mostly previously published material, including all of *Christian Science, What Is Man?,* and the title story of *Lets. Earth*, prepared by the Mark Twain Project. "Letter" numbers used in *WIM&OPW*'s corrected text of "Letters from the Earth" follow the irregularities of the original manuscript and do not match the numbers that DeVoto assigned to them in his 1962 edition; to avoid confusion letter numbers are not cited in *The Quotable Mark Twain*. By contrast, the "book" and chapter numbers used in the original edition of *Christian Science* match those in *WIM&OPW*.

WWD&OSW   *Mark Twain's Which Was the Dream? and Other Symbolic Writings of the Later Years* ed. John S. Tuckey (1st ed. Berkeley: University of California Press, 1967). Collection of previously unpublished and mostly unfinished stories. *WWD&OSW*'s most important pieces also appear in Tuckey's *The Devil's Race-Track: Mark Twain's Great Dark Writings* (1984).

Key Word and Subject Index

This index is designed to help readers locate specific quotations by listing key words and phrases taken directly from them; it also lists subjects on which Mark Twain expresses opinions. To fit as much information as possible into the available space, the index does not differentiate between key words and subjects. Moreover, the forms of some terms in quotes differ slightly from those listed here, and their meanings occasionally vary. However, readers should have no difficulty in distinguishing among forms and meanings when they consult the referenced pages. Terms printed below in **boldface** are headwords of textual entries; textual page references are also printed in bold. Some terms are enclosed in quotation marks (e.g., "Egypt") because Mark Twain discusses them as words, not as subjects.

A half dozen unattested quotes attributed to Mark Twain are discussed in the Introduction (pages xvii–xviii). In order to spare readers looking for those quotations futile searching, key words from those quotations are included in this index; they are the only quotations whose page references are given in roman numerals.

139, 141, 174, 193, 198, 232,
238, 249, 262; moral, 220;
national, 233; perfect, 53
Characters, fictional, 44, 54, 297.
See also individual character
names
Chariot of fire, 51
Charity, 44, 53, 69, 86, 217, 247,
282
Charm, 41, 101, 102, 126, 145, 271,
282, 284, 290, 292, 299;
supremest, 41
Chasteness/chastity, 191, 263
Chauffeur, 44
Cheerfulness, 45, 49, 79, 102,
203, 244, 282, 290
Chestnut, 45
Chicago, Illinois, 24, **45**
Chicken, fried, 45
Chickens, counting, 79, 225
Chief justice, 133
Childhood, 133, 176
Children, 45–46, 68, 95, 129, 160,
192, 225; burnt, 45; dying, 9;
wise, 46
Chimney sweep, 13
Chimpanzees, 242
Chinese, the, 46, 192, 245
Chloroform factory, 49
"Chloroform in print," 30
Choirs, 254; **church, 46**
Chosen of God, 139
Christ, 30, **46–47**, 129, 208
Christendom, 132, 203, 285
Christian Science, 47
Christianity, 47, 202
Christians, 46, 62, 153, 160, 185,
192, 193, 202, 207; Christian
life, 211
Christmas, 47
Chromo, 13

Church, 24, 25, **48**, 128, 183, 238;
established, 48
Cigars, 48, 274
Ciphering, 214
Circumstance, 35, **48–49**, 92, 161,
195, 276
Circumstantial evidence, 49
Circus, 43
Cities, 24, 45, 64, 87, 194, 245. *See
also* individual cities
Citizenship, 49
Civil war, 50, 108, 249
Civilization, 50–51, 134, 220, 233,
247, 257, 296, 300; American,
194; foundation of, 137
Civita Vecchia, Italy, 51
Claimants, 51
Clairvoyants, 75, 177
Clarity/clearness, **51**, 116, 132, 143,
206, 303
Class, 51, 197; cultivated, 31
Classic, 52, 131, 206
Clay, 154
Clemens, Henry (Mark Twain's
brother), **52**
Clemens, James Ross (relative), 75
Clemens, Jane Lampton (Mark
Twain's mother), **52**
Clemens, Olivia L. (Mark
Twain's wife), **53**, 96, 124,
295. *See also* Wife, Mark
Twain's
Clemens, Orion (Mark Twain's
brother), **54–55**, 131
Clemens, Samuel L. (Mark
Twain), **55–56**
Clemens, Susy (Mark Twain's
daughter), **56–57**, 102
Clergymen, 24, **57**, 215, 285
Cleveland, Grover, 57, 235
Climate, 38, 51, **58**, 121, 125, 245

Restraint, 39, 281

Retail, 148

Retorts, 236

Revenge, 40, **236**

Reverence, 46, 57, 110, 210, 226,
236, 249, 299

Revolution, 144, 161, **236–237.**
See also French Revolution

Rhode Island, 243

Rhodes, Cecil, 173–237

Rhodesia, 237

Riches, 233, 251

Riddles, 143, **237**

Ridicule, 14, 83, **238,** 279

Right, 11, 63, 64, 107, 115, 175, 185,
207, 217, 238; do, 97

Right word, 208, 300–301

Righteousness, 238

Rights, 89, 156, **238,** 300

Riots, 24, 144, 216

Rising, 238

Rivals, 239

Rivers, 12, 180, 192, 213, **239**

Robbers, 208, **239.** *See also*
Stealing; Theft

Rock, 17, 117, 148, 190, 271

**Rogers, Henry Huttleston,
239–240**

Romance, 26, 113, 171, 249

Rome, Italy, 38, 178, **240**

Roosevelt, Theodore, 240–241,
292

Roses, attar of, 122

Rough Riders, 131

Roughing It (Mark Twain), **241**

Roxy (character), **241**

Royalty, 11, 190, 238, **242.** *See also*
Aristocracy; Kings;
Monarchy

Rubbish, 176

Ruin, 239; magnificent, 131

Rules, human, 143

Russia, 72, 124, 178, **242–243**

Russians, 30, 191

Sabbath day, 26, 37, 111, 121, 202,
243, 263, 296

Sacramento, California, 244

Sacredness, 46, 97, 113, 114, 127,
147, 236, 250, 292

Saddles, 244

Sagacity, 284

Sagebrush, 244

Sailors, 244, 267, 290

Saint Bernards, 220

Saint Louis, Missouri, 244

Sainte Chapelle, 234

Saints, 51, 171, 174, 208, **245,** 259

Salary, 155

Salt Lake City, Utah, 245

Saloon-keepers. *See* Barkeepers

Salutatory, 286

Salvation Army, 98

***San Francisco Call*, 245**

San Francisco, California, xviii,
245

Sanctity, odor of, 171

Sand, 44, 164, 166, **246**

Sandy (character), **246**

Sanity, 119. *See also* Insanity

Satan, 3, 43, 45, 97, 202, 237, **246,**
253, 257

Satire, 63, **246**

Satisfaction, 81, 104, 189, 195, 204,
213, 303; personal, 84

Savages/savagery, 9, 10, 63, 80,
231, **247,** 300

Saving, 247

Savior, 46

Sawyer, Sid (character), 52